DATE DUE

JUL 1 7 2003		
	OCT 2 3 2003	

HIGHSMITH #45102

"Zemke and Bell reveal the secret for making enchantment a tool for customer loyalty."

—Ken Blanchard, Coauthor of *The One Minute Manager* and *Whale Done!*™

"Service Magic is a must-read for anyone interested in changing their customers' experience from ho-hum to Wow!"

—James Mapes, Author of *Quantum Leap Thinking*

"Two thumbs way up for *Service Magic*. It unveils the secrets to customer loyalty in a way that is both poignant and practical."

—Bob Gault, President and COO of Universal Orlando

"*Service Magic* takes service excellence to the next level, illustrating exactly how to achieve the Wow Factor. The three Ps of Place, Process, and Performance all have to be present to deliver Service Magic."

—Judith S. Corson, Cofounder and Former President of Custom Research Inc.

"A fun and valuable book to read if you are interested in service, in magic, or in both."

—Dr. Leonard L. Berry, Author of *Discovering the Soul of Service*

"*Service Magic* will be the playbook used by organizations that want to provide superior customer service. It's a must-read!"

—Paul Eckert, President and COO of United Financial Services Group

"*Service Magic* is a very innovative but practical approach for taking your service to the next level."

—John Goodman, President of TARP

"*Service Magic* provides delicious ideas for giving customers a smile on their face and a reason to return."

—Phil Romano, Founder of Romano's Macaroni Grill

SERVICE MAGIC

The Art of Amazing Your Customers

Ron Zemke AND Chip Bell

Dearborn™
Trade Publishing
A **Kaplan Professional** Company

Vice President and Publisher: Cynthia A. Zigmund
Senior Managing Editor: Jack Kiburz
Interior Design: Lucy Jenkins
Cover Design: Scott Rattray, Rattray Design
Typesetting: the dotted i
Interior Art: Douglas Oudekerk
Cover images from Masterfile® and photographer Bill Frymire (Stars) and from Getty Images Taxi Collection and photographer Scott Morgan (top hat).

© 2003 by Performance Research Associates, Inc.

Published by Dearborn Trade Publishing
A Kaplan Professional Company

Printed in the United States of America

03   04   05   10   9   8   7   6   5   4   3   2   1

Library of Congress Cataloging-in-Publication Data

Zemke, Ron.
   Service magic : the art of amazing your customers / Ron Zemke and Chip Bell.
      p.   cm.
   Includes index.
   ISBN 0-7931-6467-2 (6x9 pbk.)
   1. Customer services—United States.   2. Consumer satisfaction—United States.   3. Customer loyalty—United States.   4. Service industries—Customer services—United States.   I. Bell, Chip R.   II. Title.
HF5415.5.Z465 2003
658.8′12—dc21

                                                2003001187

FOREWORD

Service Magic is not about creating illusions. It is a powerful book that applies the art and skill of stage magic to the creation of a service experience that seems magical. What does that look like? When the service you receive leaves you with a smile on your face and a story to tell, you have just had a bona fide service magic experience. It is precisely that magic that Ron Zemke and Chip Bell now bring within the reach of any willing reader. They cleverly show us how to use Place, Process, and Performance to produce a magical result for your customers—and do it with regularity and charm.

Service Magic has an ingredient rare in other books but not surprising to me given my long acquaintance with the authors. Zemke and Bell have managed to integrate and interweave the latest research on customer care and their theory of Service Magic without faltering or boring the reader. I am equally awed and impressed at the generous way they cite the work of others. I respect their willingness to point out the shoulders on which they stand.

In the last decade, Zemke and Bell have written a number of first-rate, award-winning books on customer care and service. *Service Magic* will quickly take a place on, and likely go to the head of, this long, distinguished list. It is important, inspiring, fun, and applicable. It clearly and cleverly presents the ingredients that keep customers coming back for more, because, in the language of *FISH!*, it shows you how to "make their day."

—Stephen C. Lundin, Ph.D.
Coauthor of *FISH!, FISH! Tales,* and *FISH! Sticks*

CONTENTS

SECTION ONE

The Anatomy of Service Magic

The creation of memorable, positive customer service is strikingly parallel in structure and outcome to fine stage magic. While exemplars like Nordstrom, The Ritz-Carlton Hotels, and USAA Insurance are famous for their uses of enchantment, special practices come from organizations as diverse as Wayzata Dental, the St. Paul Saints, and the Hairy Cactus Nail Salon.

SECTION TWO

Place Magic

The service magician's role as supporting cast and elucidator of Place Magic is a subtle but critical adjunct to experience and effort. Take a lesson from the likes of Universal Studios, Sewell Village Cadillac, Old Faithful Inn, Ed Debevic's Diner, and Steinway & Sons on how the setting can be managed to leave customers with an unforgettable experience.

SECTION THREE
Process Magic

Policies, procedures, and routines from initial contact to problem solving that amaze the customer with their ease and simplicity are magical. Hotel Monaco, Aurora Health Care, MidAmerican Energy, and Byerly's Grocery Store are a few examples of service providers who craft processes with style and grace that enhance the experience.

SECTION FOUR
Performance Magic

Great service magicians, like stage magicians, are masters of audience dissection. They read customers in order to tailor their performance. Sometimes the "read" warns the service magician to replace what is planned; sometimes it simply cues a change in presentation. Café Un Deux Trois, the Peabody Hotel, and the Minnesota Renaissance Festival provide some of the unique insights into elevating the usual to the amazing.

SECTION FIVE
A Different Kind of Magic: The Virtual Realm

Service Magic is not just the realm of brick-and-mortar offerings. Successful e-service ventures are skillful practitioners of "virtual" Service Magic. Lesser known e-ventures like REI.com, Chipotle.com, Clinique.com, Godiva.com, and LillianVernon.com have developed creative ways to enchant their customers and yield impressive traffic and retention.

SECTION SIX

Where the Three Ps Come Together

There is magic in Place, Performance, and Process—and all three magics are available to the skilled service magician. Romano's Macaroni Grill, Von Maur, Children's Memorial Hospital, All-Outdoors Whitewater Rafting, and QVC are mini-case examples of organizations that use the 3 Ps to regularly create customer experiences that are unpredictable, valuable, and reproducible.

SECTION SEVEN

The Service Magician's Pocket Toolkit: Something Old, Something New, Many Things Borrowed, Nothing Blue

No magic book would be complete without a compendium of helpful tools for creating and delivering simple *magical service*. This section provides many examples of simple yet provocative ways service providers have transformed a routine service experience into one customers rave about to their colleagues.

ACKNOWLEDGMENTS

Thanks . . . to the magic of helpers.

We were sorely tempted to tell you that this book sprang fully formed from an iron caldron of swamp water, dragon wings, dictionary pages, and eye of newt with a powerful incantation at midnight of the solstice. But the truth is, no one writes a book alone. Many people gather around the authors to help transform rough words on a computer screen into polished prose on a printed page. This is our opportunity to express our gratitude to the many who gathered with us. The "thank you" task is a bit daunting, somewhat like all those Academy Award winners who we annually watch struggling under spotlight and camera to remember all the people to thank.

Chris Lee demonstrated around-the-clock commitment to this book from the beginning. She delivered her extraordinary creative strengths in a manner that usually appeared effortless and always seemed limitless. Dave Zielinski helped with the editorial "heavy lifting" on several sections of the book. Steve Miller and Sarah Fister Gale also made important contributions to research, reporting, and writing.

Jon Malysiak, Jack Kiburz, and the rest of the Dearborn Trade Publishing team demonstrated special attention-to-detail efficiency. Their professionalism and commitment to this project were matched only by their patience and zeal in nurturing a true publisher-author partnership. Andrea Pedolsky of the Altair Literary Agency in Washington, D.C., our agent, skillfully ensured that our labor of love was properly matched with a suitor who would give it the affection we believed it deserved.

Our Minnesota and Florida cheerleading team included our Performance Research Associates colleagues, Jill Applegate and Tom Connellan. Each offered helpful suggestions, unique and partially baked ideas, and never-ending encouragement. Jill typed draft after draft after draft, all the while telling us how great it all sounded. Her unique ability to blend the discipline of a drill sergeant with the diplomacy of counselor ensured we stayed on task when the special appeal of the subject enticed us to want to play.

We are particularly grateful for the five profilees whose magical practice is what this book is about—Romano's Macaroni Grill, Von Maur, Children's Memorial Hospital, All-Outdoors Whitewater Rafting, and QVC. In addition, we extend our thanks to the 100 plus companies cited in this book for their commitment to enchanting their customers—and for letting us tell parts of their stories. These companies are made up of special people. We are particularly appreciative of:

- Larry Kurzweil, Chip Largman, Russ Randall, and Denise Pizzulli at Universal Studios Hollywood, and Bob Gault, Scot LaFerté, and Richard Costales at Universal Studios Orlando.

- Bruce Kestleman, Linda Dirksmeyer, Sue Ela, Linda Smith, Becky Flink, Allen Stasiewski, and Kari Schmidt of Aurora Health Care in Milwaukee.

- Diana Hovey, Keith Rodenberg, and Vic Pisano of Romano's Macaroni Grill.

- James von Maur, Erin Marshall, and Amy Davis of Von Maur in Davenport, Iowa.

- Gordon Bass, Maureen Mahoney, and Barbara Bowman of Children's Memorial Hospital in Chicago.

- The Armstrong family of All-Outdoors Whitewater Rafting in Walnut Creek, California.

- John Hunter of QVC, Inc. in West Chester, Pennsylvania.

- Jim Marino of Hotel Monaco in Chicago.

- James Williams of the Magic Castle in Beverly Hills, California.

- Karen Walne of the Minnesota Renaissance Festival.

- Terry Ousley and Claudia Neumann of MidAmerican Energy in Davenport, Iowa.

- Brad Hayden, Stephanie Thomas, Scott Rohm, Theo Gilbert-Jamison, Greg Casey, and Rosemary Chasten of The Ritz-Carlton Hotel Company in Atlanta.

- Michael Morse of Café Un Deux Trois in Minneapolis.

- Tom Berger, Jim Cantalupo, David Finby, Rick Oglesbee, and Suzanne Rounds of the CBC Group, Merrill Lynch in Charlotte, North Carolina.

- Shannon Brennan, Dirk Herrman, Leo Horey, and Charlene Rothkopf of Avalon Bay Communities in Alexandria, Virginia.

- Carl Sewell, Neva Bell, Rick McIntire, and Allison Cohen of Sewell Automotive Companies in Dallas.

- Krag Swartz of Byerly's Foods in Minneapolis.

- John Poage and Nancy Carnes of Wayzata Dental in Minneapolis.

- Mary Jane Butters and Cece Connors of Mary Jane's Farm in Moscow, Idaho.

- Mike Veeck, Bill Fanning, and Bill Fisher of the St. Paul Saints.

- Ron Rosenberg, professional speaker, publisher of *In a Nutshell* newsletter, president of QualityTalk, Inc., and facilitator of the Drive-you-nuts.com Web site.

A special thank you to Ted Bauer of the Plymouth, Minnesota office of McCue Corporation, and Larry Kahlow of Minneapolis-based Eagle Magic & Joke Store. Although not quoted or referenced directly in the book, their thoughts and insights were nonetheless invaluable to the completed product.

"Mickey's Ten Commandments" on pages 48 and 49 was taken from *Be Our Guest: Practicing the Art of Customer Service* by the Disney Institute, Copyright 2001 Disney Institute. It is reprinted by permission of Hyperion Books for Children.

Finally, this book would not have happened without the emotional sustenance and ingenious inspiration of our wives, Susan Zemke and Nancy Rainey Bell. They never cease teaching us the art of enchantment through their love and devotion.

To all of our co-conjurers, a heartfelt thank you.

THE ANATOMY OF SERVICE MAGIC

SERVICE MAGIC
An unexpected experience with a touch of style, grace, and imagination the customer remembers with fondness and a smile.

SERVICE MAGIC
Creating an unexpected, unpredictable, and valuable experience that is both memorable and reproducible.

"Any sufficiently advanced technology is indistinguishable from magic."

ARTHUR C. CLARKE'S THIRD LAW

"Service Magic is the technology of wonder."

RON ZEMKE AND CHIP BELL

## CHAPTER ONE

The Art and Craft of the Stage Magician

Audience chatter quiets to a murmur as the houselights darken. Folds of velvet curtain become alternating pillars of crimson and night in the footlights' glow. As the house stills, a single bon-bon spotlight arcs to life and spills a magnesium circle on the stage apron. Its focus narrows to a tight beam. The pit band ends its air with a crisp flourish. The draperies part slightly. A tall thin man in white tie and elegant waistcoat, a majestic bejeweled turban atop his head, steps through the curtain. He bows from the waist and greets the audience: "Good evening, ladies and gentlemen. I am the Amazing Girabaldi. Welcome to our entertainment."

With no more introduction than that, his gloved right hand plucks a sealed pack of Bicycle™ playing cards from the air. He opens the pack, removes the cards, and spreads them with a flourish. After shuffling and spreading the deck several more times, the Amazing Girabaldi shifts the deck to his left hand and begins to pluck cards from the air with his right, much as if he were picking cherries from the branches of a tree. One, two, three—then, suddenly, the plucked cards change. In an instant, the fourth, fifth, and sixth turn into flowers. The next six cards snapped from the air are placed in a small velvet bag. After the last card is deposited, Girabaldi reaches into the bag and pulls out a dove, which immediately flies off into the theater, low over the heads of the audience. The assembly gasps and titters.

The spotlight widens and the curtain parts slightly, held open by two assistants in shimmering red evening gowns. Stagehands roll a glimmering stainless-steel cage forward, and withdraw behind the closing curtain. The orchestra begins a spirited air. A third assistant—in blue—joins the magician at the front of the cage. Girabaldi opens it, invites her to step in, closes, and locks the cage. From the rear of the cage, the other assistants quickly draw a blue drapery around its sides and hand the ends to the magician. Girabaldi fastens them in place, steps to the side, and signals to the conductor.

As the orchestra's tune fades to a single crescendoing drum roll, the Amazing Girabaldi leans toward the covered cage and makes a slow, dramatic, lifting gesture, as if willing the cage to rise from the stage. And it does! Slowly. Solidly. Without a waver. When it reaches shoulder height, Girabaldi makes a second gesture and the levitation stops. He draws a silver-plated revolver from inside his jacket, takes slow careful aim, and fires. The blue drapery falls away from the cage. The lovely assistant has vanished, replaced by a Bengal tiger that growls, paces, and eyes the audience reprovingly. The orchestra plays a fanfare as the cage descends to the stage, and the magician and his assistants bow to the applauding audience.

Watching a skilled magician at work is an exercise in awe. Try as we might to see through the sleight-of-hand and illusions taking place before our very eyes, we come away amused, amazed, and astonished. Where did those cards fly off to? Where did the dove come from? Where did the lady in the blue dress disappear to? Where did that tiger come from? How did the magician do all those amazing feats?

We know in our minds that there is a rational explanation. But in our hearts we aren't so sure. It makes us smile. It makes us shake our heads. It makes us wonder. And it leaves us with a feeling of enchantment that stays with us for a long time.

To the outsider, the professional magician is a person who must know something about physics and time and space and hidden drawers and gimmicks and secret pockets and trick cards and trained rabbits and collapsible balls and cups and glasses and hats and canes and craftily built boxes and closets and bags that aren't what they seem. That explains all, doesn't it?

Yes, everyone knows—or at least suspects—that there are mechanical devices and subtle betrayals of the senses at work in the magician's craft.

And it is true. But as important as clever physical aids are to a magician's performance, they are the lesser of what meets—and eludes—the eye.

The successful stage magician is versed in the art of practical psychology, human communication, and experience management. The magician's ability to relate to the audience—involve it in the magic and make it feel good about the surprises he brings to pass—is as important as the mechanics of the trick itself. Often the actual trick is quite humble compared to the impact of the performance. To accomplish what he does, to create those small acts of wonder and awe, the successful magician must master both the mechanics of his craft and the art of his performance.

The successful magician defines a stage persona, or professional personality, and creates or selects a bag of tricks to fit that image. Then—through hours and hours of practice—the magician masters both the mechanics of those tricks and illusions, and their presentation to an audience. Part of that preparation involves learning to match the right trick to the right audience. Another part involves positioning—doing his tricks and illusions in a way that awes and enchants his audience, fits the moment, and preserves the mystery. And part of that preparation involves subtly leading the audience to want the amazement to happen and to suspend its disbelief in magic itself.

THE MAGIC OF CUSTOMER ENCHANTMENT

The creation of memorable, positive customer service—service so good, so unique, so different, that it takes the customer by surprise and leaves him with a smile on his face and a story to tell—is often strikingly parallel in structure and outcome to fine stage magic. Just as the skilled stage magician is a master of audience enchantment, the service magician brings a touch of charm and delight to his or her customer's day, life, and world . . . even if just for a moment.

Service Magic, like stage magic, is a set of learned skills developed through desire and mastered through thought and determination. Service Magic separates the food carrier from the professional waiter or waitress who has a devoted clientele. Service Magic separates the hair cutter from the personal stylist with an avid following. Service Magic distinguishes the personal advisor from the forgettable, plain vanilla service rep.

The service magician seeks to delight, to be remembered as special, and to stand apart in the crowded room of those who only serve through necessity. The service magician takes pleasure in the pleasure of others and in the practice of skillful service. Making the difficult appear easy draws applause for the stage magician, and gratitude for the service magician. Doing the seemingly impossible and unlikely creates wonder and respect in both audiences.

Practitioners of Service Magic, like practitioners of stage magic, understand that the art of enchantment is more, much more, than a pocket full of tricks and a velvet bag of illusions. Both stage magician and service magician depend on rapport, communication, credibility, and trust. Both understand timing, presentation, and situation. And both understand and bow to the necessities of practice, perfection, and the continuous refreshment of their art. Both take pride in their special calling.

This book explores the amazing parallels between the art and skill of stage magic and the art and skill of Service Magic. Along the way we point out the unique and compelling aspects of stage magic that, when adapted to the world of service, add the same qualities to the service magician's act.

Service Magic is the art and craft of creating awe and wonder for the customer where and whenever possible. Service Magic is about creating pleasant surprises for customers weary of and resigned to bland, mundane, and impersonal service.

Consider this example: While on assignment in Seattle, Fran Sims, a St. Petersburg, Florida–based consultant, bought a bathing suit from Nordstrom's downtown flagship store. The sales rep bagged the suit and graciously accepted Sims' out-of-state check for payment—itself no small indicator of service sensitivity.

When Sims returned to her hotel room, she found a message. The Nordstrom rep had inadvertently left one of the swim suit straps out of Sims' bag and wanted to personally deliver it to her hotel. Sims asked how the rep had tracked her down.

"You remember I asked you to write the name of your company on the back of your check?" the rep asked. "I called Florida information to get your company's phone number, called it, and asked where you were staying in town." Sims thanked the rep and said she could just leave the strap at her hotel's front desk. The rep insisted that since she was responsible for leaving the strap out of the bag, personal delivery was the least she could do.

This attentive service was unexpected. The way it was delivered was certainly unpredictable. Yet it absolutely met the customer's need—and had value in the customer's eyes. And best of all it was warmly and positively memorable.

The stuff of Service Magic, which we define as:

Acts of Customer Care That Are:

- Unexpected
- Unpredictable
- Valuable
- Memorable
- Reproducible

SERVICE MAGIC VERSUS ALL THOSE OTHER THINGS

Finding ways to enchant, enthrall, and otherwise distinguish one's organization—and bring the customer back again through that distinction—is a quest that has occupied the thoughts of more than two decades of marketing researchers and operations managers. Hundreds of thousands of frontline customer service and salespeople have labored to put those ideas to the benefit of their customers.

Three well-researched approaches to pleasing customers and creating customer loyalty have particular relevance to our discussion: the R.A.T.E.R. factor view of customer satisfaction, delight management, and trust building.

According to research conducted by Leonard Berry, A. Parasuraman, and Valarie Zeithaml, the five R.A.T.E.R. factors predict customers' purchasing loyalty and willingness to recommend the company to others.[1]

Berry characterizes his findings as persuasive evidence that "Customer expectations of service organizations are clear: Look good, be responsive, be reassuring through courtesy and competence, be empathetic—but most of all, do what you said you would do. Keep the service promise."

Dozens of Ph.D. and masters' theses and several years of field application have proven these factors to be very robust indeed. As a practical matter, they are the basic pillars of customer satisfaction. They form the core content of many customer satisfaction survey systems and more than a few customer service training programs.[2]

The idea of creating "customer delight"—going beyond satisfaction—has developed a significant fan following, while the exact meaning and

The R.A.T.E.R. Factors

Reliability	The ability to provide what was promised, dependably and accurately
Assurance	Knowledge and courtesy of employees, and their ability to convey trust and confidence
Tangibles	The physical facilities and equipment, and appearance of personnel
Empathy	The degree of caring and individual attention provided to customers
Responsiveness	The willingness to help customers and provide prompt service

topography of "delight" has been elusive. In their book *The Customer Delight Principle,* Timothy Keiningham and Terry Vavra offer this definition: "Exceeding all base expectations in the performance of a product or delivery of a service (or in the servicing that accompanies a product or service)."[3] They go on to illustrate delight as part of a beyond specific expectations step in a continuum—a higher order expectation.

While Keiningham and Vavra's treatise is suggestive, it isn't specific enough for most practitioners. Further research, conducted by John Goodman of TARP, an Arlington, Virginia, customer-service research firm, uncovered the actions that lead to "delight" experiences for customers and determined the value of creating those experiences. TARP's self-report critical-incident study of 1,000 financial service customers revealed (1) what behaviors delighted customers, and (2) what effect their delight had on loyalty.

To Goodman's surprise, three very mundane classes of behavior were reported as "delightful" and as having high impact on customer retention: "consistently good service," "proactively provided information," and "tell(s) me of a new opportunity." In other words, these customers said they were "delighted" when service providers consistently

**Examples of the Range of Expectations
When Checking into a Hotel**

- *Could*   recognize me as a previous guest and thank me for returning, offering a courtesy upgrade to show appreciation.

- *Should*   have my reservation at hand, recognizing my frequent guest status and providing the accommodations I requested.

- *Will*   have a room available with the accommodations I've requested.

- *Better not*   be oversold and either send me to another hotel or offer me a substandard room.

did what they said they would, when they regularly communicated with customers, and when customers were offered something new.

These two studies make it clear that satisfaction and even delight aren't prodigious accomplishments. But there is more to the customer-retention puzzle. Research by Robert Peterson of the University of Texas strongly suggests that satisfaction, even with that "plus a little more" of delight, isn't enough for long-term customer loyalty.[4] That requires a higher level of performance. Peterson describes that highest level as an emotional connection between the service deliverers and the delighted customer who voluntarily tells love stories about those who serve. That extreme level of satisfaction-plus is what Christopher Hart, president of the Boston-based Spire Group, calls customer trust.[5] And we certainly have seen that trust is a precursor for the sort of joint risk-taking necessary for customers and servers to move beyond simple, mundane satisfaction.

We believe that customer trust, love, delight, and satisfaction all play an important role in keeping customers coming back.[6] Of course, if the customer's basic expectations of a product or service aren't being met, the customer won't be satisfied or delighted or willing to trust. But once the customer's basic needs and expectations are met, once there is a trusting and competent relationship between server and served, that is where Service Magic serves a purpose. It takes a little magic to keep the relationship intriguing, surprising, and enchanting—and the customer not just coming back, but happily coming back.

WHAT SERVICE MAGIC IS NOT

If customers consider a "blow-your-mind" act of service to be pure happenstance or fluke, it's not Service Magic. While customers may be truly awed by an experience, they will not return for another "show" if they think it is simply serendipity. And customer loyalty is an important by-product of Service Magic.

Service Magic does not depend on an extravagant gesture. While there may be the occasional over-the-top component to Service Magic, that's not what leaves the customer enchanted. Nordstrom didn't need to throw in a $100 gift certificate with the bathing suit strap to awe Fran Sims. In fact, it would have detracted from the uniqueness of the experience. Service Magic is the manifestation of ingenuity, not excess.

Service Magic is not a complex set of practices. Its power lies in its simplicity. But that simplicity comes from a skillful and thoughtful application of resourcefulness. Service Magic can occur by accident, but it takes competence to repeat it "show" after "show."

Service Magic is confident, not boastful or arrogant. The Nordstrom clerk insisted on delivering the swim suit strap because she assumed personal responsibility for Sims' experience, not because she believed she was the only person who could perform this service. Successful service magicians, like successful stage magicians, leave a customer charmed by the experience rather than astounded by their distinctive stage presence.

Service Magic is not a pseudonym for good, value-added customer service. Ask customers what actions they consider value added, and they will focus on taking the expected experience to the next step—"they gave me *more* than I anticipated." Value added is a predictable linear response—the upgrade, the extra helping, the complimentary dessert, or the baker's dozen. Service Magic is unpredictable and unique. It's the response that leaves you more amazed than simply delighted, more awed than wowed. When you are left thinking, "I wouldn't have thought of that," you have probably witnessed Service Magic. Bottom line, Service Magic is service with imagination more than service with generosity.

THE SERVICE MAGIC PLAYING FIELD

Service Magic has a context: It takes place somewhere, somehow, and is done by someone. These are the Three Ps of Service Magic: Place, Process, and Performance.

Place Magic is associated both with naturally occurring magical places like Yosemite National Park or the Grand Canyon, and with man-made places of magic like a thrilling theme park or a special restaurant or simply a place that has a special meaning for a single customer. The service magician can enhance this quality when he or she knows the rules of Place Magic.

Process Magic is simply the way things are done—the processes, pro-cedures—even the rules of conduct—for serving the customer. There are rules as well for making the process of being served—and serving—a little more magical.

Performance Magic is the live, face-to-face—even phone-to-ear—serving of a customer in a way the customer finds surprising, memo-rable, and positive. Here also are rules and tools for the service magician to learn and follow to create a little magic for his or her customers.

We will look at each of these magics in depth shortly. But first we will examine the tricks and techniques the magician employs to enter-tain and awe an audience—tricks and techniques that are equally ap-plicable to the creation of Service Magic. We call this The Service Magic Method™. Next, we open that box, and reveal all.

## CHAPTER TWO

The Service Magic Method™

An Architecture for Practical Amazement

A METAPHOR FOR A METAPHOR

For 25 years, Karl was the chief engineer of Smallville Power. A buy-out by Allpower Consolidated brought new management, new ideas, and early retirement for Karl. The following spring, Smallville's largest turbine ground to a halt and stubbornly refused the ministrations of Allpower's engineering SWAT team. In desperation, Karl was called in to consult. After a few minutes of careful consideration he went to the tool room, selected a small hammer, walked to the malfunctioning turbine, and gave a large bolt in the base three firm taps. Seconds later, the balking machine coughed twice and whirred to life.

The next day Karl delivered a handwritten bill to Allpower's local manager.

> Repair to #7 Turbine $1,500.00

The plant manager was incredulous. "Fifteen hundred dollars? All you did was tap the turbine three times with a hammer. That's ridiculous! I need an itemization for that kind of money." Without hesitation Karl went to the manager's desktop, typed up a new invoice, and pushed print:

Consultation Invoice

Tapping #7 Turbine 3 times with
number 2 ball peen hammer . . . . $ 1.00
Knowing where to tap #7 Turbine
3 times with number 2 ball peen
hammer $1,499.00
Total $1,500.00

Practicing Service Magic is adding a little surprise, charm, or enchantment to a perfectly competent, but mundane and forgettable service experience. It is very often a matter of knowing where, when, and how to do those small but brilliant acts that can make all the difference in the customer's eyes. On one level, Service Magic is about taking carefully constructed, competently delivered services and service transactions, and adding some zest, color, and memorability to them—knowing just where a small tap will reap big results.

But make no mistake, Service Magic is not about tricking customers into seeing value where none exists, or appreciating differentiation that is inconsequential. Service Magic is not a marketing "gimmick." Service Magic is not manipulation, exploitation, or sophisticated con artistry. Service Magic is about finding unusual and unexpected ways to add value to a customer's experience with your organization. Service Magic is about creating enchantment through little differences in performance that make big differences in the customer's eyes. The Service Magic Method is a technology and a set of tools derived in part from the art and science of stage magic, and in part from the art and science of service management.[1,2]

THE MAGICAL TWO-STEP

The Service Magic Method is a two-step process—two very large steps.

Step 1: Opportunity Quest

Customers can come into contact with your organization in many ways. Seeing your advertising, calling your offices, buying your products, or engaging your services are obvious. But seeing your equipment on the street, observing your sponsorship of a community event, and even word-of-mouth are ways your organization can also be brought to the customer's mind.

All of these touch points are *potential* points of impact. They are opportunities for the customer to observe, assess, and evaluate your company and your service. These *points of impact,* instances in which the customer comes into contact with your organization, are *moments of truth.* We have developed an opportunity assessment system that includes the Cycle of Service Mapping™ and the Moment of Truth Impact Assessment™ (described in detail in Appendix A). This process for blueprinting customer experiences with an organization is one of several that have been used extensively for purposes ranging from developing strategy to establishing standards.

The cycles of service and moments of truth approach can help you document and dissect your service delivery, and search out opportunities for adding magic. Regardless of the type of scan or assessment or audit you use, we recommend adopting an approach that will help you identify those points of opportunity where a little magic can make a big difference to your customers. These points of opportunity should meet one or more of the four following criteria:

1. This point of contact is necessary and important, but lacks any distinguishing attributes. Checking into an establishment (hotel, restaurant, resort, hospital, etc.), demonstrating qualifications, producing credentials, placing an order, listening to instructions, and trying out or trying on a product are examples of the *necessary but undistinguished routine.*

2. This point of contact or frequent experience is perceived as unappealing, if not annoying. Waiting in line, being kept on hold, being sent to a waiting area for extensive periods, experiencing complex and/or slow decision making, answering the same questions several times during the same visit, experiencing a slow download time, and having to sort through the same long menu of choices with each call are typical customer experiences that fall into the category of the *annoying or unappealing contact.*

3. This process, procedure, or experience can and frequently does go somewhat—but not critically—astray for the customer: getting lost, misreading or misunderstanding an instruction or procedure, ignoring or missing a step, and encountering a situation that is vague and easily misinterpreted. Think of them as

processes or experiences that are aggravating or out of "spec"—like getting lost trying to find the radiology department of the hospital or clinic during your annual physical—but that aren't bad enough to prompt a move to another physician. Characterize these as *creaky operations* or *perilous processes*.

4. The procedure or process already has a value-adding feature that has become undistinguished because so many competitors perform the same function the same way. When airline pilots began thanking customers for their business over the in-plane address system, then stood in the cockpit doorway to thank them again as they deplaned—both gestures were novel and noteworthy. After the majority of airlines adopted first one and then the other of these practices, the original value-adding performance became an *undistinguished* or *value neutral add-on*.

It is also important to know where and when to avoid the impulse to add magic to your organization's customer service act. Steer clear of changes in situations that meet these four criteria:

1. When custom and propriety would be dislocated or disturbed adversely by the change. The jazz band procession is a proud tradition of New Orleans funerals. Perfectly wonderful. Perfectly acceptable in context. The same experience would be incompatible and unacceptable transported to an Amish funeral in Bucks County, Pennsylvania.

2. When customers would view the change as peculiar or puzzling rather than pleasing and endearing. A nature center or arboretum guide could don red nose and clown face, but guest perception would likely be one of puzzlement. The costuming doesn't fit the setting, nor does the performance expectation of someone in a clown costume match the acceptable performance parameters for a day spent communing with nature.

3. When safety and welfare could appear compromised. The old M.A.S.H. television series not withstanding, doctors and nurses in Halloween costumes addressing patients in sideshow patter are more likely to put off than put at ease. Don't joke around or attempt cuteness where life and limb—and purse strings—are perceived to be at stake.

4. When the delivery system is unequivocally and obviously broken. No amount of magic and pizzazz can make up for non-

performance. The automobile service operation that fails to fix problems gains nothing—save perhaps increased enmity—by adding a gourmet coffee bar and a flat-screen television to the waiting area.

Step 2: Matching Technique to Opportunity

Magic is composed of tricks and illusions—what magicians do to amaze and amuse us. Those tricks and illusions are composed of techniques—what the magician does to make the tricks work. Some of those techniques take advantage of basic facts of nature: the way gravity and electricity work; how numbers behave when they are added, subtracted, multiplied, or divided; and the psychology of perception and misperception. The magician's crafts take advantage of the very natural way humans create patterns in their minds, make choices, and fill in missing information based on their experience.

Other techniques of the magician are the result of carefully practiced skills. The ability to manipulate coins or balls or cards without looking at them or drawing the audience's attention to the manipulations are important skills in the art of the magician. Body control, the ability to move about the stage, and chat amiably with the audience while performing a difficult manipulation, and the ability to plant objects on volunteers and remove them at will are equally important in creating mystifying effects and stunning illusions.

The world of magic, like so many trades and crafts, has an extensive body of language, concepts and ideas, tools and techniques—many of them overlapping. Tricks, for example, are also referred to as "effects" and "illusions." A trick that has gone awry is referred to as having "flashed" or "talked" or been too "busy" or having "busted." Among the hundreds of items in the magician's bag of techniques, three have a direct corollary to the creation of Service Magic: (mis)direction, pattern interruption, and force.

You will see these techniques used and referenced throughout the book in a variety of ways. As you read the various applications in the context of Place, Process, and Performance Magic, you'll come—as we have—to appreciate their power. Here they are defined and illustrated in their most straightforward and simplest form.

(Mis)direction. Misdirection—or direction if you prefer—is the art of establishing a frame of reference or stating a premise that occupies audience attention while something completely different is happening. Misdirection is a fundamental of magic: the magician who gestures and looks off to the left or right of the audience is almost always moving the audience's attention to where the trick is not happening—to be precise—away from where the effect is subtly being set up or staged.

Misdirection in everyday life is a frequent phenomenon, although—of course—we usually don't notice it. The nurse asks about the patient's weekend while giving a flu shot; the bellman calls the guest's attention to a beautiful plant or painting opposite the site of new construction; the dentist chitchats about his latest ski trip or the weather while the patient has a mouth full of stainless steel and goo—all are instances of misdirection. We even practice misdirection on ourselves. Listening to the radio while mowing the lawn or turning on the television while paying bills are ways of distracting ourselves or redirecting our own attention.

Francie Johnsen is a pharmacist in an Eckerd Drug Store in Dallas. She is also a master of redirection. When a familiar customer chooses to wait for a prescription, Francie has, for instance, been known to put a customer to work: "Nancy," she asks, "can you do me a big favor? My nephew's birthday is coming up in a couple of days and I haven't had time to find him a card. Would you mind picking out a cute card for him? I'll pay for it before I leave the store tonight." A simple, but flattering and effective, misdirection.

Pattern interruption. Also referred to as pattern alteration or "breaking set," pattern interruption is based on a simple psychological principle: Humans are perpetually and automatically in search of patterns to make sense out of what they see and experience. Reinforce a pattern so the person is confident with it, then alter that pattern, and you have the basis for insight, humor . . . and magic. Groucho Marx was a master of the art: "Next to a dog, a book is man's best friend. Inside a dog, a book is next to impossible to read."

Two-card monte is a simple but well-known trick that relies on pattern interruption. It begins with two supposedly "normal" playing cards: one held face up, the other face down in the magician's hand. The magician turns his hand 180 degrees to reveal the other sides and to "show" that they are indeed two cards—for instance, a three of clubs and a queen of diamonds. The cards are returned to their start positions, the "up" card is separated and moved away from the viewer's line of sight—held under table edge or simply palmed. The viewer is now looking at the back of the "down" card, and assumes it is the opposite card of the removed card. The magician asks the person to name the "down" card. Since the viewer saw the three of clubs moved away, he names the queen of diamonds. The magician brings back the removed card and reveals that it is the queen of diamonds. The magician usually repeats the effect several times and each time the viewer's guess is wrong.

The magician is relying on the viewer's misperception that the cards in use are two normal playing cards. In fact, one card has two faces and the other has two backs. The "trick" works because of a misperception of what is being shown and the assumptions that follow—and a little verbal adroitness on the performer's part.

Pattern interruption in Service Magic is not a shifty ploy or an attempt to dupe or confuse the customer. In fact, pattern interruption is a routine part of our lives. Pattern interruption is at play, for instance, when we successfully stage a surprise party, or when we are delighted by the speed or ease with which a customer service rep fixes a problem we thought would be a hassle or lead to a confrontation.

Pattern interruption was at play on the automated call forwarding system of a bank we recently called. The recorded voice was bankerly formal and professional. "For new accounts press 1. For information press 2. . . ." And so on—until the very end of the menu where a little pattern interruption was lurking. "If you'd like to hear a duck quack, press 7." And sure enough, there was a duck quack at that address. According to an official of the bank, the duck quack option was selected more than 1,000 times a day when first added to the otherwise easily forgettable menu.

Force. Force is a technique in which an audience member is offered what seems to be a fair and free choice (like a playing card), but in reality the magician has predetermined the outcome. Force can be programmed or guided.

A programmed force is one in which the spectator is seemingly given a choice but some factor strongly tilts the choice in a predetermined direction. There are riddles that rely on a quirk of arithmetic that guarantees the teller of the riddle will seem clairvoyant. Programmed forces are used in the service world in a number of ways. An angry customer calls a company and gets the call center. "Let me immediately speak to the manager," he demands. The call center rep uses a programmed "force" and responds with, "Certainly, sir, what seems to be the problem?" In the great majority of the cases, the customer will vent to the rep as if he just got his wish and is speaking with the manager.

Guided force is indirect or subtle influencing of the outcome. The magician says words that entice the audience member to make the choice the magician has predetermined. Similarly, when a restaurant hostess asks a customer, "Would you prefer a table near the entrance or a table by the window where you will be able to watch the fireworks as you enjoy dessert?" she is guiding the choice. She is making the window table seem a special treat. Had she no window tables available and only a table near the entrance, she might say, "I have a very nice table where you can see all the action."

MANAGING SERVICE MAGIC

Although not techniques in the same sense as the above examples, five performance and audience management tools play a major role in stage magic—and in Service Magic.

Inclusion. Audience members are more than observers of magic acts—the stage magician makes them part of the action through volunteers. The volunteer who steps up on stage vicariously represents every individual in the audience. Inclusion doesn't require personal, active participation from everyone in the audience—it's a state of mind that engages observers in the experience. The audience watches, enthralled, as the magician plucks flowers or coins or cards from the volunteer's person, and wonders "How would I react were I on stage?"

Magicians use inclusion as a tool to form an emotional connection with the audience—as if they are all fellow travelers along the road to enchantment. In the words of illusionist Jeff McBride, "A good magician does not say, 'I'm a magician and you're not.' A good magician says, 'I'm a magician—and you are too.'"

Inclusion is based on the psychological principle of reciprocity—a person will give to you if you give to him. And what might be the payoff for the volunteer? It could be as simple as a good story to share with friends, attention, or the fun of being in on a secret.

A hotel in San Antonio, Texas, used inclusion to cope with an unexpected service predicament. A hand-printed sign in the lobby explained the situation to customers: "Dear guests: We need your help. The aunt of one of our housekeepers passed away and today is her funeral. Since the aunt was a special person in our housekeeper's life, we all felt we should be at the funeral. Consequently, there will only be one employee on site . . . at the front desk . . . between 2 and 3:30 PM. We appreciate your understanding. Thanks!" Guests served other guests coffee in the lobby cafe. Guests greeted arriving guests and explained the situation to them. Everyone demonstrated great patience and tolerance. Inclusion created a touch of magic and sense of camaraderie that even carried over to the following day.

Personalization. In the world of stage magic, personalization can be the second part of a one-two move—first include, then personalize. The magician uses inclusion when inviting a volunteer to join him on stage and then personalizing the encounter with "May I ask your name, sir?" Then the magician invites the volunteer to get more personal. "And where are you from, George?" The magician is, in effect, introducing the volunteer to the audience, personalizing the experience by making him an acquaintance of all.

Personalized service is particularly powerful today because of its contrast with the pervasive "one size fits all" standard so many organizations rely on. Still, personalization is not innately magical. Customers of Amazon.com log on to the Web site to find a screen containing their name and a collection of new books that fit their unique buying patterns. Is it delightful? It is for most customers. Is it magical? Not after the first few times. Personalization is magical only when it is unexpected.

As it was in this situation: A customer traded in an older model car for a new one. A week after owning the car, she turned on the radio for the first time to discover the dealership had programmed the radio stations from her old car's radio into the new one. That bit of unexpected and thoughtful personalization created a small thrill of magic for this customer.

Patter. Patter is the story the magician tells and the words he uses while performing a trick. The story or patter ties the trick to the observer's personal experience in some way. "Patter gives the trick a meaningful place in the magician's show and in the spectators' daily lives," observes Robert Stebbins, a social psychologist who studied the work of magicians. "The trick may actually be impossible to do without patter, in that the patter justifies the bodily movements and positions, shielding the magician's maneuvers."[3] After learning a new trick, magicians decide upon some catchy patter to go with it. Most often it is outlined, rather than scripted, allowing the magician to extemporize between points.

Patter works with misdirection to enhance its impact. The magician directs a volunteer to select a card. Then, as if absentminded, he asks the volunteer, "Now tell me again where you're from, Mary." The audience attends to the conversation, not to the magician manipulating the deck of cards to make certain Mary's chosen card is on top.

Patter should have relevance. It is not idle chatter to fill air space. While a magician performs the familiar rope trick (in which three seemingly unequal lengths of rope are made to appear first as the same length and then as one rope), his patter might relate how problems in life come in different sizes. Working up to the finale, where the lengths of rope become one piece, his patter unfolds in parallel, ending with ". . . if we all work as one."

Patter adds allure and intrigue to a service experience. Most guests on the Jungle Cruise attraction at Walt Disney World know the tour guide at the helm is neither driving the boat (it travels on an underwater track) nor really shocked as crocodiles suddenly rise from the river bottom. But the magical ride would not be the same without the guide delivering the carefully crafted script that reinforces the drama of the experience.

Using confederates. A confederate is a helper the audience does not suspect. It may be an audience member whom the magician has briefed before the show or a member of the magician's staff. Regardless, the confederate is the person who enables the magic to work and amplifies the enchantment.

A doorman at the Ritz-Carlton Buckhead in Atlanta not long ago used a guest as a confederate to choreograph a bit of magic. The guest had arranged to meet his wife at the hotel. He had flown and she was driving. He had already checked in and stood in the lobby, waiting for her to arrive, and passed the time chitchatting with the doorman.

Eventually, the doorman asked, "You're pretty excited about her coming in?" The traveler acknowledged that he was. "May I ask her favorite drink?" the doorman asked. "Ice cold Absolut with extra lime," he replied.

"Why don't we surprise her?" suggested this service magician, making the guest a confederate in an impromptu trick. "I'll go get her a drink from the bar. I'll put it on a silver tray, and I'll go out and serve it to her as soon as she pulls in. You just let me know which car is hers when she pulls up out front." Five minutes later, the traveler's wife drove up. As she stepped from her car, the doorman was in front of her, proffering the drink on a silver tray, addressing her by name, and saying, "I believe you're looking for this. . . . oh, and your husband is waiting for you in the lobby. Have a great weekend."

Outs or escapes. All good magicians have "outs" for their magic. Outs give magicians an escape route when something goes amiss: "I forgot to take into account the rotational force of the earth." Or "That's strange; it worked at the magic store." Magicians also use these alternatives to tailor the act for the audience. At a magic show in New York, for example, the first two rows of the theatre audience got up to leave as the magician was completing a trick. The clever magician built their sudden exit into his patter: Instead of moving to his next trick, he informed the audience that the first two rows had been completely empty when the show started. The newly materialized people leaving were members of his pit orchestra and were departing to rehearse for the next show. His repartee left the audience delighted, and the departing patrons regretful they were going somewhere less charming.

Service magicians use escapes or outs in two ways: as a part of *magical service recovery* and as alternatives that tailor the magic to the audience. Escapes for recovery are the worked-out-in-advance ways to turn temporary disdain into long-term delight. The waiter who proffers a complimentary dessert when a diner's entrée disappointed is using an escape, as is the front desk clerk who upgrades a late-arriving guest to a suite when the guest's requested corner room is unavailable. (Magical Service Recovery will be covered in detail in Chapter 11.) Service Magic matched to audience—the drive-up bank teller who provides a free lollipop if Junior is along or a free treat if Fido is on board—is also a pre-planned out.

Outs give service magicians a sense of security. When customers are irate, when service is unfolding differently than expected, service magicians need confidence—and planned recovery "outs" can bolster their confidence. Planned outs also can help service magicians retain focus during monotonous routine service. If they have several alternatives for the same service encounter, selecting the best approach requires attentiveness and creativity—both helpful tools for keeping service magicians "on their game."

The Service Magic Method will help build customer amazement into the service you provide—no matter how mundane it might be, you can make it magical. Use the opportunity assessment system in Appendix A to identify the points of contact or Moments of Truth amenable to magic. Apply the magician's tools and techniques to your brand of service. Don your spangled costume, grab your magic cane, hop up on stage, and get ready to amaze your customers.

## CHAPTER THREE

Place, Process, Performance

The Three Ps of Service Magic

There is a feeling of awe and wonder, of pleasure and delight in Service Magic. When it is present, the customer perceives that something special and unique has been done to, for, or with him or her. It can come from a word spoken, an experience observed, a process experienced, or the context in which the service occurred. And while many customers simply evaluate an encounter with your organization as "acceptable" or "disappointing" or "marvelous," it is the components of the "marvelous" experience that can lead to a level and style of service your customers will describe as "magical."

There is magic in Place, Process, and Performance—and all three are available to the skilled service magician and the organization determined to create consistent Service Magic for its customers:

- *Place Magic* is a venue—natural or manmade—with physical attributes that attract and please, and that are subtly enhanced by human endeavor. We vacation at national parks to enjoy the great out-of-doors and visit theme parks for fun and thrills. And we remember most the vistas and the rides, but without a little Service Magic, those pleasures would be greatly diminished, mundane, or nonexistent.

- *Process Magic* is the often thankless, almost always invisible effort that makes the difference between policies, procedures, and routines that are difficult, confusing, maddening, and frustrating—and those we experience as surprisingly easy, positive, and memorable. No waiting where once lines were long; sign-ins, sign-ups, and renewals that are hassle-free and even interesting—if not fun—are the result of a little well placed Process Magic.

- *Performance Magic* is at work in the surprisingly positive interaction with someone from an organization during the acquisition of a service or product—or even when a problem with a product or service is being resolved. The waitperson who makes the dining experience "work" for you by correctly reading your mood and engaging you in light-hearted banter or by leaving you to your solitude is a card-carrying, practicing, professional service magician.

Each of these three "magics" is powered by a set of principles. The rules of carpentry and construction create palaces and houses—not symphonies and sonatas. Yet the combined efforts of carpenter and composer can create magnificent concert halls where the composer's symphonies and sonatas, under a skilled maestro's baton, sound their very best and form a memorable, magical experience for the concert goer.

Metaphorically, the service magician knows when and where to apply the rules of carpentry, and when and where to apply the rules of musical composition and performance—and how to make them work together to create an unforgettable evening. Place, Process, and Performance must be harmonious for maximum impact on the customer's perception of the experience you are delivering.

THE MAGIC OF PLACE

A cocktail served at sunset on the veranda of a Maui restaurant overlooking a tranquil bay is as magical and memorable as a cold sandwich from room service on a chilly rainy night in Seattle is forgettable. Newlyweds sailing the Maid of the Mist through the moist veils at the foot of Niagara Falls, a family watching the sun set behind the western wall of the Grand Canyon, and a father and son sharing a ball game at Wrigley Field are experiencing the magic of place. That special feel to special places is Place Magic: the hip intimacy of a Hotel Monaco, the swank luxury of the Ritz-Carlton Laguna Nigel, the rustic rightness of the Old Faithful Inn.

The service magician's role as supporting cast and elucidator of the experience is a subtle but critical adjunct to Place Magic. The waiter who slides smoothly on and off the stage, honoring the quiet ambiance of the softly fading sun and tranquil sea is unobtrusively supportive of the Maui restaurant's magic. The Wrigley Field grandstand peanut vendor who whistles, shouts, and lofts bags of hot goobers to waiting fans ten rows away is a critical part of the "take me out to the ball game" ambiance. Each set of actors and actions adds its own unique texture to Place Magic and helps complete the experience for the customer.

Place Times Three

Place Magic has three faces: natural, constructed, and virtual. Nature's Place Magic is intrinsic to those wonders of the physical world that thrill and awe us by simply existing. The Grand Canyon, Yellowstone National Park, Victoria Falls, Mt. Kilimanjaro, the Amazon River, and a thousand other large and small wonders of the world—the stuff of National Geographic specials—create magic through their natural grandeur. Our primary memories of these places will always be of the magic of the natural wonders themselves. Just the same, our experience of Place Magic is subtly—but measurably—enhanced by skillful service magicians.

A Fort Lauderdale, Florida, couple celebrating their 25th wedding anniversary selects Burt and Jack's, a local restaurant with a wonderful view of Port Everglades for this very personal, intimate event. The husband calls many days in advance and requests a 7:45 PM reservation— and casually mentions the special occasion the dinner will commemorate. The hostess suggests an earlier reservation—7 PM—when "a very good, waterside table will be available." Not mentioned, but well understood by the hostess, is the fact that sunset on the date in question will be waning at 7:45 PM, but will be a spectacular sight at 7:15 PM. The service magician's role as supporting cast is often such a subtle, but critical, adjunct to the enjoyment of natural Place Magic. Some things can, of course, detract from the enjoyment of natural wonders: a traffic jam in Yosemite or Yellowstone or the roar of dune buggies in the Mojave can override the natural splendor the visitor anticipated. A fly fishing outing along a pristine Montana trout stream can be diminished by the presence of trash or an encounter with a pack of inebriated revelers with rowdiness rather than fishing and the Isaac Walton experience on their minds. Likewise, a table of loud-mouthed partiers can ruin that Maui sunset or that Fort Lauderdale anniversary dinner. An important behind-the-scenes role for the service magician is to seek out and prevent as many

potential experience detractors as possible. That balancing and blending is key to creating consistent Place Magic and showing off the main
attraction at its best.

Manmade or constructed Place Magic comes in a greater variety
than does nature's Place Magic. The skylines of New York, Paris, Rome,
São Paulo, and a dozen other cities—viewed from an observation deck,
scenic overlook, a city central park, or a fine restaurant in the sky—are
breathtaking and memorable. A sunrise view of the Taj Mahal from the
far end of its reflecting pool, the pyramids of Egypt from the Sheraton
Royal Gardens Hotel, a Nile River dinner cruise, the Eiffel Tower at midnight from a floating bistro on the Seine are magic moments at man-
made wonders of the world that have memory-making qualities as awe
inspiring as the greatest of natural wonders. And here, too, the work of
the service magician can make an important difference.

Few manmade places are palaces, castles, or world icons. But the
most mundane can also be magical. There are hotels and grocery stores
and retailers and automobile dealerships and hospitals and dental offices that stand above others and sparkle—just a little magically.

"A visit to the dentist." Hardly words you would associate with "a
wonderful experience." Yet that is exactly how Phyllis Jones describes
her first encounter with Wayzata Dental, a 54-year-old, 20-person dental
clinic in Wayzata, Minnesota. And well she should. Since 1999, when
John Poage, DDS, decided to transform the practice founded by his
father-in-law, Wayzata Dental has worked to become a leader in cus-
tomer-centered dentistry.[1]

Though a successful practice by any measure, Poage wanted Wayzata
Dental to be "first class in technology, first class in customer service, and
a great place for talented people to work." He began with a complete
physical overhaul, hiring experts in dental office design to create a
highly efficient, high-tech, and customer-pleasing environment. "He
challenged us to make Wayzata Dental the Nordstrom of dentistry," says
Brian Denn, the clinic's operations manager.

They succeeded. The reception area—not waiting room—is reminiscent of the commons area on the concierge level at a Ritz-Carlton or
Peabody hotel. Three television options (listened to via headset), video
games, a virtual aquarium, and a refreshment bar complete the anti-
dentist-office feel. "Concierge," by the way, is exactly the attitude Poage
wants clients to experience. "People should feel attended to and comfortable here," he says.

Traffic flow moves guests—not patients—in a circular pattern from
reception through the treatment areas, to a separate "checkout" area
that allows for maximum confidentiality and undivided attention at

every step. The nine operatory suites—where the actual dental work gets done—are a high-tech marvel. Patient records are all online. X-rays are stored digitally as soon as they are taken—reducing radiation exposure and development time. Flat screens in each treatment area can flash up enlarged color X-rays for patient-dentist consultation. The same screens can display images from an intra-oral camera that allows the dentist or hygienist to show the client what he or she is looking at real time, or to demonstrate a proposed procedure.

In a separate area of the clinic, designated the "Smile Spa," clients can have their teeth whitened using the Lasik's BriteSmile™ system while receiving a massage, resting on a heated neck pillow, or taking a mini-vacation via video glasses. Creating "a smile to last a lifetime" is an important theme at Wayzata Dental, explains Nancy Carnes, clinical director. Accordingly, the clinic co-sponsors bridal galas and other events where the value of a smile—Carnes refers to it as "the joy of smiling"—can be showcased.

Beyond the technology and in-office amenities is a dedication to patient comfort, convenience, and well-being. Carnes spends much of her time making sure that customer experience exceeds customer expectations. "We constantly work on making the little things work right for our guests. For instance, the doctors do follow-up calls to guests who have had a particularly difficult procedure. We make sure every guest has the doctor's business card, which includes the doctor's home phone number. There is a consultation area where the doctors can take our guests and discuss treatment in detail if it is going to be complicated or take several visits. We don't think lying on your back with your mouth wide open is very good for communication or decision making," says Carnes.

Poage's experiment in patient-centered dentistry paid off well. In the six months after the transformation began, there was a 72 percent increase in business. Subsequent growth has been a remarkable and steady 30 percent a month.

Virtual Place

Place is not always a physical location. Not since the World Wide Web made Internet commerce and communication a reality. As many would-be dot-com entrepreneurs have learned the hard way, there is more to online success than simply opening up a portal, giving it a memorable name, buying a database, and lining up some products.

A successful e-organization must have a presence, a story, and a sense of the experience—and magic—it wants to create for the customer.

Walk into the Godiva shop in Water Tower Place shopping center on Chicago's Michigan Avenue and you know you've entered a special space. With your first breath you inhale the rich, decadent smell of chocolate. The curved golden walls, art nouveau design, and elegant display of chocolates all work in concert to say, "Come in," "Browse," "Take something home." You know you aren't just buying candy—you are experiencing Godiva.

Click to Godiva.com and you know you have entered an equally magical space. While the fragrance isn't there—yet—the look, the feel, and the ambiance are just what you would expect of a site dedicated to the expensive, high-quality, melt-in-your-mouth, special occasion chocolates and truffles that bear the Godiva name.

As important, the look and feel of Godiva.com reflect the look, feel, and ambiance of a brick-and-mortar Godiva boutique. Just as the physical Godiva stores exude quality, taste, and a touch of indulgence, the Godiva Web site sends the same subliminal "Go ahead. You deserve it." message. It is exactly what we mean by imbuing a virtual place with a touch of magic.[2]

Distinctive and eye-catching design is only one part of the formula for creating a virtual place with magical properties. It is also about building trust and creating a unique service experience. There are thousands of mediocre Internet places, Web sites that do little more than offer a list of items for sale. The successful ones imbed themselves in shoppers' memories by instilling an effortless feeling of being well served. From the first click, shoppers are drawn in, made curious, and delighted by the display of offerings. When every link works—and help is given if and when it's needed—the experience is secured in trust. Whether shoppers buy on the first visit or not, the visit is branded in their memories, and they will return to experience it again.

Lands' End is another company that knows the importance of making every e-space touch point—the look and feel, the ambiance created, and the personal care provided—exude a little magic. Specialized tools, live access to customer service representatives, and multiple ways to browse and shop work in concert to convey LandsEnd.com's dedication to customer service and desire to please the customer.[3]

Organizations like Lands' End and Godiva design virtual places with distinction and magic. They take the time to evaluate their customers' desires and present their goods and services memorably, reliably, and consistently. Shopping at these sites feels real to the consumer—whether she's a housewife in Utah or a purchasing manager for a Fortune 500 firm in Philadelphia. A well-branded site with a touch of magic attracts a loyal and profitable following that guarantees its online success and bottom-line performance.

The word "virtual" has come to be associated almost exclusively with the Internet. But there are other ways for the essence of reality to be imbued in unsubstantial form. It is at the heart of literature and animation. One of the most overlooked of virtual places is the humble mail order catalog. A good catalog displays and showcases desirable products. A magical catalog enfolds the reader in a fantasy world woven around the products it displays and sells. Two of the best are the *Vermont Country Store* and *Mary Jane's Farm*. Pick up either catalog and you are drawn into a world of country living, organic farming, and old fashioned country storekeeping. Indeed, the catalogs themselves are more magazine than catalog. Of the *Vermont Country Store* catalog, first published in 1945, the *Saturday Evening Post* wrote:

> Some bright morning the mailman may hand you an unusual and surprising kind of mail-order catalog. You may well mistake it for a *New England Almanac* of 1888. Its archaic title reads "The Voice of the Mountains" and it comes from the Village of Weston in the Republic of Vermont.
>
> Printed in black and white and embellished with woodcuts, this old-fashioned pamphlet advertises products varying from Vermont Indian pudding and Bearpaw popcorn to a convertible rubber-tired buggy. And salted in between the salable items you'll find bits of poetry, an editorial on "Getting Up Early in the Morning" or a fervent plea for cleaner mountain brooks.[4]

Those words were written in 1952, but the *Vermont Country Store* catalog still weaves its virtual magic web of old-fashioned cracker barrel nostalgia around its customers, many who have been loyal readers—and buyers—for two generations. The red-heel cotton work socks, cold-weather hand creams, flannel nightgowns, and bags of hard candies—where else can you find a chocolate Brazil nut–stuffed trout called a Turkey Joint—they sell are unique and nostalgically reminiscent of another era.

Mary Jane's Farm, 57 years younger and published half a continent away in Moscow, Idaho, enfolds customer/readers in a virtual world of organic farming and New Age, old-fashioned values so richly, they can almost smell the straw of the hen house and the back-country breakfast frittata cooking over an open fire. Founder Mary Jane Butters describes her mail order publication as "one part catalog and two parts magazine." The color photos of her cuisine are coupled with unique articles, interviews and tips, photocopies of reader letters, and nostalgic sepia-tone pictures of kids and cows. On one page is an article on how to make a camp stool, on another how to stack 39 bales of hay on a regular pickup truck, and on yet another how to get really great customer service. The stories and letters interspersed among the ads elevate the buying process to the part–barter, part–banter ambiance of the 21st century version of the old country store—or a direct–from–the–grower transaction. You only see Mary Jane in the photographs, but a quick leaf through her "magalog" leaves you feeling you have found not just a merchant, but possibly a friend for life and a great source for organic trail mix.

Virtual Magic doesn't just occur through the manipulation of a mouse or the thumbing of pages. Virtual Magic can be live and spontaneous as well. QVC, the West Chester, Pennsylvania–based television shopping network creates an "intimate" and "personal" community of half a million members—viewers—each and every day of the week. The QVC shopping channel—the initials stand for Quality, Value, and Convenience—has fashioned a virtual mall that generates $4 billion in annual sales, and feels as homey and personal as a backyard fence relationship among a group of friends. Truly an act of Virtual Magic.

THE MAGIC OF PROCESS

The hotel guest met at curbside and ushered rock-star-like directly to his room and the new car buyer amazed to find the stereo of her new car preprogrammed to the same stations as her trade-in are experiencing the magic of thoughtful process. Such Service Magic is performed in a pre-planned way that amazes the customer and creates a positive impression.

USAA, Inc. is an organization well-known for such procedural prowess. Originally United Services Auto Association, USAA was founded in 1922 in San Antonio, Texas, to provide automobile insurance to U.S. Army officers (now serving all ranks and their families) who had trouble obtaining insurance because of their transient life style. Over the years, USAA has distinguished itself through policies, procedures, and electronic automation focused on servicing customers better—not just keeping costs in check. USAA insurance members returning from the Gulf War were surprised to receive prorated refund checks on their automobile premiums, along with a note: "We're sure you couldn't have been driving your car a lot while you were in the

Persian Gulf, therefore we don't want to charge you for carrying insurance you didn't use."[5]

So it is that USAA's technology allows it to routinely perform small bits of impressive Service Magic for its customers. But not all Process Magic is about computers and complexity. Process Magic is at work when an organization—large or small—creates a standard operating procedure that seems just the right thing to do. Case in point: The Hairy Cactus Nail Salon in Cincinnati, Ohio, a full-service salon that also provides manicure services. Knowing that time is valuable and that many a woman has ruined her "not quite dry" nails immediately upon leaving the salon, the Hairy Cactus came up with a solution. They take the customer's purse and keys, open the salon door, escort her to her car, open the car door, put her belongings securely in the car, start the car, assist her into her seat—and voilà—she's safely on her way—not a chip or smudge to be found!

Practices, policies, and procedures from initial contact to problem solving that amaze the customer with seeming ease—are magical. The service magician who implements those practices with style and grace enhances the experience yet again.

THE MAGIC OF PERFORMANCE

A considerate act by a thoughtful service person creates its own charm and magic: the hotel employee who, when asked for directions to the Eisenhower Ballroom responds, "Sir, it would be my pleasure to guide you there"; the waiter who advises, "That is a wonderful choice of appetizer. Might I suggest that since it is an ample serving, you consider sharing it with madam?" Both these service magicians are practicing the subtle art of customer reading and direction, two skills that are critical aspects of successful Performance Magic. The Duke Energy call center employee who volunteers a wake-up call to the cell phone of a doctor caught in a power outage—is creating Performance Magic through the art of surprise.

The empowered employee who confidently goes above and beyond for a customer in despair or confusion is a practitioner of Performance Magic par excellence. Consider this simple car rental arrangement that turned into an opportunity for National Car Rental to turn on a little magic.

Ray Brook, a product-supply market manager at Procter & Gamble and a frequent National Car Rental customer, was more than a little puzzled when a remote rental machine at the Portland, Oregon airport rejected his request for a car and directed him to see an agent at the main terminal. The National Car agent quickly found the problem: Brook's Washington-state driver's license had expired on his birthday just the week before. Due to some sticky liability issues, National couldn't rent him a car without a valid license.

With the prospect of meeting a customer in 30 minutes and a full day of business 600 miles away in Sacramento, California facing him the next day, Brook was frantic. Wayne Ranslem, National's on-duty manager, was summoned, and confirmed the company's policy on licenses. Ranslem could have let the exchange end there. Instead, he offered to have a National employee drive Brook to his customer meeting—20 minutes away—and then to the Department of Motor Vehicles to renew his license—another 30-minute drive. Brook gratefully accepted the generous offer. But his travails weren't over. The DMV office was closed. Back went Brook and the driver to the Portland airport, where National's Ranslem laid out Plan B. National would transport Brook to his hotel where he would take responsibility for his own transportation for the rest of the day. Another National employee would pick him up early the next morning and take him back to Vancouver, Washington, for the renewal, after which he could rent a car—at a discount—for the trip to Sacramento. This time, at long last, everything went according to plan.

In a follow-up letter to National's CEO, Brook wrote: "It's apparent this kind of persistence in customer service only happens as the result of very strong leadership, clear direction, and discipline. My sincere thank you to you and your organization for providing that."[6]

WHERE PLACE, PROCESS, AND PERFORMANCE MEET

Perhaps the most magical of service experiences are those where Place, Process, and Performance come together so seamlessly that they seem inseparable to the customer, patron, client, and user. The ballpark without the teams, the game, the lights, the crowd, and the peanut vendor is only mildly interesting . . . even if it IS the house that Ruth built. The great resort destination without the easy check-in, simple room-charge system, and thoughtful service people is, at best, half a loaf—regardless of the beach, the vista, and the hammock. And the trek up the mountain of your dreams, without the knowledgeable guide, the fellow travelers to share the experience, and the evening campfire to reminisce around, is a greatly diminished adventure.

That synergy is obvious at Midway Stadium in St. Paul, Minnesota, home of the St. Paul Saints, a Northern League baseball team. Some fans of professional baseball consider the major leagues "the show," but everyone in the packed stands at a Saints home game knows they're watching a much more gloriously entertaining version of the national pastime—and their enjoyment has only a slight connection to the quality of the baseball being played on the field.

The Saints have been drawing fans—more than 2.26 million of them since 1993—to this funky, old stadium by following a simple slogan: "Fun is good." That's a phrase that defines the organization's marketing plan, that is written on the tops of dugouts, and that describes the philosophy of the team's part owner and president Mike Veeck.[7]

Fun abounds at Saints games, and it keeps the fans coming. They come to get a haircut or a massage in the stands. They come to applaud as the team mascot, a pig, trots out to deliver balls to the umpire. They come to cheer the wisecracking announcer and jeer contestants in a multitude of dopey between-innings events from fans dressing in inflatable costumes for sumo wrestling matches to blindfolded base-running competitions. They come to experience the magic of the tailgating, the contests, and the Saints' quirky charm. They come because they never know quite what to expect—except fun.

The carnival atmosphere that seems effortless is the result of a dedicated staff of ten that spends the off-season coming up with goofy ideas and themes for each home game: Halloween in July, Irish night, Groundhog Day (a riff on the Bill Murray movie, not the holiday). "I hope it looks effortless because we work hard at it," says Bill Fisher, assistant general manager. "It's not as easy as just announcing a 'Halloween Night.' You've gotta know someone who has coffins." Which Fisher did, as it turned out. A buddy, who is "into Halloween in a big way, let me know he had a whole yard full of coffins we could use."

The Saints make a point of knowing their customers. Players show up before games to sign autographs. The staff works every home game. Veeck, Fisher, and everyone who can, spend time in the stands, talking with the fans. The result: They deliver value to their mostly blue-collar, working-folk fans by keeping ticket, concession, and parking prices low so families can afford the night of live entertainment a Saints' game provides.[8]

The 6,329-seat ballpark has no stadium seating. The aluminum bleachers are so uncomfortable that experienced Saints' fans bring their own cushions, a habit the team encourages with regular giveaways. The 2002 giveaway—cushions depicting Major League Baseball Commissioner Bud Selig on one side and Major League Baseball's Player

Association representative Donald Fehr on the other—was a clever pro-motion that inspired sports writers to bad lines about turning the other cheek to both sides in the big league's 2002 labor dispute.[9]

In 1998, the city of St. Paul proposed building a new stadium for the ball club, so the Saints surveyed their fans. They responded with a re-sounding "no," and the team passed on it. But the stadium question hasn't gone away: once again, there's talk of building the Saints a new home on the Mississippi riverfront on the west side of St. Paul.

Most fans don't like the idea of leaving the old stadium, Fisher ad-mits, but seem resigned to the idea that it might be time—especially after waiting in a long line at the inadequate restrooms or spending a butt-numbing night on cold, aluminum bleachers. "We've reached the point where we're talking about a new stadium or a major update to this one," he says. Fans, nonetheless, insist that there is a magic to the rick-ety, old, industrial-park venue. "Where else," they ask, "can you go to a ball park with an active railroad track?" Somehow, a game without a passing train has become a disappointment. Perhaps the concierge that is being added next season will help overcome the loss.

Even so, the St. Paul Saints will continue to awe and delight because they've perfected their ability to deliver enchantment to customers. As general manager Bill Fanning says: "The fans are the magic. Our job is to provide a fun, fan-friendly, personalized atmosphere that encourages their collective personality to come out. Win or lose, we want the fans to leave with a smile on their faces."[10]

AND FOR OUR NEXT TRICK . . .

What follows, further develops the three Ps of Service Magic—and the emerging technology for putting these magics to work. Whether your orientation is organization—that is, you'd like to put a little magic to work for your company, division, department, store, or association—or your orientation is personal and you'd just like to spruce up your personal magic act—there is something here for you. Sections 2 and 3 of *Service Magic* expand on the practice of adding magic to Place and Process. And while the focus of these two sections is largely organiza-tional, there is guidance aplenty for the individual service magician as well. Section 4 explains in detail the philosophy and practice of Performance Magic. This section is dedicated to those who come face-to-face with customers every day. The four chapters of this section, plus the Service Magician's Pocket Tool Kit found in Section 7, are chock-full of tips, tricks, and ideas for putting a little more Performance Magic to work for those customers.

Section 5, is dedicated exclusively to those who practice service in the virtual realm and want to separate their province there from the mundane tone of Place, Process, and Performance that characterizes so much of what exists in the virtual space of the World Wide Web. Along the way we will introduce you to organizations—Section 6 showcases five of them—and individuals for whom Service Magic is a way of life and who can serve as role models for your organizational and individual aspirations. If your desire is to elevate the service you deliver, to add a little magic to your customer encounters, to raise the experience above the din and beyond the humdrum, we invite you to turn the page, lift the curtain, and let us share with you the fascinating secrets of *Service Magic.*

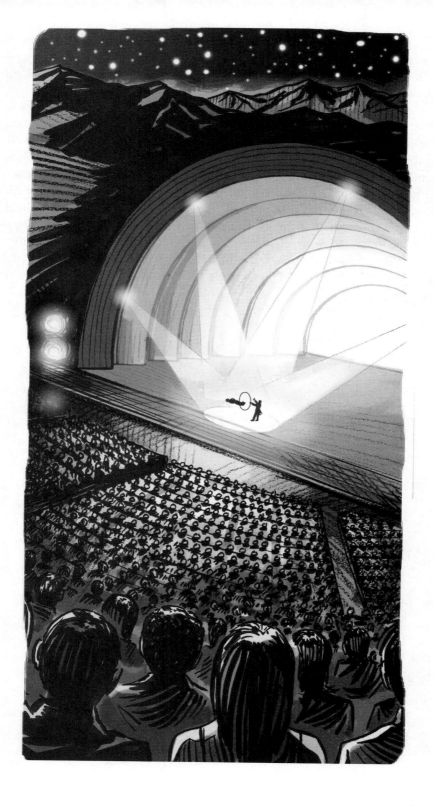

PLACE MAGIC

PLACE MAGIC
Environments that delight, support, and enliven.

MAGICAL PLACES
Venues with physical attributes that attract and please,
subtly enhanced by human endeavor.

*"We are children of our landscape; it dictates behavior and even thought, in
the measure to which we are responsive to it."*

LAWRENCE GEORGE DURRELL
BRITISH POET, NOVELIST

Great magic is staged. That is, it is performed in real space and real time. Whether that stage is Liberty Island, where David Copperfield vanished the Statue of Liberty before a national television audience, the showroom of Las Vegas's Mirage hotel where Siegfried and Roy transport and levitate their magnificent white tigers for thousands, or simply a table top where a master of card and coin illusions is performing for a group of intimates—the performance space must be managed and mastered with care and skill.

The best of the best stage magicians combine physical space management, engineering, lighting, pyrotechnics, and more to make their effects succeed and amaze. What would simply be an interesting trick if performed on a bare stage, becomes an eye-popping illusion when accompanied by an orchestra and surrounded by moving colored lights, smoke, and sparkling tinsel. It is the "gestalt"—the totality of the performance—that awes and amazes.

Illusions like sawing a woman in half, passing swords through an assistant in a woven basket—even the venerable pulling a rabbit from a hat trick—are, in fact, quite simple tricks. They amaze time after time, because the magician creates the illusion that much more is happening than meets the eye, giving the audience more to look at, think about, and be amazed by than simply the trick. Case in point:

Rabbit from the Hat

Pulling a rabbit from a top hat is actually a simple trick. Typically performed atop a small black table, the key to the trick is audacity: the magician places the rabbit in the hat right before the viewers' eyes. It works like this: The rabbit, a voiceless and docile animal, is hidden away in a small black bag suspended from the edge of an on-stage table immediately in front of the magician, but out of the audience's line of sight. The magician makes an elaborate—and convincing—show of demonstrating that the hat is empty, and places the hat back on the table, usually opening side down. Sometime later the magician picks up and inverts the hat—simultaneously sweeping the bunny—bag and all—off the hidden hook and into the hat. He is now ready to simply reach into the hat, loosen the ties on the bag, and pull Mr. Fluffy out into the light and the view of the audience.

Simple, even boring, when you know the trick. But the staging—the music, the lights, the patter, the story the magician tells—all converge to make the moment the rabbit is plucked from the hat, special.

Playing to—and on—the customer's senses of sight, sound, smell, touch, even taste—and doing so with style and class, and a little suspense and surprise, is key to the most memorable Place Magic.

CABELA'S: FISHING GEAR AND A LITTLE PLACE MAGIC

Last year six million people visited one of the eight mid-western Cabela's stores. Most of them . . . men, the world's most reluctant shoppers. The magic that lures so many to this small chain of sporting goods stores is the *magic of place*. Cabela's stores not only sell fishing gear, tents, and guns and ammunition, they create a dazzling "guy-oriented" experience that makes their stores magnets for the hunting and fishing enthusiast. They are virtually theme parks for the outdoorsman.

Visitors to a typical Cabela's are greeted by an extraordinary array of nonretail features to which 40 percent of the floor space is dedicated. Every store features a miniature mountain vista and is dotted with stuffed trophy animals from buckhorn sheep and mule deer to mountain hare. Every store also features gigantic fresh-fish aquariums stocked with championship-sized specimens of game fish most anglers have only seen in their dreams.

The larger stores, the 150,000- to 200,000-square-foot behemoths, even feature African plains dioramas complete with indigenous game animals in lifelike scenes.

Every Cabela's store is a learning-rich environment. Interactive touch screen kiosks answer questions on thousands of topics from fish identification to mountain-gear purchasing advice. Every Cabela's also features a restaurant—usually on a second story level with an open view of the entire store and all the animal displays—a Gun Library filled with collectible firearms, a live-bait shop, service departments for firearms, archery equipment, and fishing gear; a Cabela's Outdoor Adventures and Travel Service; and an interactive firearms and archery laser-training system.

Natural Place Magic

Nature's Own ... Plus

Natural Place Magic is a collusion between the world around us and our desire to experience, appreciate, and be awed by it—our desire for a magical experience. A shimmering sunset on Kenya's Masi Mara plain and the wonder of a moonlit Alpine evening are incomparable. At their most enjoyable, both are—more often than not—subtly and clearly enhanced by human intervention.

The safari guide who knows where—and when—to park the Land Rover Discovery so his touring charges can best absorb majestic Kenyan nature makes all the difference between a memorable, exotic, sundown experience and the simple passing of another day. Likewise, the Swiss chalet with the observation deck overhanging a pristine snow field creates an illusion of mountain solitude despite the number of guests simultaneously captivated by the clear night and the glistening view.

Although the natural wonder is what we remember most, the carefully planned enhancers are often what make the creation of that memory—and the unencumbered enjoyment of nature—possible.

THE SUBTLETY OF SIGNAGE—AND A
WELL-PLACED OBSERVATION DECK

The Grand Canyon of the Yellowstone River in Yellowstone National Park—the world's first and oldest preserve of natural jewels—is one of nature's most magical wonders. The canyon varies from 800 to 1,200 feet in depth, from 1,500 to 4,000 feet in width, and is 24 miles long. The upper 2½ miles, where the Yellowstone River cascades 1,000 feet, is purely spectacular.

Hot springs have actively bubbled through the ages, altering lava rock in the canyon to produce the lovely colors (largely due to varied iron compounds that paint the canyon wall). Steam vents and geysers in the canyon walls give the views from the various observation decks and overlooks a primordial feel.

This *National Geographic*-like tour of the Grand Canyon of the Yellowstone comes courtesy of the carefully crafted educational signage and walking tour literature developed by the U.S. National Park Service. Knowledge is an important attribute of natural Place Magic. Both are an expected part of the national park experience—and an important part of the magic. The secrets—we the audience are privy to—personalize the experience.

Southwest of the Grand Canyon of the Yellowstone is the park's best known icon—Old Faithful—the largest and most dependable geyser in the world. The physical setting is well kempt. The geyser field, of which Old Faithful is but one of 25 spectacular features, is crisscrossed with carefully constructed, handicap-accessible, boardwalks and vantage points. The boardwalks, observation platforms and each of the individual 25 geysers, paint pots, and boiling hot water caldrons, offer detailed explanatory signage telling the tale of their discovery and nature. A geyser that erupts on average once a week is just a steamy mud hole—unless and until you know that at any minute, without warning, it could flare into action.

A two-story information center sits less than 50 yards from Old Faithful. Knowledgeable, well-trained park rangers conduct mini-seminars on volcanology and walking tours of the geyser field. The story of this natural wonder—how Yellowstone sits atop a giant lava field, the geysers' role as petcocks for the heat of the subterranean world—makes the site more than an interesting curio and enfolds the visitor into the many layers of wonderment. The information explains the inner magic of Yellowstone and its many amazing attractions.

ADDING CONVENIENCE TO NATURE'S MAGIC

Natural Place Magic is enhanced by making visits convenient and comfortable. A visitor's first walk up from the drive through the subdued entryway and into the soaring great room of the Old Faithful Inn is unforgettable. The experience is a prime example of enhancing natural Place Magic by design. Opened in 1904, the inn reflects the ruggedness and grandeur of Yellowstone National Park and its signature attraction, Old Faithful Geyser—just as architect Robert Reamer intended. Along the way, Reamer created a signature architectural style referred to today as "park-itecture," a style that consciously creates human spaces in harmony with their natural setting. And that indeed happens in Old Faithful Inn.

The inn's Place Magic lies in the way Reamer reflected the outdoor wonders inside in obvious and subtle ways. The rock chimney of the 76.6 foot story atrium lobby's fireplace is 500 tons of volcanic rhyolite, quarried right in the park. It draws the visitor's eyes upward just as they are when Old Faithful erupts. The timbers of this largest of log structures are lodge pole pine, harvested eight miles south of the inn and sledged across the snow by mule teams in the winter of 1903. Reamer hand selected the gnarled wood that accents the entire inn. As quietly magical is the play of shadows across floor and walls, reflective of the changing patterns of light and dark in the surrounding forests, an effect created through strategically placed, differently shaped windows in the east and west faces of the inn. Old Faithful Inn has rightly been described by design experts as "both primitive and magnificent."

And though the inn itself is a passive architectural enhancement of natural Place Magic, the interaction of staff with guest is not. Indeed, waiters, waitresses, bellstaff, maintenance people, and grounds keepers are all schooled in the lore of the park and the inn—and in the art of sharing their knowledge with guests. Restaurant staff wears tags advertising both name and home state—an automatic conversation starter. Staffers are encouraged to ask guests where they traveled from to visit and what they've seen so far in the park. And, of course, staffers are schooled in all the park wonders so they can give knowledgeable information. The goal—though never stated this way—is to create a temporary haven of warm humanity amidst the experience of natural grandeur. Personalization at work.

That same goal of enjoying natural magic in the magical comfort of manmade convenience exists at Treetops Hotel in Aberdares National

Park, Kenya. And has since 1932. The 50-guestroom lodge, originally a three-room treehouse in a giant wild fig tree, overlooks two watering holes and a natural salt lick that draw rhino, elephants, bush buck, lion, and hyena. Especially magical is the way the hotel has made the sight's nocturnal visits by Africa's great animals available to guests. Special soft lights illuminate the watering holes throughout evening hours, rendering them and their wild kingdom visitors visible from all of the hotel's viewing balconies and ground level photographic hides. Every room in the hotel has a buzzer that, upon request, is rung to alert guests that something special—like a lion pride or an elephant herd—has arrived at the watering holes.

Meals at the lodge are served at long tables with bench seating to encourage camaraderie and the feel of being on safari and roughing it—if only just a bit. Naturalists and professional hunters are on duty in the inn's lounge around the clock to chat up guests about the facility, the wild life, and what they've seen at the watering hole. "Just two nights ago a family of lion made short work of an unfortunate wart hog off the edge of the western hole," is a typical revelation. And of course the entire staff knows—and at some point in a visitor's stay will reveal—that this very lodge is where a young English girl climbed the tree as a princess the afternoon of February 5, 1952, and descended the following morning Queen Elizabeth II—her father, Britain's King George VI, having died during the night. Guests leave Treetops feeling they've been at a unique hotel where they became members of a special family, privileged to have been enfolded in a rare experiencing of nature.

WHEN NATURE IS AT YOUR DOORSTEP

Few of us have one of the seven wonders of the natural world at our doorstep. But even the proximity of a favorite local fishing lake, biking trail, or sunset overlook can serve as a platform for creating a little magic—if you know the rules enhancing natural Place Magic:

1. *Find your "natural" story.* Is your operation near an interesting geographical site, or the site of a special happening—such as a volcanic eruption or great fire or dinosaur migration trail or an alleged spotting of Sasquatch? Avoid references to tragedies and disasters unless you are certain you can avoid crossing a politically correct sensitivity (or think you can handle the inevitable heat). Did an interesting piece of history unfold nearby? Hint: If others in your locale have created a compelling "theme" or

motif, you can capitalize on it as well—as long as you do it in a creative and unique way.

2. *Educate yourself.* If there is a genuinely compelling natural story—or even a plausibly interesting one—steep yourself and your associates in the details. Remember that people love to feel "in on the trick" or owners of "little known facts" they can relate to others.

3. *Create an "elevator story."* Senior managers in large corporations are schooled these days in the art of being able to explain their organization and its mission in the time it would take for an elevator to go from the 10th to the 18th floor—thus the name. You and your associates can create an "elevator story" about your locale and its uniquesses. A restaurateur on a northern lake might create an elevator speech around the formation of the lake and the kind of fishing it supports plus any local details. At a restaurant on a lake we know, the story goes like this:

    "Well, this lake has some pretty good small-mouth bass, and some great walleye fishing. The state record on walleye—17 pounds—was set near where we are standing. The lake was formed over two different glacial periods so there are spots over 100 feet deep and a lot of shallows and weedy spots as well."

    Visitors, who egg on the teller by perhaps asking if anything interesting ever goes on there, will hear:

    "Well, in the early '60s, the Rolling Stones played down at the old amusement park dance pavilion. One of the local characters claims to have sat at the soda counter next to Mick Jagger and when Jagger ordered a kipper sandwich, the old boy said, 'You know you can't always get what you want,' to which Mick replied, 'But if you try sometimes you can get what you need.' Of course nobody knew how true that might be."

4. *Dabble in décor.* If you are near that great fishing lake, photos of the strings of the local catch might enhance your place feel, as well as a little memorabilia that suggests the fishing motif. If the locale was once home to buffalo or dinosaurs or just has great sunsets, include visual representation of those distinctions in your décor, and in printed material as well.

5. *Create conveniences.* As a service magician, there are wonderful opportunities to enchant your customer by providing services that are practical, logical, and take the burden off your customer. Without fail, customers with cameras in tow will be fre-

quenting your establishment. Make it convenient for your customer to get film developed quickly by offering a 12-hour drop-off service. If customers are visiting your locale on the way to other famous locations, offer legible maps with simple directions to all points of interest, or shuttle busses to carry guests to their ultimate destination. Sharing services—like tours or offering discounts to neighboring businesses—can be a mutually beneficial arrangement—for businesses and customers alike.

6. *Sensory congruence.* The smells and sounds need to be in sync with the sights and feel. Realtors advise homesellers to bake an apple pie right before an open house to enhance the nostalgic, homey ambiance. Smart cab drivers know that while they may enjoy acid rock waiting at the cab stand, their passenger might be more soothed by classical music on the trip to the airport. Make sure the senses you touch are cut from the same cloth as the motif and ambiance you are trying to create. Part of Place Magic is the congruity—the way it all fits together.

## CHAPTER FIVE

High-Level Man-Made
Place Magic

There is no better contemporary example of building magic into man-made places than the world of the theme park. These modern day versions of the venerable old amusement park business—the first one was opened in 1583 near Copenhagen, Denmark—are created and peopled by on-stage and off-stage magicians gifted in the arts of sight and sound, action and movement, psychology and performance. The forte of the modern theme park industry (referred to as the controlled entertainment business by some insiders) is taking guests out of their everyday world, hiding them away from as many reminders of that day-to-day life as possible, and transporting them to an environment that invites them to suspend disbelief and enter into a safe, carefree total entertainment experience for a few hours. Whether the venue of focus is Disneyland, Universal Studios, Walt Disney World, King's Dominion, or Islands of Adventure, theme park designers must achieve a level of detailed experience engineering seldom attempted elsewhere, but holding lessons for us all. The masters of these modern entertainment complexes clearly understand that they are first and foremost in the business of illusion, amusement, and delight. They have created a marvelous model for Place Magic management in its most complete form with lessons for organizations of any size.

IT STARTS WITH DISNEY

In 1955, when Walt Disney opened the first of his "magic kingdoms" in Anaheim, California, he created an entirely new approach to the concept of entertainment, a business obsessed with the customer point of view and the precise management of the customer's experience. Disneyland, the seed from which a thousand flowers have blossomed, was deliberately (and with careful forethought) engineered to deliver a safe, clean, family-oriented entertainment that appealed to the five senses and avoided the disquieting and seedy side of what the amusement park business had become. Martin Sklar, chairman of Walt Disney Imagineering, recalls: "When Walt first told Mrs. Disney he wanted to build a park, she said, 'Oh, my goodness, why would you want to do that? They're so dirty and the people who work in them are terrible.' Walt replied, 'That's just the point. Mine isn't going to be that way.'"[1]

The essential magic of the theme park, whether a Disney, Universal Studios, or Busch Gardens park, is having a clear vision of the desired or intended customer experience and a methodology—or simple obsession—for anticipating and controlling every detail that will support—or detract from—that vision.

Walt Disney called that obsession, that methodology for managing the place side of the experience, "imagineering," and defined it as "the blending of creative imagination and technical know-how."[2] Disney's Sklar, codified the imagineering approach to Place Management in a set of principles he dubbed "Mickey's Ten Commandments."[3] They reflect Walt Disney's moviemaker view of the world and the enterprise he was creating in its image:

1. *Know your audience.* Before creating a setting, understand who will be visiting or using it, in some depth.

2. *Wear your guest's shoes.* Evaluate your setting from the customer's perspective by experiencing it as a customer.

3. *Organize the flow of people and ideas.* Think of setting as a story and tell that story in a sequenced, organized way. Build the same order and logic into the design of customer movement.

4. *Create a "wienie."* Borrowed from silent film slang, a wienie was what Walt Disney called a visual magnet. It means a visual landmark is used to orient and attract customers. Sleeping Beauty's Castle is the "wienie" of Disneyland.

5. *Communicate with visual literacy.* Language is not always composed of words. Use the common languages of color, shape, and form to communicate through setting.

6. *Avoid overload—create turn-ons.* Do not bombard customers with data. Let them choose the information they want when they want it.

7. *Tell one story at a time.* Mixing multiple stories in a single setting is confusing. Create one setting for each idea. Disney's "It's a Small World" attraction is a simple story with seven chapters—each continent has a "room" along the ride's route—and 100 themes—a scene for each of the 100 peoples represented in the attraction.

8. *Avoid contradictions, maintain identity.* Every detail and nuance of a setting should support and further the organizational identity and mission.

9. *For every ounce of treatment provide a ton of treat.* Give your customers the highest value by building an interactive setting that gives them the opportunity to exercise all of their senses. A cookie shop with elf bakers cooking up easily identifiable treats—like chocolate chip cookies, for example.

10. *Keep it up.* Never get complacent and always maintain your setting. The horse's head hitching posts outside City Hall on the Magic Kingdom's Main Street are rubbed and patted by hundreds of guests every day. So a maintenance crew repaints them every night.

Consistent with Disney's moviemaking motif, entering guests see the "movie posters" of the park, colorful announcements of current park attractions. They smell the atmosphere; fresh popcorn is always popping. In general, they encounter all the accoutrements of a movie theater lobby including a bank of payphones and a row of restrooms. Just as in a movie theater, the guest will always know where to find a phone or a toilet—near the box office. In that same vein, the four "lands" of Disney—Fantasyland, Frontierland, Tomorrowland, and Adventureland—correspond to the backdrops or settings in which Disney movies and animations took place. Each of those "lands" was separately conceived and physically demarcated from the others and the experience staged as a separate performance. Walt Disney and his "imagineers" worked to make the look and the "feel" of each land unique. They even varied the texture of the walkways in each land under the supposition that a guest's foot tread was a part of the experience. They created transitioning protocols, rules for the way one land's look would meld into another's as the guest moved between them. Likewise, imagineers worried over the grounds immediate to an attraction such as *Pirates of the Caribbean* or the *Haunted Mansion*. How should the approach to a haunted house look? How does the landscape change as one enters bayou country? All part of an effort to make the approach to a ride or attraction an enfolding part of the experience. Place Magic management with amazing precision.

THE ORGANIZING EFFECT OF STORY

The concepts of "story" and "back story" are important organizing principles of theme park experience and Place Magic engineering. Illustrative is Walt Disney World's MGM Studios' *Twilight Zone Tower of Terror* attraction—a 130-foot forced drop from the top of the tower to the "basement" below. The ride itself is housed in a building designed to look like an abandoned 1930s Deco high-rise hotel called the Hollywood Tower Hotel. The back story—or mythology of the ride that enriches the attraction and enfolds the guest—is designed to both evoke the spirit of Rod Serling's *Twilight Zone* television series and to remove the guest mentally from the amusement park thrill-ride mind-set.

The Back Story

Something strange happened in this one-time hangout of Hollywood's social elite. On a dark and stormy night in 1939, two glamorous movie stars, a bellhop, and a budding young child star and her governess entered the hotel elevator. At the exact moment the doors closed, a bolt of lightening struck the hotel's tower with such force that the five passengers disappeared. Word of the horrible event spread, the hotel lost its clientele and was forced to close.

The Story of the Experience

Park guests are invited to enter the long-abandoned hotel and visit the sight of the mysterious tragedy. The lobby is blanketed in dust. Suitcases and steamer trunks remain unchecked beside the front desk. An "out of order" sign hangs askew on the elevator doors. The ride queue winds through the lobby and down into the basement of the abandoned old hotel. At one point, guests stop in the hotel library where a black and white TV jumps to life—with the familiar "Welcome to the Twilight Zone" narration by Ron Serling. Following the welcome, bellhops lead groups of park guests to the hotel's dark, creepy boiler room to see the haunted elevator. Guests step into the rusty—and until now—inoperable freight elevator. The doors suddenly close, and the guests experience the 1939 ride rising slowly to the 13th floor—then plunging back down to the basement. Riders may drop two or three times—depending on how the ride has been programmed—another mysterious element.

THE UNIVERSAL STUDIOS APPROACH

While all theme parks owe a Garden of Eden debt to Walt Disney and his parks, not every theme park follows the imagineering canons of Place Magic. Universal Studios Hollywood creators pride themselves on successfully defying some of those standard theme-park truisms.

Universal's approach has evolved from the company's history as a movie studio tour and a specific geography—the first park was built on the side of a mountain. Universal's special approach has produced three audience-pleasing theme parks that, according to some surveys, regularly outstrip the Disney theme parks in guest delight scores—and repeat visits. And while Universal holds to some of the same basics as all theme parks—simple parking and litter-free walk ways—the Universal approach is noticeably unique.

Total Immersion

Universal Studios Hollywood's meta-concept—its overarching goal —is to create an interactive environment that feels like a familiar movie—plus. Everything at the park is about a balance between looking back and what might be. They seek to hook your sense of familiarity, yet take you beyond. They want guests to say the *Jurassic Park* ride was more thrilling than the movie; that *ET* was more heartwarming; that *Terminator II:3D* and *Backdraft* were more exciting.

Toward that end, the entrance and exit of a Universal Studios Hollywood attraction are designed to feel like a walk into and out of a sound stage—plus. The plus is that the attraction contains elements that were only in your imagination when you watched the film. The *WaterWorld* attraction looks similar to the floating city in the movies. It is hot, as if baking in the sun in the middle of the ocean. It smells fishy and of gasoline—as a movie viewer could only imagine the scene would, but of course could not have actually experienced in a theater. The attraction greeters have an edgy, nervous, even suspicious—some might say malevolent—manner about them, just as the *WaterWorld* residents did—and they look evil and smell bad to boot.

The queues, the lines all guests go through to reach the rides and attractions, become part of the entertainment. At *Jurassic Park* the queue is set in jungle terrain, just like the ride. Guests get to touch the car used in the *Back to the Future* movie as they are going in for the *Back to the Future: The Ride!* At the *Studio Tour,* guests wind through a series of movie billboards with TV screens playing excerpts from award-winning Universal Studios movies. Having just seen a short clip from *The Ten Commandments,* while waiting in the queue, makes the "parting of the Red Sea" portion of the tour more powerful.

Do the Unexpected

Other Universal Studios Hollywood Place Magic rules differ from theme park "norms" by creating surprise where others encourage smooth and secure sameness. Three examples: Other theme parks obey the concepts of "connected tissue," "same plain," and "transition area." Specifically, the normal park attraction area is built entirely on one level, side by side, shops and attractions are similar—if not identical— in height, color, and architectural look.

But Universal Studios Hollywood turns this rule on its head. While it honors the goal of being immersive, interactive, and experiential, this counterintuitive theme park does so in an unpredictable fashion. Side-by-side attractions may have wildly different looks and clashing colors, and there are un-Disneyesque, even jarring, transitions between areas.

The unique mishmash works well because it feels real, authentic, and very comfortable. The visual, audible, and tactile experiences tend to surface "I've been here before" reminiscences in guests that cause them to want to return again and again. One executive explained the Universal Studios Hollywood version of eclecticism as being similar to the difference between leather and Naugahyde. Naugahyde is perfect, with no flaws, and a balanced symmetry. But you'd rather have leather because of the realness.

They even ignore the "all-on-one-plain" rule and have attractions at dramatically different levels. A virtual *Cat in the Hat* approach to place design. Speaking of which, Universal's newest domestic park (opened in 1999)—Islands of Adventure—features Seuss Landing, a kind of composite of characters and themes from the stories—and looks—of the Dr. Seuss children's books. There are quite literally no straight lines in Seuss Landing. Even the palm trees—salvaged from a hurricane site—are bent and crooked. Roads in and out of Seuss Landing are a dizzying spiral. Rides on the bright and colorful *CaroSeussEl* feature animated interactive characters who move up and down the atypical curvy pole. The *Cat in the Hat* attraction takes place on moving couches while guests are assaulted by Thing One and Thing Two.

High Interactivity

All Universal Studios theme parks use the key design principle of high interactivity between the park and the guest. All their parks continually talk to the guest. Every sight is eye candy; every view entertains. There is an unmistakable connection between the guest and the park that is perpetually animated, alive, and entertaining. Toward that end, all Universal parks have costumed characters like Lucille Ball, Laurel and Hardy, the Blues Brothers, Rocky and Bullwinkle, Beetlejuice, and Marilyn Monroe, roaming and entertaining guests.

At the *Amazing Adventures of Spiderman* 3D thrill ride at Universal's Islands of Adventure Park in Orlando, guests see a live Spiderman character performing and posing for pictures before they ever see the ride entrance. The queues are in constant motion and always entertaining. At the end of the ride, guests are exited into the Spiderman souvenir store—also designed to be memorable. Taking the guests on a larger-than-life thrill ride and then dumping them out in a chintzy little retail store would feel dissonant and subconsciously off-putting. Instead, Universal ensures that the retail experience is not only bigger than life—like the attraction—but is also crafted to be a part of the total experience. This interactivity is also subtle and often tactile. In addition to characters to interact with, there are "touch me" statues, waterspouts, and automations with whirring and whirling, constantly moving parts in the "strolling street" areas of the parks.

EAT IT AND GET OUT!

The concepts of story, back story, and the unexpected experience work equally well outside the theme park world. A perfect example: Ed Debevic's Diner, Inc., a Chicago-based chain of four Ed Debevic's restaurants. Created by Ed Debevic in 1984, the back story is a heart warmer. From their Web site:

Those of you fortunate enough to have passed through Talooca, IL during the 50s and 60s probably remember Lill's Homesick Diner on Highway 50. The Homesick knew how to feed you: fresh-baked bread and pies, homemade chili, real beef burgers (no soybeans) and plenty of good, hot coffee. And Lill knew how to treat people right—eat and get out, that was her motto. Unfortunately, when a fast food franchise moved in down the road, Lill closed the Homesick and moved to Florida to sell fruit at her sister Estelle's roadside stand.

The Homesick is where I learned the short order business. And while I'm no Lill, I think I've made this place something she'd be proud of. So as Lill always said, 'If you like what you're eatin', order more. If you don't—there's the door.

The *story* is that guests are being welcomed into a 50's diner to experience the ambiance of those days of a misty yore, complete with bobby sox, saddle shoes, and juke box. The surprise "twist" on the experience is that the servers are professional entertainers as well as wait staff, trained to create a rollicking, in-your-face experience—as well as perform the odd musical entertainment—dancing and singing on the counter.

Adhering to the motto, "Eat and Get Out," Ed Debevic's service is anything but service with a sweet and dimpled smile. Dressed in mismatched orange and green floral prints that should have been lost in the attic, the comedic cast does more than take orders. It gives them— to guests.

One of the stock cast characters in an Ed Debevic's, LouLou Lewis, tells guests to finish all the food on their plates, otherwise they'll get no dessert. LouLou will also demand guests stop dawdling and talking and order a meal—"NOW!" Wait staff are frequently heard reciting Lill's famous refrain to diners, "If you like what you're eatin', order more. If you don't—there's the door." But their attitude—complete with foot-tapping, gum-smacking, watch-checking, eyeball-rolling hesitation—provides a quirky, magical charm that keeps customers coming back for more of their insults and meat loaf.[4]

PLACE MAGIC—WITH A TOUCH OF CLASS

Not all the magic of place is about entertainment and splash. It can be subtle, inferential, and quiet as well. Steinway & Sons of Long Island City, New York, makes grand pianos . . . the finest in the world. The pianos themselves are an act of magic over 150 years old. Equally magical are the Steinway & Sons showrooms. That Long Island City factory showroom, as well as Steinway Hall on West 57th Street in Manhattan, weave a subtle magic that expresses the Steinway concern for quality and exactness in a way no brochure copy or marketing material could. The showrooms match their history, story, and mission. Floors of marble, chandeliers of crystal, chairs of teak. Impeccably dressed salespeople chosen for their musical knowledge and understated manner. Stationery—weighty parchment with embossed gold logo and a gold piano in the upper right hand corner. On the walls, why of course, photos of the great pianists who made a living at the keys of a concert Steinway. Each Steinway Hall—there are seven—has a piano "bank," a lower-level room with dozens of pianos—where prospective purchasers can try out every model. In the Dallas Steinway Hall, visitors report they have encountered the likes of Van Cliburn practicing on different models. The Steinway story—the history and success of its products is captured—and quietly told—in pure Place Magic.

Putting Magic into Man-Made Place

Much of high-level Place Magic comes from the hands of architects and design specialists—like the Disney imagineers and the Universal Experience engineers. But there are important things service magicians can do to enhance the sense of Place Magic on a more local level—just as Ed Debevic's has. It starts with discovering the organization's back story.

Find or develop a strong back story. Every organization has a proud history or founding vision or unique mission to use as a back story. For instance, Science Diet®, a product of Hill's Pet Nutrition, traces its ancestry to Dr. Mark Morris, a veterinarian who, in 1943, saved a German Shepherd named "Buddy" (the world's first Seeing Eye dog) from death, by kidney failure, through a carefully crafted, diabetic diet. Morris's dietetic approach to disease management became a hit with other veterinarians and a company was born. Everyone at Hill's knows the "Buddy" story and takes great pride in being part of the tradition. Customers are carefully folded into the tradition of companion animal care through salespeople and company literature. What is your organization's back story? Is there a compelling person, event, or vision in your history?

Develop and use a customer experience story. Porsche automobiles have a long history—their back story—that begins on the racing circuits of Europe. The typical Porsche showroom "tells" the tale of that racing tradition through photos, décor, and written materials. The front story—Porsche as worthy of the fast-car afficienado's attention—is further suggested by both an emphasis on performance data and a long list of available racecar driver-like accessories. Many salespeople enfold the customer even further into the magic of the high-performance sports car fraternity by pointing out a unique Porsche engineering feature—the car's ignition switch is on the left side of the steering column. The reason? So drivers in cold start races, like the 24 hours of LeMans, can turn the ignition with their left hand while simultaneously shifting into gear with the right (an advantage where tenths of a second count). That "tidbit" of Porsche lore brings the would-be purchaser into the Porsche story in a personal, vicarious way.

Dress your "set" in concert with your story. The story of a quick service restaurant is usually some version of decent food served up in a hurry. Speed. The entire set should facilitate that concept. A McDonald's, Burger King, or Wendy's with sit-down dining accoutrements—silverware, plates, table service—would make no sense—and indeed would have a "not right" feel to it. On the other hand—a fast-food restaurant on the shore along a popular vacation lake dressed with antique fishing gear, "fun-in-the-sun" sepia tone photos, and posted info on current fishing conditions takes clever advantage of the local Place Magic. A particularly nice "pocket trick" is equipping counter staff with a little information on what the "big ones" are biting.

Dress the cast to fit the story. Dressing cast members to fit the place story is straight forward in a theme park or entertainment venue. Even in professional settings there are customs that dictate dress—doctors in white coats, nurses in scrubs.

- Is there a natural costuming for your cast?

- Is there a way of dressing that will create commonality or comfort for your customers?

- Would an actual or approximate uniform make the service magicians in your organization more easily identifiable to your customers?

CHAPTER SIX

Applying Little Magics
in Big Places

A cautionary tale: A decade ago, Seattle, Washington–based Nordstrom department stores—thanks to an aggressive expansion plan, an industry leading sales per square foot metric, and the notoriety gained from being mentioned in several best-selling business books—became the focus of considerable industrial tourism, a place to visit and learn from.

Executives of other retail chains—as well as from over a dozen other SIC codes—began trooping into Nordstrom stores up and down the Pacific Coast, in an attempt to discern the genius behind the company's lofty customer service reputation. One easy to see differentiation was the grand piano in the lobby played virtually nonstop by a small legion of well-turned-out professional musicians. Soon grand pianos began appearing in other retailers' lobbies and atria, automobile showrooms, and—yes—even a hospital or two. Twenty months later, most of those "monkey see, monkey do" imitations had vanished. A place amenity, a simple nuance, had become confused with Service Magic.

The *magic of place* is not found in trappings. In fact, the simple aping of décor and amenities, the transportation of physical features from one setting to a totally different context has a derogatory name, several in fact: cute, kitsch, retro, and—in its worst form—tackiness. However, one must be wary of absolutes. The difference between tacky and appropriate Place Magic is often very much in the eye of the beholder.

57

The Midwestern Native American casino with a tropical island theme can seem silly, corny, or tacky to the same person who raves about the mini-pyramids of the MGM Grand Resort and imitation Eiffel Tower of the Paris Resort in Las Vegas. What is seen as an eyesore in one context—a sweeping Midwestern prairie—is evaluated completely differently in another—a blaring, bustling entertainment strip—by the same customer. There are those for whom Las Vegas is a study in garish excess and sensory overload. For them, venues such as the New York New York, Excalibur, the Luxor, and the Venetian, no matter how lavish and well done, are simply seen as studies in taste gone awry.

Just the same, the lesson of the Nordstrom piano has two important cautions. The first: Mistaking the amenities and décor of a place for Place Magic itself, or expecting significant results from the transportation of place amenities from one context to another, in hopes of borrowing the magic of the original place, can and generally does lead to disappointment. The second lesson is not understanding your target market's place parameters. The customer who loves to be challenged, the customer who loves having his or her senses assaulted, and the customer who responds instead to the familiar, safe, and comfortable are seldom part of the same target market—at least where Place Magic is concerned.

At the same time, amenities and nuances, properly conceived and fitted, can change a physical location from humdrum and plain-Jane to something at least approaching magical. The difference between quizzical—and positively memorable—is often in the outcome envisioned by a site's creator. Trimmings without solid underlying tenants are tinsel; physical space magic is a by-product of mental space imagining.

Case in point: Carl Sewell is chairman of Sewell Automotive Companies, a multibrand automobile dealership group headquartered in Dallas. Sewell and his associates have made the showrooms, customer waiting areas, and service bays of his Cadillac, Saab, Hummer, Lexus, Pontiac, GMC, and Infiniti dealerships a positive example of the right way to employ amenities to distinguish what is—most often—a drab and mundane setting. Sewell's avowed vision is to engage customers in a specific kind of sensory overload. Sewell says, "While they come to see and test drive a car or truck, we want them to hear great music, see elegant lighting and terrific artwork, taste gourmet coffee, and feel luxurious leather and fabrics on the chairs. We want their memories to be filled with far, far more than engines, sticker prices, and sales talk. We sought a way to create a consistent, well-thought-out sensory plan. Every object, amenity, and look comes out of a plan for their experience. You've got to know what you're trying to communicate to develop such a plan. You must be clear about the memory you're trying to engrave in your customer's mind. Our plan was to create a look and experience of luxury . . . after all, we sell the best upscale brands in the world—Lexus, Infiniti, Cadillac."[1] Any visitor to one of Sewell's showrooms—or service bays where the floors are as clean and spotless as the showroom floor— would tell you the plan succeeds.

The "plan" Sewell refers to doesn't necessarily have to be a "from the sidewalk to the service desk" masterpiece to work for your customers. Sometimes an approximation of that thoroughness can succeed as well. At Grace Presbyterian Village, just south of downtown Dallas, a few carefully selected amenities play an important role in the treatment of Alzheimer's patients. People with dementia, the most common form of the disease, regress in thinking and behavior to their childhood and early adulthood. That characteristic led Goodwin Dixon, Grace's executive director, to take stock of the facility's physical look. "We keep forcing residents to be in our reality, but they are more comfortable in their own, living in the past," Dixon told *Dallas News* staff writer, Kendall Anderson.

Consequently, Grace did a four-month renovation that restyled the facility in a way that downplayed the square, institutional look and, instead, appealed to the comforting memories of Grace's residents. From posters of '49 Fords to baking classes held in a '50s-style kitchen and an old-time front porch with rocking chairs, the décor at the new Grace is purposely constructed to evoke memories of an earlier era when residents had a more positive self-image. Although research on this concept of place familiarity for Alzheimer's patients is as yet inconclusive, the children of residents and the staff at Grace are convinced that the anti-institution design and memory evoking amenities make a difference in the comfort and mental acuity of the residents. Their measure? The enthusiasm of the residents baking cookies in the kitchen with the 1955 Maytag oven, the chatter of those eating lunch in the '50s diner-like cafeteria, and the toe tapping of those attending an afternoon matinee of the 1962 movie *The Music Man,* just down the hall.[2] Place Magic in the service of human dignity.

GUIDELINES FOR CREATING PLACE MAGIC THROUGH DÉCOR AND AMENITIES

Our initial warning still stands: Do not expect the copying of amenities and features of one locale—be it man-made or natural—to transform a second setting into a magical space. Place Magic, unlike the magic of the stage, is seldom so easily portable. But you can indeed learn from others' successes and begin to transform a limited and mundane space in a magical way IF you . . .

Begin with a vision of what you want the customer to experience. Start by revisiting what you know about your customers; what they have told you about their expectations. Whether your knowledge is informal, gleaned from off-hand customer remarks and comments, or gathered through formal avenues (like customer surveys and focus groups), you already have some of this intelligence. Write down what you think you already know. Ask your colleagues for their impressions and observations of customers. What have customers asked for or commented on while making appointments, waiting, being served, and paying for the service? In particular, probe those memories and data for clues to customer expectations of place. These will be your starting point. You are looking for clues to the look and feel customers expect of physical locales like yours. Whether one customer at a time, or in a more organized fashion—through focus groups and surveys—ask your customers to tell you about place features of other companies or organizations they have enjoyed.

You need to amass enough information to form a vivid description of what your customers see as an ideal place for doing business. Your own ideas and creativity will eventually have to come into play—but your first step should be to tap into your customers' view of place. Once you know their place expectations, it will be easier to play with what you can do to amaze and surprise them—and avoid the "piano in the lobby" mistake. What you will hear initially when quizzing customers may be about process or performance—it often is. Place can easily become transparent to customers once they are comfortable with it. But you can steer the conversation to place features that have impressed them in other settings. Questions like:

- What specifically did their facility look like?

- Was there anything about the lobby/waiting room/check-in/parking lot/drive-up window/dressing rooms—that impressed you?

- Did anything about the signage or furnishings or décor stand out and impress you? Was it easy to find what you were looking for? What made it easy?

Often questions like these will evoke a "Now that you mention it" response that can lead to a wealth of "What if we . . ." ideas.[3]

Fit your amenities to your target market. In addition to being in sync with your vision of place, the amenities need to fit the needs, goals, and expectations of the target market. As mentioned earlier, customers at fast-food restaurants don't expect cloth napkins or glassware. Paper and plastic are just fine and are often in sync with their expectations of speed. If you try to force the issue by substituting china and silver for plastic and paper, you can find yourself violating other, non-place expectations. The typical fast-food luncher, for example, is more interested in "eat-it-and-beat-it" than in a lengthy social transaction—the experience more universally identified with dress-up, sit down, china-and-silver dining.

Ask yourself: How will my customers use this experience to meet their needs? How can I provide them exactly what they need . . . with a magical surprise that fits the experience and adds memorability but doesn't conflict with another expectation? A simple example: Courtyard by Marriott Hotels found that its target market (the budget-minded business traveler) wasn't terribly interested in an array of free toiletries in the hotel room. Soap and shampoo would be just fine. In fact, a broad range of extras—mouthwash, hand lotions, shoe shine cloths, and so on—appeared wasteful. They did not, however, want the hotel to cut corners on the quality of the desk, work chair, and desk lamp. And the surprise? Guests wanted washers and dryers, coffee pots and hair dryers in the rooms—and a vending area with a microwave for popcorn.

Be comprehensive rather than selective in your choices. Think of décor and amenities as supporting structure in a movie or play—costume design, set layout, theme music, an actor's accent, or background weather. All are carefully chosen as a part of a whole, not in isolation. Think about the famous flubs and faux pas—the breaks in continuity—you've heard about in well-known movies. The digital watches worn in the lifeboats awaiting rescue in *Titanic*, the eyeglasses worn by stunt men in *The Ten Commandments*, or Darth Vader's backwards chest plate while in battle with Obi Won in *Star Wars*. If your amenities are selected in isolation, rather than as enhancements of a unified concept, they will appear similarly dissonant to the customer . . . even if there is no conscious recognition of that discord.

All the amenities, taken together, should form a single impression for the customer. Do you want the customer to feel pampered? Then ask yourself and your customers what parts of the experience—and particularly what place amenities—will lead them to that pampered feeling.

Do you want customers to feel a shopping experience with you is efficient and respectful of their time limitations? Then ask them about that experience and the place cues that say efficient and effective to them.

Review the amenities periodically to ensure they continue to work. Carl Sewell Village Cadillac opened in 1957. At that time, free coffee in the waiting area of an automobile dealership was a novelty. People were not critical of the taste of the vending machine brew, they were just happy to get a paper cup full of a hot, caffeinated beverage. Fast forward to 2003. Thanks to Starbucks, Caribou, and a dozen others, the easy availability of a premium cup of java has outmoded standard vending-machine coffee. Today, no self-respecting major-brand automobile dealership waiting room would be caught dead without a phalanx of air pots filled with multiple blends of freshly brewed brand-name coffee. The relevance and value of such amenities is a moving target and must be constantly assessed to ensure they work with your vision, as well as with your customer's definition of those little magics that make them say "wow." Another caution: Trying to linearly advance the last experience, even as customers' expectations climb, has a terribly low ceiling. The "one-up" effort deadends easily. Sooner or later, you will run out of room to improve on the basic cup-o'-coffee. Instead, consider amenities like coffee as a category. That mind-set gives rise to doing different things, not just assumptions to ratchet up the impressiveness value of a single variable. You don't have to spiral up from vending-machine coffee to gourmet-percolated coffee to a waitress taking orders for a custom-designed cup of coffee from a menu of world coffee blending options. "Would that be Jamaican, Columbian French Roast, or Sumatran breakfast blend with hazelnut scent, madam?" Great coffee can be laterally enhanced by adding a hefty mug to the plastic cup options, gourmet cookies, napkins that occupy the customer with interesting facts about the coffee, or recipes using coffee. Think of coffee as one item in the category: "Things to occupy the waiting customer and cater to his or her personal tastes."

Get ongoing customer feedback on the value of the amenities. The Western Warehouse—with four stores in Dallas and the surrounding area—is famous for its wide selection of western gear, especially boots. Western-wear fans in Texas take their boots seriously, often spending a considerable amount of time getting a perfect fit, the right heel and toe, and the best quality material—be it basic steer leather, alligator, kangaroo, ostrich, or goat. A great fit requires trying on many pairs before finding just the right one. At one time Western Warehouse customers being fitted for boots were asked, "How about a cup of coffee or a soft drink?" The most common customer retort: "No thanks, but I could sure use a cold beer!" The customers were really reflecting an attitude more than an actual request. Today the store starts the customer refreshment query with, "Can I get you a cold beer?" Sure enough, there is a large barrel of ice-cold beer in the store—not for sale, but for the refreshment of customers. Most customers opt for the coffee—but their reaction to the more generous gesture clearly telegraphs their delight.

Examine your amenities through all five physical senses. AvalonBay Communities, a Virginia-based company that develops, builds, and manages luxury apartments throughout the United States, includes permanent wine racks in some of the kitchens of its units. "We found a way to use what otherwise would be vacant space in the kitchen area that added a taste of class," explains Shannon Brennan, VP for customer service. The company also includes gas grills in the courtyards of many of its garden-style communities. Brennan explains, "The smell of someone grilling helps residents feel they are residents in a community, not tenants in a complex." The key is to use the five senses as tools to review and renew amenities. If your setting is pleasing to the eye, ask yourself: What should it sound like, smell like, taste like, feel like? The change in perspective can generate ideas for important amenities.

If you were in the automobile repair business, would you want your waiting customers to focus their attention on the repair bay or a television soap opera? It depends—again—on the impression you want them to leave with and their basic expectations. For instance, if you want to emphasize efficiency and speed as part of your lasting image, then placing your customer waiting area above the shop floor with a panoramic view of the service bays might do the trick. But if you want your customers to feel that you're concerned with not inconveniencing their daily life flow, then TVs, courtesy phones—perhaps even a fax machine and an Internet hook-up—might serve that purpose.

Amenities play supporting roles and are not the main attraction. It is crucial to remember that amenities are not what brings the customer into your door—or portal—initially. Rather, amenities add an enchantment dimension. They serve you poorly if they are used as camouflage for a shabby product or lackluster basic service. When the novelty wears off, and the amenities are no longer unique or intriguing, what is left is the quality of the product or service the customer came for in the first place.

A company in Dallas purchased a classic 500-seat theatre in an up-scale neighborhood as the site for a chic new playhouse. The goal was to bring in live performances that would appeal to a 50-plus audience. The velvet seats, curtains, and gilded wallpaper were elegant, the lobby bar was well stocked with top drawer beverages, the ushers were clad in tuxes. Opening night was a successful gala complete with a live concert by the Platters. The theatre closed after a few months. The company had overspent to create the perfect setting with amenities to appeal to every sense—and had little budget left for the quality talent that would draw and sustain an audience.

Any restaurant manager will tell you that a new physical setting covers a lot of sins. At the same time, that physical setting does not remain new and novel forever. Once the customer has become accustomed to the look of the restaurant, the ambient buzz of a room full of diners, the feel of the napkins and silver, and the novelty of the menu—the taste of the food, the quality of the service, and the price of the experience are what remain—and must be at the core of what you manage most carefully to bring the customer back again. To paraphrase an old adage: "Don't confuse the sizzle for the steak."

CHAPTER SEVEN

Third Place Magic

Not all effective Place Magic is so highly engineered as a theme park, as riotous and theatrical as Debevic's, or as formal and upscale as a Steinway showroom. For most of us, there is—or has been in the past—a place beyond home and work we remember fondly for its conviviality and character, its warmth, and friendly and comforting nature. This "third place," as sociologist Raymond Oldenburg calls it,[1] may have been a soda fountain or a pool hall, a coffee shop or a corner bar, a barber shop or a beauty parlor. Even a neighborhood grocery or hardware store could serve the purpose.

A *third place* is an inviting venue where people like to "hang out" and is more noted for its sense of commonality and camaraderie than for its commerce—although the majority of third places are indeed as commercial as they are convenient for socializing. Think "Floyd's Barbershop," "Arnold's Drive-In," "Cheers," and "Central Perk," each a prototypical third place. And while many Western sociologists lament that the American migration away from core cities to suburbs has lead to a decline in third place opportunities, others point out that most shopping malls, many chain restaurants like McDonald's—as well as chain coffee shops like Starbucks—are coming to serve much the same purpose. Indeed, as anyone who has ventured into a "Golden Arches" around 9 AM in an older suburb on a Saturday morning can attest, the spirit of Klara's Koffee Korner has simply moved down the street to Big

Mac's dining room. The coots and gaffers, the characters and cutups who inhabited the corner diner cum java joint of old have found a new hangout. So have a sizable constituency of early morning jogging buddies, recreational bicycle groups, best girlfriends stoking up on Egg McMuffins and O.J. before a trip to the mall, and any number of young dads taking a turn at breakfast and quality time with a pair of curtain climbers.

And while the neighborhood McDonald's and Starbucks and the area mall may lack the picturesque quaintness of a small Parisian café, a Liverpool pub, or a German beer garden, many of the key characteristics that lead to Third Place Magic are in place.

Oldenburg has observed four fundamentals of successful third place venues—places that succeed both as commercial ventures and community crossroads. Tweaked with a little imagination and creativity, many otherwise mundane settings can take on third Place Magic.

Third places are relatively inexpensive to enter and purchase food, drink, or services. Many sociologists argue that $3 cups of coffee and $30 haircuts impinge on third place development. "Who can really afford to linger and socialize in such environments?" one writer complains. We contend, however, that "expensive" is relative and market segment specific. A Bally's membership may be expensive relative to a YMCA or community recreation center membership, but all three can function equally well as convivial meeting and socializing venues—within their target market segments.

Third places are highly accessible. Some sociologists argue that "accessible by foot" is a critical variable for third place building. Yet we've all seen how area malls and drive-ins—venues accessible primarily by car—successfully serve as meeting places for young adults and teens. Easy access is also in the eye of the beholder—and a matter of travel habit. The key to transforming a place to a third place is linked more to frequency of attendance than to method of arrival.

Third places have regulars. Habit is habit. Whether the coffee outlet of choice is Starbucks or Klara's Koffee Korner doesn't really matter, as long as it is a convenient crossroads for people in search of a cup of coffee, can become part of a routine—and has a little space conducive for people to meet and interact on a regular basis. We've seen Starbucks, Caribou, and Java Centrale coffee shops in strip malls across America easily serve as third place venues for adjacent office complexes. In the same way, chain sports bars like Champps and ESPN Club seem to be functioning fairly well as contemporary corner pubs—frequently with a third place feel to them.

Third places are welcoming and conducive to conversations with old and new friends. We would agree that a sports bar with blaring wall-to-wall television sets and deafening music is more conducive to shouting than conversation, but other contemporary venues pass this test with flying colors. Chain bookstores like Barnes & Noble and Borders have successfully installed coffee bars and comfortable conversation areas. Casual observation suggests—where attached to a shopping mall— these venues have also quickly become congenial gathering spots for the less retail oriented during family shopping junkets. In a word— hangouts for trailing husbands and kids, while the matriarch is off in search of bargain-priced pelts.

CONSIDERING A THIRD PLACE MAKEOVER

If the idea of morphing a physical locale where you currently serve customers into a third place is intriguing—the act itself is relatively easy. It is a matter of adding amenities and conveniences to an existing space where people can congregate comfortably—and encouraging them to come in for more than a simple transaction. A sporting goods store with a basketball court, a gun shop with a firing range, and a fishing gear store with a stocked pond and fly-casting lessons—are simple examples of place extensions that can lead to Third Place Magic. We know of many Harley-Davidson dealerships that have set space aside for Harley Owners Group (HOG) meetings and repair and maintenance classes. The stores have literally turned into third place hot spots for recreational bikers.

Five Questions to Think Through before Taking the Third Place Magic Plunge

1. Do you have the temperament for managing a third place—a "hangout"—no matter how specialized it may be? If you are more comfortable with a transaction trade and prefer your customers "buy it and beat it"—don't toy with Third Place Magic. You could conjure up a devil of a mess.

2. Is your market area—your wider commercial community— going to accept your commercial space becoming a third place?

Neighbors can be supportive—or throw obstacles in your path. If you don't know which is likely, find out first.

3. Is your clientele likely to accept your offer to extend the nature of your offering? (All magic needs participants and an audience.)

4. Is it possible that the creation of a successful third place will endanger—rather than enhance—your commercial viability? A third place has regulars and those who—usually inadvertently—provide a less hospitable environment for transient customers.

5. Are you willing to let your customers become participants in shaping the destiny of your business? Third place denizens—comfortable with you and your business—seek to extend their psychological "ownership" of the magic by lobbying for changes that will enhance the third place viability—but not necessarily your profitability.

In the End, the Audience Decides

Third Place Magic exists when people come together in a spirit of conviviality and common interest. As the magician in charge, you can set the stage and plan the act—but for the show to succeed, the audience has to show up, buy the premise, and participate. You can't force your customers to take part in the magic, but you can invite them to come and play along.

PROCESS MAGIC

MAGICAL PROCESSES
Policies, procedures, and routines that make transacting business with an organization easy, positive, and memorable.

PROCESS MAGIC
Filling the space between "customer need" and "customer need met" with experiences of awe and memories of amazement.

"Think left and think right and think low and think high.
Oh, the thinks you can think up if only you try!

DR. SEUSS

Some of the most entertaining magic comes from little understood, easily observed processes that are as regular and predictable as sunrise and sunset. But because of the magician's skill they seem paranormal acts of mind reading and prescience. Part of the effect is the sociology of the setting—the audience has come to be entertained, not to think logically. Also, the rapidity of the magician's patter discourages pensiveness and analysis. Most of all, Process Magic depends on our willingness to be enchanted. Case in point:

Nine Steps to Amazement

To best appreciate this piece of mental manipulation, take pencil in hand and follow along with the magician's instructions to see what happens—just as an audience member would:

Ladies and gentlemen, we are all familiar with the concept of synergy and collective energy. Each and every one of us has the ability to tap into that cosmic unconscious we all share and use it for problem solving and decision making. Relax, clear your mind, and listen to my instructions, and I will demonstrate the phenomenon for you.

On that television screen in your mind's eye, picture the following steps:

- Think of any number from one to ten.

- Now multiply that number by nine. I'll wait. Got it? Good.

- Now, if the product of your multiplication is a two-digit number, add the two digits together. Good!

- Now, subtract FIVE from the number you are thinking about.

- Now, think of a letter in the alphabet that corresponds to the number you are thinking about. 1 = A, 2 = B, 3 = C, and so forth. Good!

- Now, think of a country that starts with that letter.

- OK, now, carefully spell that country in your head. Then think about the second letter in that country's name. Visualize it clearly.

- Now, quickly, think of an animal whose name begins with that letter.

- And, finally, visualize the color of that animal.

> Ladies and gentlemen, there are no gray elephants native to Denmark, but there are in your mind's eye, aren't there?

This wonderful little trick works because of the nature of base ten numbers—and shared common knowledge. It works every time for every person—save for those audience members who are arithmetically challenged or geography mavens who know that there is a country called Djibouti.

Fortunately, the service magician doesn't need to be a mathematician or even be aware of the peculiarities and anomalies of base ten numbers to create Process Magic. Take, for instance, the service magicians who work the front desk of the Hotel Monaco in Chicago at a very mundane task—the process of checking a guest into the hotel. After filling in the registration card, verifying the stay and method of payment, the Monaco's desk clerks change the process in a unique, fun, and unexpected way:

> **Clerk:** "Mr. Guest, the Monaco is a pet friendly establishment. Do you have a pet with you?"
>
> **Guest:** "No, I don't."
>
> **Clerk:** "Mr. Guest, it would be our pleasure to loan you a pet for your stay if you'd like. Specifically, we would be delighted to deliver a companion goldfish to your room. At no charge. Your only responsibility would be to give your fish a name. Housekeeping will take care of everything else."

Of course, when guests return, they are asked if they would like Goldie—or Fluffy or Charlie—to join them again for their stay. And they remember a simple process to which a little magic has been added.

Service magicians, like those at Hotel Monaco, know where and how to add a little magic to mundane practices. Most of all, they know how to capture that magic and communicate it to others in their organization.

The following three chapters reveal the amazingly simple secrets of transforming everyday processes into little acts of magic.

## CHAPTER EIGHT

Process Magic

Blending Comfortable Consistency with Surprise

To the stage magician, the surprise ending is the zenith of the art. The rabbit from the hat, the rose that becomes a dove, the unexpected and astounding—these are the magician's stock in trade. Surprise is what audiences love about magic: something unexpected and unexplainable happens—something magical that is enchanting.

Transport members of that same audience to the check-in counter of a hotel, the checkout line of a grocery store, or to a doctor's office—and surprise has a significantly lower value in their minds. Indeed, researchers repeatedly confirm[1] that customers use "consistently good" as their gold standard for service. The customer's sense of reliability, security, and comfort hang on service promises—real or implied—being kept, and being kept with a high degree of precision and consistency. That "steadfastness" is so important that most organizations take care that their processes come with rigid standards and stern rules.

If customer confidence depends on most processes occurring with great certainty, how does Service Magic gain any leverage at all? Simple. There is a difference between an unpleasant surprise and surprising delight: Customers are willing to alter their expectations of a process or to be surprised by process alteration—but only if they can expect a positive payoff.

For example, airline customers are accustomed to assigned seats (which they generally get when making reservations) and the process of boarding by row numbers—first class first, then back-to-front coach class in groups. Southwest Airlines changed that process. The airline does not preassign seats. Instead, it rewards those who arrive at the airport early by giving boarding preference to the first 45 customers to arrive at the gate.

Southwest managed this breach of custom by creating an eminently fair process—and communicating the new process up front. In addition, the carrier loudly proclaims that its "best on-time record in the industry" is due in part to the no-reserved-seat boarding process. The privilege of boarding early became an equitable game of chance; the likelihood of on-time arrival at one's destination, however, was greatly enhanced. In other words, this altered process created a positive trade-off and a predictable, acceptable outcome for Southwest's customers.

The "payoff" for a process that varies from the customer's preconceived notions or expectations need not have such a clear-cut trade-off to be acceptable. A change that is simply a pleasant surprise addition to the core of consistency can make a mundane process magical. Chicago's Hotel Monaco's complimentary companion goldfish program is a perfect example. Hotel manager Jim Marino: "We ask our guests if they'd like a goldfish delivered to their room. When they say 'goldfish?' We say, yeah, we're pet friendly, and if you don't have a pet, we'll provide you with one. It will keep you company, and it won't talk back to you. When the guest returns for a second or third visit, we say 'Hi, Mrs. Jones, welcome back. Would you like us to send Matilda back up to your room?' Mrs. Jones replies, 'Yes, and make sure it's Matilda, she was great.' Hotel staff feed and care for the fish, all the customer has to do is name it." Marino continues, "We probably get 50–60 requests a day for a goldfish. We have a tank in our housekeeping office that probably has about 200 fish." Customers relish the unique feature of its check-in process. Hotel Monaco and Southwest Airlines are two quite different, but useful, examples of process-change strategies. Southwest changed the rules and the outcome in a way that was acceptable to its target market. Hotel Monaco simply attached a surprise enhancement to the end of an existing core process and left the process largely unchanged.

THE NATURE OF PROCESS

All processes fall into one of two categories: algorithmic or heuristic. *Algorithms* are step-by-step processes. Think of them as "rules of law" that focus on precision, replication, exactness, and dependability. The hospital lab technician who tests a patient's blood sample for cholesterol levels follows an algorithm to ensure a reliable outcome. The desk clerk at the Monaco checking in a guest follows an algorithm as well. But there is an important difference between the desk clerk and the lab tech's algorithms. If the lab tech doesn't follow her algorithm carefully, the test is likely to go bad and will need to be redone. If the hotel desk clerk does not precisely follow his algorithm, the check-in process may look bumbling and take more time, but the outcome is still likely to occur: The guest will be checked in.

The lab tech follows an algorithm that, through trial and error, has proven to be the most effective in creating a reliable—that is, accurate—reading of the patient's cholesterol levels. This is a "Red Rule" algorithm, designed to maximize effectiveness, safety, and predictable outcome. The hotel's check-in process follows a step-by-step logic that the organization determined is the most efficient way to check in a guest. It is a "Blue Rule" algorithm, designed to maximize efficiency and sameness. As we will see later, the difference between the two is critical to deciding where and when to add a little magic to a process.

Heuristics are "rules of thumb" for doing work. "Give each arriving guest a warm greeting," "Listen to the customer before you try to solve his problem," and "Treat patients with respect" are all rules of thumb for behavior rather than step-by-step guidance.

Ritz-Carlton Hotel employees follow a heuristic code of conduct called "The Ritz-Carlton Basics," 20 guidelines for dealing with customers, service, safety, and quality that all employees are expected to memorize and follow. They include such guidance as, "We are ladies and gentlemen serving ladies and gentlemen" and "Use the proper vocabulary with our guests and each other (eliminate Hello—Hi—OK—folks)."[2]

Implicit in the guidance offered by these "Basics" is an in-context judgment call. For example, another Ritz-Carlton Basic says, "Smile—We are on stage. Always maintain positive eye contact." Reasonable guidance, but a smiling and cheerful countenance may be inappropriate while serving a wake. And at times, excessive eye contact could be interpreted as leering or just plain odd. When organizations try to make algorithms of rules of thumb like these, the attempt to create uniformity is likely to backfire because of the judgment-call nature of heuristics.

A good example: Safeway Stores learned that customers come back more frequently when checkout clerks are perceived as friendly, smiling people—so far so good. But when the stores imposed rigidly defined rules requiring employees to make eye contact and smile at all customers, the "service with a smile" policy became the subject of a formal grievance filed with the National Labor Relations Board by Safeway workers. Some male customers misinterpreted such attentiveness from female employees as flirtatious, rather than friendly, and the women—required to smile, at all costs—felt powerless to use their natural self-defense mechanisms to set the occasional creep straight.[3]

The lesson: When complex judgment calls are a part of the service situation, creating complex guidance seldom results in either improved impact or anything resembling Process Magic.

ADDING MAGIC TO RULES OF THUMB

Rules for adding magic to an established process—or for transforming a process entirely—depend on the process being addressed. Putting magic to work with a heuristic or set of "rules of thumb" requires a different approach than rewriting a "Blue Rules" algorithm or a "Red Rules" algorithm. Once you know what type of process you're dealing with, you can decide on just the right touch of magic that will make it a pleasantly surprising experience for customers. Here's what a common heuristic would look like:

When a customer walks into a white-tablecloth restaurant on a Tuesday evening without a dinner reservation, the hostess greets him and asks a programmed question, "Would you prefer smoking or nonsmoking?" She enters his name on her wait list. She invites him to go to the bar, and tells him that she will come and get him when a nonsmoking table is available. After a 20-minute wait, she fetches him from the bar, has the bartender switch his bar bill to a dinner bill, and escorts him to a table near the front of the restaurant. "The scallops are terrific if you're thinking of seafood," she informs him. Shortly thereafter a waiter brings a menu and a complimentary scallop hors d'oeuvre. It is a dining experience repeated in heads-up, customer-oriented restaurants every night.

Behind this encounter is a heuristic process—with magical contingencies attached. The hostess knows that a short wait increases the perceived value of a meal and directs the customer to the bar rather than seating him immediately at an undesirable table by the kitchen. She notices his dress and targets him for a table in the front, one seen by arriving guests, to reinforce the restaurant's "curb appeal." She has been instructed that dinner guests often pay by credit card and do not like having to charge two bills (bar and dining) at the same location. A seating chart allows her to seat the customer at a table that balances the workload (and tip potential) of the wait staff. She also has been informed by the kitchen staff that the scallops are not moving as fast as expected. She alerts the wait staff that a single customer has been seated at table B-14—returns to the host station to greet the next guest.

All of these frontline practices are driven by a heuristic process—a worked-out-in-advance set of procedures that helps provide good service to guests while taking care of the internal demands of the restaurant. The hostess is expected to honor these "rules of thumb" when taking care of guests. However, any number of variations are perfectly acceptable: The customer may get a table straight away if one is available and in sight. The customer may prefer to remain in the waiting area and bypass the bar. Should that be the case, the hostess may take care to keep the customer informed of her efforts to seat him ("I should have a table in another five minutes"). She might recommend the sea bass if the scallops are selling well.

"Rule of thumb"—or heuristic—processes are not lockstep, exact, or precise. They may be guidelines borne of the folklore of an industry and conventional wisdom learned only through experience. They may be the "thou shalt's" sent down from mahogany row. They may emerge from unwritten secrets of success quietly spoken from master to novice after closing time. Regardless of their origin, they inform consistent, masterful behavior.

What would these rules of thumb look like with the addition of magic? The hostess might surprise the guest by saying, "We normally have a 20-minute wait, but this is your lucky night. We have a table available right now in our nonsmoking section." Or she might reward him for waiting for a table by making his first drink "on the house." She might cue the waiter that the customer has already consumed a Jack Daniel's with a splash of water at the bar, so the guest can be pleased by the advance knowledge of his waiter. She might present him with some item as a take away—a logo shirt, a coupon for a free appetizer on his next visit, or a complimentary take-out menu—as he leaves the restaurant.

Several universal principles are important to keep in mind before tinkering with heuristic processes. Remember: Consistency is the overriding quality of both heuristic and algorithmic processes, so exercise great care and thoughtfulness before tampering with them. Better to have plain vanilla that leaves the customer secure and comfortable than to attempt magic that leaves someone insecure and anxious!

Never tinker with the customer's core expectation. A customer goes to an upscale restaurant expecting a nice meal and attentive service. If the meal is inferior or the service too mechanical, the customer concludes, "I could have gotten this at a fast-food restaurant."

The customer's core expectation also includes a mental picture of great service. If the magic attempted is too extreme, the customer will remember it as disruptive, artificial, or as some aberration not likely to recur on a future visit. The energy wasted on the gesture will fail to yield the ultimate payoff—greater customer loyalty. If you plan to get quirky, the customer needs to come with full knowledge that quirkiness might occur. At Ed Debevic's Diner, for example, customers could be greatly offended if they didn't understand the humor. The '50s diner atmosphere, the wait staff's costumes, and the spotlighting of the "Eat and Get Out!" slogan all prepare customers to expect the eccentric treatment that is Debevic's special brand of magic.

Make sure the alteration in the process fits. Service Magic enchants because it is unexpected and positive, yet it needs to be appropriate to the context and the relationship. A customer would not expect the waiter to know his drink preference in an economy restaurant, but that personal touch fits perfectly in an upscale restaurant. At a St. Paul Saints baseball game, fans love it when a pig carries out the game balls. This same act would not be appropriate at Yankee Stadium. The question to keep in mind: Is it reasonable to incorporate this particular brand of magic and assume it will not disrupt existing relationships?

Ensure the alteration is a team effort, not an isolated gesture. If the change is carried out unilaterally by one individual, the customer won't see it as reflecting the attitude of the whole staff or the organization. The customer also knows single-relationship magic when he sees it and knows it is vulnerable to turnover. It does not ensure long-term loyalty.

The Charlotte, North Carolina office of Merrill Lynch is known for delivering Service Magic. It assembled a team, the CBC Group, to ensure that several financial advisors would have detailed knowledge of every client. When the team learned key clients enjoyed around-the-clock service, it decided to provide them with online access to their accounts. But the team also realized that a client's late-night review of account activity might trigger questions. The magical alteration it came up with? Like physicians in a medical practice, one of the team members is "on call" at all times. Clients have the home phone numbers of these financial advisors—along with instructions to "call me anytime." The usual process that assured clients of 8 to 5 EST, Monday through Friday service was made magical—especially when clients can call their stockbroker on Sunday morning!

REWRITING "BLUE RULES" ALGORITHMS TO INCLUDE MAGIC

Algorithmic processes are precise, lockstep means of getting the service the customer expects from the service provider to the customer. Algorithms can be dictated by law (airline safety briefings, for example), but more often they are specific to the organization. When magic is the goal, process reconstruction requires careful guidance since customer trust is at stake. Reinventing an algorithmic process without carefully anchoring it to customer's immediate expectations can be costly; it's one reason ATMs took ten years to catch on—customers had to learn why they needed and wanted automatic access.

Here's an example of a common algorithmic process: Many sit-down restaurants offer take-out service. A customer calls the restaurant and a designated person takes down the order. The order-taker is instructed to read back all orders for customer verification, check for special customer requirements (dressing on the side, sweetened or unsweetened, hot or mild, etc.), and to give the customer an approximate number of minutes required for the order to be readied. When the customer arrives, he or she enters the restaurant, picks up the packaged meal, pays, and leaves. If the wait staff or cook skipped a requested item or included coleslaw instead of a lettuce salad, the customer learns of the error after arriving at home, changing clothes, checking mail and messages, and, finally, unbundling the take-out order—too late to go back for correction.

Romano's Macaroni Grill uses an algorithmic process for take-out that ensures consistency, responsiveness, and—most important—accuracy. But Macaroni Grill added a little magic to the process as well. When take-out customers call in their orders, the order-taker gets the food order and asks for the type, model, and color of the customer's vehicle. When customers arrive at the restaurant, they pull into special close-to-the-front parking spaces. A video camera alerts a runner inside, who delivers the order to the car window and picks up payment—just like an old fashioned drive-in restaurant. The customer never has to get out of the car. Take-out orders are checked for accuracy before the customer arrives. They are re-checked with the customer when delivered to the car. The process has proven effective and is non-negotiable in how it is performed. "It may be improvisation inside the restaurant," says Marketing Vice President Diana Hovey, "but the take-out process is all about precision and accuracy."

Call the typical insurance company to follow up on the letter you sent three weeks ago, and you'll likely be shuttled through a dozen telephone menu choices and then put on hold for 20 minutes. After you get through to a live human, chances are you'll explain why you're calling, and get passed off to four more clerks (who each ask you tell your story) until you find one who agrees to get back to you within four to six weeks.

Contrast that scenario with the service provided at USAA. Customers contact a service rep who can see their letter immediately, since on arrival it was scanned into a computer system every customer-contact employee can access. No wait, no passing customers along to a "we'll let you know" dead end. The lockstep process is as predictable as a military unit parading for review. Service reps successfully handle 86 percent of all customer requests on the first contact. No wonder when customers speak of USAA service, they frequently use the word "magic" in their accolades.[4]

Helpful rules for adding magic to "Blue Rule" algorithms include:

- *Select a process the customer must endure and enrich it with a little magic.* Some processes are crafted exclusively for the convenience of the service provider. Magical process architects make processes customer-friendly as well by zeroing in on the feature or attribute that is most important to customers. Checkout lines at grocery stores are designed for the stores; express checkout lines are largely for customers. Bank lobbies with lines and tellers are designed for the bank's convenience; drive-up banking is largely for customers.

  USAA understood that its primary customers, military officers and enlisted personnel, often had no time to spend being shuffled through a bureaucratic process. Macaroni Grill seized upon absolute accuracy and ease of pickup as important features to guide the reinvention of its take-out process.

- *Don't alter a part of a process without examining the whole experience.* The *magic of process* depends on the whole experience being magical. If only a part of the process is enhanced, a bland or negative part left unimproved can erase or negate the enchanting memory for the customer.

  A major hospital, seeking to completely revamp its admission process into one customers raved about, neglected to address the parking shortage at the hospital. No matter how pleasurable the check-in was, patients were still stewing over spending 20 minutes looking for a place to park before they entered the front door. Ultimately, the hospital purchased a large parking lot three blocks away and provided several fun buses to transport customers from the lot to the hospital. The colorful transportation impressed the hospital's customers, coming and going.

- *Include props to reinforce consistency.* Consistency is a prerequisite for all algorithmic processes. However, retaining the required uniformity can be challenging. Service providers get distracted, bored, or simply adventurous in administrating a service through a process. Magical "rules of law" come with devices aimed at ensuring—or at least promoting—the precision of the process. Devices take many forms—reminders, checklists, job aids, guides, cueing devices—to help the service magician remain disciplined and focused.

TURNING "RED RULE" ALGORITHMS INTO MAGICAL MEMORIES

The more challenging arena of service processes is the unalterable algorithmic process. Most of these algorithms originate with the discovery of a method or procedure that yields the desired results—the steps a lab tech follows to measure blood cholesterol levels correctly, the procedure a FedEx driver follows to ensure overnight delivery, the routine McDonald's employees follow to serve fast-food items that are always the same.

The service magician, unable to alter Red Rule processes, must find ways that will yield a magical experience for customers. This entails finding actions that effectively run alongside a "rule of law" process without tampering with it directly. The Mayo Clinic, headquartered in Rochester, Minnesota, has found a way. Mayo treats some of the most famous patients in the world, yet anyone is welcome—no physician referral is required. About 80 percent of patients come to Mayo on their own initiative—many without having a prior appointment. Once they arrive, they're continually surprised by another magical addition to a standard health care process: At Mayo, no one mentions money until the patient has been treated. Forms are filled out when you leave, not when you arrive.[5]

An automated e-mail message that assures customers their order has been received is standard procedure for most Web retailers. Shortly after customers place an order, they receive a confirmation by e-mail. Proflowers.com doesn't want customers worrying about whether their flowers will arrive on time, so they put *three* assurance-builders into every transaction. The first message goes to the customer when their order is received. When a delivery truck picks up the order from Proflowers, a second e-mail update is sent. But it's the third message that's the magic charm: The customer gets a message saying when the flowers were delivered and the name of the person who signed for them. The third e-mail twist eliminates the concerns of gift-givers and has lowered the number of worried calls Proflowers receives.[6]

Rules of thumb for altering Red Rule processes:

- *Alterations must be delivered in matched tones.* While consistency is important in any process, it is what makes the algorithmic process. The "lockstep" nature is present because absolute replication has been deemed key to value. Therefore, alterations must be made with the experiences that surround the process, not the process itself. Any surrounding experience must be kept in the same tone, style, and manner as the process itself. Proflowers sends three e-mail messages to assure customers that their orders have been received and delivered—it doesn't place phone calls or send snail-mail postcards.

- *Alterations must be subtle.* The key is to not tamper with anything that causes the customer to question the core values imbedded in the process. This means alterations should not call attention to themselves. The Mayo Clinic doesn't require patients to fill out insurance forms when they arrive, but it doesn't give away its medical services either.

- *The magic can operate alongside the process without upsetting requirements.* Since tinkering with an algorithmic process is a "no-no," sometimes the magic can occur alongside the strict, algorithmic process. At Wayzata Dental, for example, patients can watch the procedure they are undergoing on a screen in the operating suite. The "add on" is surprising and memorable, but doesn't interfere with the step-by-step nature of the dental procedure.

- *Value addeds should be of the same nature as the core offering.* Adding value can be the seat of great magic. We all are enchanted by the unexpected "extra helpings" of life. However, adding value to an algorithmic process must be done with meticulous care. It works best when understated and cut from the same cloth as the core offering: Proflowers' extra e-mail assurance, for example, or Mayo Clinic's willingness to treat patients with or without a physician referral.

HANDLE WITH CARE

Service processes are not naturally magical. Magic occurs when the process is transformed or contains an unanticipated dimension—the more "sparkly" the transformation, the more magical it is. Yet care is required: Magic depends on identifying a process alteration that will be permissible by the customer, and then crafting its expression into a form unexpected by the customer.

That "permissible by the customer" caveat is important. Be thoughtful in choosing the process to be altered. Be careful in transforming the process. Remember that some processes are so sacrosanct to the customer that any alteration provokes uproar and rejection, and your customer "storms out of the theatre." But select the right process, alter or enhance it the right way, and you can turn dull into delightful and mundane into magic.

## CHAPTER NINE

Magical Scripts

Walk in the door of your local Home Depot and you'll invariably receive a greeting tailored to customers of the big orange warehouse: "Hi. What project are you working on today?" Thus encouraged to launch into travails with a balky toilet or the symptoms of an ailing water heater, you immediately know this place and this person can provide help, advice, and comfort (if necessary), as well as hardware or replacement appliances or even installation service. Home Depot knows its customers are often contemplating, planning, or stuck in the middle of a home-improvement project, so this short script is a fitting—and encouraging—replacement for the generic opening line, "May I help you?"

> **SCRIPT:** The written text of a stage play; a plan of action.

An organization that knows its customers can create scripts that make it "easy to do business with." Words so right, so appropriate, and so effective for the situation appear magic to impressed recipients of the carefully crafted words. What might appear to be clairvoyance to the do-it-yourselfer—who just crawled out from under his kitchen sink and staggered into his nearest Home Depot to find just the right pipe-fitting—is the predictable outcome of a transaction in which a service magician confidently delivers a simple line known to fit the situation for a majority of the organization's customers. It is a *scripted* greeting.

Of course, some situations call for more elaborate scripts. Here's an algorithmic process that creates a magical outcome for customers.

Cable television people know that one of the most common causes of service calls is a television set inadvertently tuned to the wrong channel for the cable box to work. This is called "operator error" in the repair trade; it's expensive to send a technician to a subscriber's home for such an "oops" problem. The dilemma: How to ask a customer to check the channel setting without embarrassing him? Several companies have evolved a simple patter that saves everyone's face.

"Mr. Smith, would you mind helping me do a simple diagnostic so I can properly brief the service technician? Turn on the TV set and cable box. Is the problem still there? OK. Turn the TV set to channel nine, wait a few seconds, and then turn it back to channel five. Now try one of your regular cable channels. Is there sound and a picture? Great. I think that's taken care of the problem. If it doesn't stay fixed please call me back and let me know. My name is Marge and my direct number is. . . ."

One company we know sets up the conversation by saying, "Before I dispatch a service technician, I'd like to try and solve the problem from here," creating a perception that the phone rep can remotely diagnose and correct the subscriber's problem. Regardless of approach, the intent is the same: To check for an operator error problem without embarrassing or upsetting the customer. The tool of choice is a carefully scripted conversation.

SCRIPTED PATTER

Service people in organizations ranging from retailers to hotels to hospitals rely on scripted lines—and sometimes stage directions to accompany the words—to work their magic. In addition to using their specialized greeting for do-it-yourselfers, Home Depot service magicians walk customers to the location of the product they need—they don't point the way. Employees of the Cincinnati Marriott Northeast reply with a distinctive, "It's my pleasure," to a guest thank-you, instead of a mundane, "You're welcome."[1] The Ritz-Carlton Hotels use some specific word scripting to reinforce its service credo, "We are ladies and gentlemen serving ladies and gentlemen." Employees are asked to use guest names whenever possible, along with a slightly formal greeting such as "Good morning" or "Good evening" as opposed to "Hello" or "Howdy" or "Hi folks."[2] Housekeepers at Aurora Sinai Medical Center in Milwaukee carry laminated cards that remind them to knock before entering a patient's room, smile, introduce themselves, and ask, "Have I missed anything?" before departing with, "Thank you and have a nice day."

These simple touchstones lend a predictability and consistency to the quality of every service encounter. The challenge is to prescribe words that will help provide a consistently high level of service, without falling into the trap of impersonal language delivered robotically. Telemarketers have used prewritten, scripted conversation for decades. That singsong voice on the other end of the phone is a dead giveaway that a dinner-interrupting call is scripted. That's the kind of rote delivery that gives the whole idea of scripting a bad name. But it needn't be that way.

A Little "Feeling" Please

Consider this line, scripted for delivery by cashiers in a grocery store checkout line:

"Did you find everything you were looking for today?"

Delivered in a bored monotone, or in a rapid run-on "Didyoufindeverythingyouwerelookingfortoday" manner, it would hardly be comprehensible, much less magical.

However, delivered in a pleasant, well-measured, properly metered way, it is much more likely to result in something like:

"Oh, now that you mention it, I never did find the salsa I was looking for. I guess you are out or something."

Which gives the checkout person an opportunity to make a little magic:

"Let me call someone who will know for sure if we're out. If he finds some, we can add it right in."

A well-delivered, scripted opener can start a dialogue that leads to a small delight for the customer and an add-on opportunity for the store. (See Chapter 14 for more about customer-pleasing dialogues.)

The service magician's performance—the way he or she performs the lines—is as much a part of the customer experience as the words said. Enthusiasm, willingness, and sincerity add the magic that turns a mundane, forgettable service encounter into an occasion memorable for the warm glow it leaves with a customer. "It's one thing for a script to come from the head, but if the words don't also come from the heart, it's going to backfire," observes Allen Stasiewski, director of service management for the metro area of Aurora Health Care in Milwaukee, Wisconsin.

MAKING A MAGICAL DIFFERENCE

Scripts created with care and delivered with feeling—online or face-to-face—are not mind-numbing, robot-creating endeavors. Indeed, concise and well-considered scripts enable organizations and their service magicians to capture a sort of lightning in a bottle. At MidAmerican Energy, a gas and electric utility serving four Midwestern states, customer service associates in the Davenport, Iowa call center ask every caller, "Is there anything else I can help you with today?" That question, designed to ensure utility customers don't have to call back shortly on another matter they may have neglected to address on the first call, also uncovers critical problems on occasion. "We've had customers say, 'Oh, and I smelled gas the other day.' We've actually discovered gas leaks from simply asking this question!" says Terry Ousley, MidAmerican Energy's manager of customer contact.

Gail Boylan of the Studor Group, a Gulf Breeze, Florida health care consulting firm, and former chief nursing officer of Baptist Health Group of Pensacola, Florida, is a convert to the power of scripted conversations. "I hated the idea of scripting people. It seemed like an insult to their intelligence," she admits. Nonetheless, encouraged by the customer raves she'd heard as a result of scripting instituted at Holy Cross Hospital in Chicago, Boylan and her colleagues wrote a series of simple scripts for Baptist's most critical interactions with patients.

Customer surveys had told them that a sense of privacy was an important issue for patients. Nurses came up with a line designed to acknowledge and reinforce that expectation: "I'm closing this curtain to help protect your privacy." Almost immediately, patients started rating nurses higher on thoughtfulness and consideration. After tidying up a room, cleaning people started asking the scripted question: "Is there anything else I can do? I have some time right now to help you." Patients began asking room cleaners to close window shades, shut doors, or lower television volume—all things they had previously been ringing their call buttons to ask nurses to do. Nonmedical calls to nursing stations declined by 40 percent, and patients began remarking about how helpful and considerate the cleaning people were.

Likewise certain seemingly insignificant actions—the stage directions that accompany scripts—can make a magical difference to customers. Aurora Health Care's Allen Stasiewski tells of interviewing a customer who had been a patient in the emergency department to find out what service experiences made an impact. "I expected her to tell a dramatic story of her life being saved by doctors who cracked her chest and massaged her heart or something. But what she really remembered was that every time the doctor came into her curtained, emergency room cubicle, he knocked. Every time." The action demonstrated the doctor's respect for the patient and it made a lasting impression.

Owning the Script

Service magicians look at scripts the same way actors and stage magicians do—as tools for creating the right impression and precisely communicating a message to an audience. Just as actors mold, internalize, and personalize the delivery of their scripted lines to create a sense of spontaneity in each performance, service magicians work to personalize and "own" their scripts. They find a balance between meeting the organization's required service standards consistently—and delivering their lines with a verve that feels fresh to customers. Employees of Southwest Airlines, the Dallas-based carrier that routinely appears on airline industry's "best" lists as well as *Fortune* magazine's "Most Admired Companies" list, are renowned for their mastery of this art.

Southwest flight attendants deliver the standard airline announcements and FAA-required information with a distinctive—and often wacky—panache. Passengers may be treated to embellishments such as, "Smoking is not allowed in the restrooms. If you're caught smoking in the restroom, we'll ask you to step outside, where the movie showing this week is *Gone With the Wind*" Or "In the seat pocket in front of you, there's no telling what you'll find, but you'll also find. . . ." Or "Please pass all the plastic cups to the center aisle so we can wash them out and use them for the next group of passengers."[3] The result of such improvisation: passengers who are delighted by these entertaining personal touches—and who actually may hear safety information that often becomes so much white noise because of repetition. Of course "zany" doesn't play to every audience or every occasion. But Southwest Airlines prides itself on its renegade, "different kind of airline" image, and the slightly off-kilter announcements and recitation of the FAA rules reinforce that image quite nicely.

A major telephone company in the Midwest discovered the value of encouraging the improvisation of lines after first implementing a rigid script designed to meet a uniform standard. The public utilities commission required the company to advise every residential customer who reported a phone problem that the customer would be charged a repair fee if an on-site inspection revealed the problem was with the telephone or the wires in the wall. To ensure it met the requirement, the telephone company gave telephone operators in its customer-inquiry centers a script to follow when customers requested an on-site repair. That satisfied the utilities commission, but customers invited to focus groups complained that they felt "Mirandized" by the cue-card reading—to them, it sounded like a police officer advising a criminal of his rights. Not the impression the company intended to leave with customers!

Anxious to improve its customer-satisfaction ratings, the company altered its standard from "read this cue card" to one that encouraged employees to use their own approach when advising customers about a possible charge. Customers treated to the more adaptable, less robotized approach responded with higher service satisfaction ratings.[4]

WRITING MAGICAL SCRIPTS

The best service scripts—scripts that are flexible, customer-focused, and aren't embarrassing to use—are written by the people who must deliver them. Truly magical scripts come from people on the frontlines who have identified a need and sit down together to brainstorm through situations that are difficult to handle, instructions that are hard to give, and conversations with customers that have a history of going wrong.

Consider the hospital maintenance workers who were extremely uncomfortable going into patient rooms to repair some faulty bit of hardware or other problem. They didn't know what to say when a patient was very ill and the family was sitting at the bedside. The workers themselves took the matter in hand, says the Studor Group's Boylan. They got together and wrote a simple script: "Hi, I'm John from the maintenance department. I'm sorry to disturb you right now, but I want you to be as comfortable as possible so I want to fix. . . ."

MidAmerican Energy's senior frontline customer service associates (CSAs) helped develop the manual of procedures for the most frequent customer calls. For example, the manual provides suggested questions to ask customers who call about a higher-than-usual gas bill: "Has anything changed in your family?" "Are more kids living at home?" "Have you added a pool?" Although MidAmerican relies on its philosophy of

treating customers with dignity and respect in lieu of tightly scripted patter, these questions are designed to help a CSA get the most out of a discussion with a customer during what might be a touchy conversation.

In most situations, Service Magicians need to be able to modify
scripts as their read of the audience dictates. Some customers appreciate a formal, "Good Morning, Mrs. Smith," and others are much
more comfortable with an informal, chatty, "Hi, Jane. How goes it?"
MidAmerican Energy CSAs are trained to listen for cues that will help
them quickly identify customers' needs and match their pace. If CSAs
recognize they're speaking with an elderly customer, for instance, they
won't talk as quickly or as casually as they would with a 20-something or
a Gen Xer.

Scripted Recovery

The savviest use of scripts comes into play in situations where something has gone amiss for the customer—calling for *service recovery*.
Dialogue that responds to service gone awry—the computer isn't fixed,
the dry cleaning isn't ready, the soufflé collapsed—can test the skills of
even practiced service magicians. Service recovery is a special challenge
in health care, points out Aurora Health Care's Allen Stasiewski. "We're
dealing with a microcosm of every experience in life from 'How did my
mother die?' to 'Why are the beans cold?'"

Aurora Health Care employees once followed a standard complaint-
handling procedure that directed them to call a customer back, with list
in hand of what went wrong and why. Not, they slowly concluded, a productive approach to magical recovery. The problem, says Stasiewski, was
that employees were inclined to start spewing out the list immediately,
and failing to listen to the customer. "Our philosophy was, 'If you see a
problem, you own it, you fix it.' We changed that to, 'You see it, you own
it, you recover from it, you fix it.'" The change, he says, reflects the understanding that "an explanation will always sound like an excuse to a
customer with a complaint, and a correction will always sound like you're
calling the customer a liar."

Recommended recovery conversations were modified as well. "Now
we say, 'Don't do research. Your job isn't to explain the company's action
or correct the customer's understanding.'" Instead, Aurora employees
follow a six-step process[5]: Apologize and offer to help. Listen, empathize,
and ask open-ended questions. Fix the problem quickly and fairly. Offer
atonement. Keep your promises. Follow up. At Aurora Health Care, that
process now appears on cards kept next to telephones or in pockets to remind staff to listen before even beginning to fix a problem.

Service recovery scripts aim to help service magicians be at their most confident when the customer is most insecure. The planned and practiced patter—and processes—of the recovery script provide the confidence and competence to turn distress into delight.

Certain time-tested phrases are (almost always) guaranteed to work a little magic on customers—or at least to calm them down long enough to give dedicated service magicians a chance to show their stuff. For example:

An irate customer announces, "I'm very upset. Let me talk to a manager." One disarming response is: "I'll be delighted to let you talk to my manager. What seems to be the problem?" That line tends to stop customers in their tracks and enables them to let go of their resistance; they can take a step back from a combative stance because, suddenly, there's no need to fight. When a customer uses other methods to question the service person's knowledge or competence ("Is there anyone around with more experience?"), another useful phrase is, "Please give me a chance to assist you." Few people are unwilling to give service providers a chance if they simply ask for it.[6]

Customers confused or intimidated by a new process or new technology often ask, "Why did you change it? I liked the old way." One way to respond is to help the customer feel involved in the change. A good script that addresses this situation: "Changing was a difficult decision for us. We did an extensive customer study. You may even have received a phone call or a survey. We based this change on what we learned. I think you'll be surprised at how much easier this is."[7]

Some customers ask for assistance by using the "rescue-me" maneuver or the "I'm-so-stupid" ploy: "I'm probably just an idiot, but I can't seem to empty my delete folder." Savvy service magicians *don't* agree with the customer—no matter how tempting it might be. A more skillful response: "I've had the same problem myself. It's easy to get confused. Let me explain to you how I remember."[8]

THE RULES OF MAGICAL SCRIPTS

Part of what is magical about *magical scripts* is improvisation, and the service magician's ability to fit a script to the wants and needs of individual customers. But there are a few rules of thumb that will help you develop effective scripts:

- *Magical scripts should square with the organization's service strategy.* At MidAmerican Energy, call center employees are dedicated to one goal: Doing the right thing for the customer. Their ability to personalize every customer contact, while still getting key information and using a few key phrases, reflects that goal.

- *Discover what customers value, and develop scripts around those issues.* Baptist Hospital nurses developed the script telling patients "I'm closing this curtain to help protect your privacy" as a direct result of surveys that indicated patients value privacy.

- *The script maker would be wise to get input from the people who will be delivering the lines.* As we mentioned, this is how the best scripts are written. "Supervisors are sometimes clueless about what will work," says Aurora Health Care's Stasiewski. "We have to get the people who will be saying the words involved in creating the words. Then they know the words will work in most situations."

- *Keep it simple.* The most effective scripts are simple. They directly address the comfort or concern of customers or service providers. That's why Home Depot's opening line, "What project are you working on today?" is effective, as is MidAmerican Energy's memory-jogging closer, "Is there anything else I can help you with today?"

- *A script is a performance.* The way a script is performed is as important as the choice of words. When cashiers are directed to say, "Thank you for shopping at XXXX," but the line comes across as a run together, meaningless space-filler—someone has failed to communicate the importance of tone, feeling, and pace in performing the script in a way that adds to the customer's experience with the organization.

- *Make some allowance for improvisation.* If some people are more comfortable asking customers "Can I help you?" than "May I help you?"—so be it. Personalization, within agreed upon and clear limits, is desirable; people who imbue the words with their own spark put magic into their performance.

- *Develop scripted procedures that service providers can fall back on when service recovery is necessary.* Recovery scripts act as a security blanket when dealing with service breakdowns—the users don't have to worry about what to say because the basic script has been established. That gives them the confidence and the mental energy to concentrate on working magic for this customer in this unique situation.

## CHAPTER TEN

The Six Secrets of
Magical Service Recovery

The skilled stage magician often creates magic from the illusion of a failed trick. The failure could be either a part of the setup, preparation, and presentation of an entirely different trick or an escape the magician has thought through in the event an out was needed. But when the magician turns those broken eggs into turtle doves, the effect is more awe-inspiring than had he not had a "problem" at all.

So too with service magicians who take upset customers and deftly return them to a state of satisfaction—even awe—by virtue of their sensitivity, quick action, and follow-through in the face of service breakdown.

Magical service recovery is about keeping customers coming back even after the worst happens, and making them even more loyal to your organization along the way. To the most skeptical customer, the true test of an organization's commitment to service quality isn't its cutting-edge advertising or marketing pledges, but the way it responds when something goes awry. What becomes of those "we care" promises when that time-sensitive product shipment arrives a day late, the external server crashes during online rush hour, or when the drive-thru order is sans the French fries and salt? Magical recovery isn't simply about effective damage control and efficient problem resolution. It's as much about fixing the customer—repairing the disappointment caused by the breach of faith—as it is about fixing the customer's problem.

Nothing creates a stronger bond between provider and customer than when a problem is fixed with empathy, speed, and competence. Such recovery ensures the pieces that have been "glued back together" after a mishap are even stronger than the original, unshattered versions. That's because prior to any problems, customers operate on hope—hope that in the event of a breakdown, the company's service magicians will respond in good faith. In the aftermath of good recovery, they have proof of that commitment—and surging confidence in the organization. Studies by the Arlington, Virginia research firm TARP show that customers who have a problem satisfactorily resolved are more loyal to the company than had they not experienced any difficulty at all.[1]

Magical recovery, like a stage magic escape, happens not through steely resolve, but through preparation and practice. There are six secrets, or behind the scenes principles, that prepare service people to become *recovery magicians*. Some of these secrets concern the support organizations must provide frontline magicians, while others are about the psychology of betrayal management. Implemented together they can turn aggrieved customers into committed believers who evangelize about your organization to colleagues, friends, and family—and who stay loyal to your organization for life.

SECRET #1: RECOVERY MAGIC BEGINS FAR OFFSTAGE

The kind of *magical service recovery* that transforms at-risk customers into walking billboards for your organization isn't the result of random acts committed by a handful of Good Samaritan employees. Magical recovery is the result of a planned, systemic process that begins far off-stage. The process includes creation of: (1) a clear problem-resolution process, (2) a subsystem that captures and analyzes customer disappointments, and (3) a "recycling" of that information back into the system to reduce repeat mishaps. The magic is delivered by employees who are trained in the quick-thinking tact and diplomacy—the performance skills—necessary to convert irate or frustrated customers into happy, repeat buyers.[2]

Just as seasoned stage magicians can exude confidence because of a well-devised "out" for a failed trick, service magicians act out of the certainty that they have a well-designed tactic and are empowered to take action when something goes wrong for the customer. They know they can work with their customer to find creative solutions rather than defer to managers. At Ritz-Carlton Hotels, for example, all associates from the general manager to the housekeeper have blanket authorization to refund or spend up to $2,000 to solve a customer problem. That empowerment allows everyone to perform acts of memorable recovery magic for customers.

SECRET #2: CUSTOMERS HAVE A CLEAR VISION OF HOW YOU SHOULD FIX THEIR PROBLEMS (AND IT DOESN'T ALWAYS MESH WITH YOURS)

All service recovery begins with the expectation of fairness. Customers enter a service experience with clear ideas of how you should react in the event of a problem—be it a defective product, incomplete product delivery, or undercooked entree. Recovery expectations can vary by geography, customer demographics, and even the recovery process of a competitor familiar to your customer. If a large percentage of your customers also are customers of service-magical organizations like Federal Express or Amazon.com—or even the stellar mom-and-pop dry cleaner on Main Street—their experiences with those organizations will inform their expectations of you.

All upset customers want personalized treatment—"Here's how we're going to fix your *particular* problem, Mr. Ramirez." Just the same, those individual visions usually include similar basic expectations. The longtime bank customer with multiple high-balance accounts and the month-old customer with a minimum balance checking account may have similar recovery expectations if there's a significant error on a bank statement. *Fix it fast—and don't let it happen again.* But the longtime customer may expect—and indeed requires—some personal hand-holding as well as a call and apology from a bank executive. The new customer, on the other hand, will probably be satisfied with an e-mailed form letter and evidence in his online account that the problem has been resolved.

SECRET #3: FIRST FIX THE CUSTOMER— THEN FIX THE CUSTOMER'S PROBLEM

The first response of most organizations to service breakdown is to do what's necessary—often minimally so—to fix the problem, then send the customer on his or her merry way. But customers also have a need to be "repaired" psychologically. Service breakdown threatens the very glue of any business relationship—trust in the service provider's ability to deliver what was promised. The first step toward recovery magic is to let customers vent about the problem, and for service personnel—like it or not, and regardless of who caused the problem—to apologize and grovel a bit before moving on to the business of fixing the problem. Letting the customer tell his tale, provide his take on the problem, and release the pressure valve a bit helps advance this emotional repair. How that apology is handled makes all the difference. It's important for service workers to take full responsibility—not blame the problem on a "misunderstanding" or "miscommunication" or place the burden on a third party. A direct and simple "I'm sorry this happened and I'll make sure it's fixed right away" is as close as you can come to a magical incantation in service recovery.

Customers do make mistakes, and know those mistakes often cause or contribute to their problems. But they assume their view of what should happen to atone for that mistake—whether they or the organization caused it—is the only right course of action. When the Service Magician challenges that view—when the endgame becomes determining who's right—the customer assumes he is being coerced, patronized, or even lied to. Focusing on who's right puts the long-term health of a business relationship in jeopardy. Far better to focus on collective discovery and problem resolution with the customer—not on finger-pointing. Because even if you're ultimately right in your position, you still lose.

Tony Iyoob, a training specialist with Harris Teeter Inc. grocery stores, handled an irate customer in a way that offers a lesson in self-control for us all. An angry customer had returned a spoiled chicken to Tony's store. The problem: It was one of his competitor's chickens. "But the customer proceeded to tell me how slack our store was in selling spoiled meat, and wouldn't let me get a word in edgewise," Tony says. "The yelling didn't let up for a second."

Tony let her finish venting. When she finished, he apologized, letting her know his company cared about her concerns. He then gently pointed out her chicken was purchased from a competitor, but that he would be happy to replace it with one of his own. "She was mortified and felt bad about giving me such a hard time," he says. "I insisted she let me replace the chicken, but she refused. She then left the store."

About an hour later, Tony noticed her shopping in his produce department, and when she saw him she ran up and gave another heartfelt apology. She went on to explain the reason she was there was, "If you can back up a product from another chain as well as you did, then I can only imagine how you would back up one of your own products." She said she was committed to doing any future shopping in Tony's store, and he's indeed seen her several times since the day of the infamous "chicken lickin'"—she gave him.[3]

The need for such emotional healing is especially acute when customers feel they lack:

- Information, or when they're in the dark about the cause of the problem or how long it will take to fix it.

- Recourse, or a lack of options for fixing the problem aside from dealing with you. In other words, the customer feels you're his or her only hope.

- Expertise, or the ability to fix a problem with their own know-how or experience.[4]

SECRET #4: OFFER A FAIR RESOLUTION TO THE PROBLEM—THEN ATONE FOR ANY INCONVENIENCE

While apologizing and showing empathy are crucial to fixing customers' emotions, they are only the opening salvos in a magical recovery effort. Plenty of organizations think their recovery work is done with an act of contrition—when the damage inflicted actually requires some further atonement or compensation to the customer. Understanding that need separates magical recovery efforts from those that leave customers with a lingering sense of being coerced or marginalized. In short, it pays to remember that for many customers, a brusque refund beats a smiling rebuff any time.

To wit: A colleague rented the hit movie *Lord of the Rings* from a local video store for his family's Friday night entertainment. After fighting traffic to and from the store, he arrived home only to open the box and find the wrong DVD had been inserted—and the R-rated movie inside hardly seemed a suitable replacement.

Steamed, he drove 30 minutes back to the store through the still-lingering gridlock, while his family put its plans on hold—and an accompanying meal back in the microwave. The store clerk offered an appropriate but rote-sounding apology—"We're sorry about that"—but the recovery effort ended there. No waiving of the rental fee, no coupon for a free rental—nothing to compensate the customer for the hassle of having to drive back to the store and disrupt his Friday night plans. The seeming indifference suggested such foul-ups were status quo around there—and the customer better get used to it. Our colleague vowed not to darken the store's door again—and warned any in his large circle from doing the same.

Contrary to popular belief, most customers bring a sense of fair play to the table when the situation calls for atonement. Our aforementioned colleague didn't expect the video store to offer a roundtrip to Orlando and a pass to Universal Studios for his inconvenience, or to force the offending clerk to sit through repeated showings of the movie *Glitter*—only some form of "symbolic" atonement like waiving a $4 fee or providing a coupon for a free rental. These are the small, reasonable gestures that say "We understand your frustration or disappointment, and want to do something to make up for it."

The good news is that research shows, in the majority of cases, what customers expect by way of atonement costs less and is easier to deliver than you might guess.

Consider Domino's Pizza and its original service guarantee of "delivery in 30 minutes or your pizza is free." Although the pledge more than achieved the company's marketing goals, Domino's discovered the number of customers taking it up on the guarantee was far less than the number of "more than 30 minute" deliveries. Follow-up focus groups unearthed the reason. Most customers thought a free pizza was excessive atonement for pizza arriving only five or ten minutes late. When Domino's shifted its guarantee to $3 off the pizza price for missing the 30-minute window, a far greater number accepted the offer.

When and how to offer atonement can be one of the hardest things for budding service magicians to learn. We've found the best approach to sorting it out is to draft a series of recovery cases—real ones from the organization's own files—and hold a number of short, one- to three-hour training meetings to discuss the handling of the cases. By proposing and discussing solutions, participants in the discussions develop the skill of looking at both the nuances of a problem and the ramifications of possible solutions.

Involve the Customer

Research also shows that customers who participate in the problem-solving effort tend to find the problem resolution more magical. This doesn't mean you shift the burden to them to fix the problem. It *does* mean asking them what they would like to see happen next to fix the problem, which gives them a sense of regaining control. And that con-

The Service Recovery Process

Once a customer problem is identified, the service recovery process should begin. Not all of the six steps described here are needed for all customers. Use what you know about your company's products and services, and what you can discover about your customer's problems, to customize your actions to the specific situation. One size doesn't fit all.

Apologize/Acknowledge   Positive service recovery stories begin with some version of "I'm sorry."

Listen, Empathize, and Ask Open Questions   Listening is an active process; empathy shows you understand what the customer is saying, and that you care. Asking open questions helps you gain and keep control.

Fix the Problem, Quickly and Fairly   Develop and implement solutions; involve the customer to reaffirm partnership and build trust.

Offer Atonement

Go the extra step!

Follow Up   Confirm that what went wrong has been put right, and that you care.

Remember: Keep Your Promises   Customer expectations—stated or unstated, reasonable or unreasonable—form a promise between you and your customer. Be realistic about when and what you can and can't deliver.

Each episode of service breakdown is different. Sometimes you will need to use all six service-recovery steps, at other times only a few. How you use the recovery process will depend on the emotions of your customer and on the specifics of the individual situation. Only you are in a position to evaluate and act.

trol can be essential to customers who feel they've just been abused by an organization.

SECRET #5: MAKE "RESPONSIBLE FREEDOM" A CORNERSTONE OF RECOVERY TRAINING

Although the goal is to thrill customers with recovery responses, proportionality must come into play as well. The customer whose T-bone steak arrives rare instead of well-done might be impressed with an offer of free steaks for a year, but making a practice of such atonement puts an organization on a collision course with bankruptcy. The goal is to put a smile back on customers' faces, but with one eye on the organization's interests—and with the knowledge that most unhappy customers quickly get beyond their anger given a heartfelt apology and a little atonement.

Equally critical to *recovery magic* is giving service workers autonomy in solving customers' problems. The last thing any organization needs is for frontliners to have to run to managers every time a recovery situation arises. Yet you also need to ensure your people make prudent recovery decisions. You do that by combining smart guidance with "responsible freedom."

SECRET #6: NO ACT IS COMPLETE WITHOUT FOLLOW-UP

Nothing enchants a customer like a follow-up call at home or the office following a service problem. The organization that takes the time to check back to ensure the solution is still satisfactory—that the repaired laptop is still working well, that there are no complications from the laser or cataract surgery, or that the newly-patched roof isn't leaking—makes a powerful, magic-imbued statement. The return on investment from such phone calls is huge in terms of goodwill created and loyalty captured, making customers more immune to the gravitational pull of your competition.

Following up serves another important purpose. There are some breakdown situations where customers feel that voicing upset or frustration during the transaction or experience may put them at risk. Research in the health care field, for instance, has found that due to fear of retaliation, many elderly hospital patients keep quiet about service problems, particularly regarding nursing issues, until after their discharge. Following up with a phone call or survey gives an organization a second chance to resolve the customer's problem, and potentially win back their trust and loyalty.

Responsible Freedom in Action

At Byerly's, a Minneapolis grocery store chain, employees are empowered—given explicit permission—to do what it takes to solve customer problems, regardless of how those problems come about.

When Matt McCalley, a 19-year-old on a Byerly's overnight crew, received a call for help from the set of a movie being shot nearby at 1:00 AM, he didn't hesitate to take action. It seems someone on the movie crew forgot to order food, and they needed 220 box lunches by 4:30 AM or risk a revolt. Hanging up the phone and rushing to the store's deli, Matt found only a dozen pre-made sandwiches on hand. He proceeded to wake up the store's deli manager at home, who called deli managers at three sister stores, who called yet other employees to action. By 4:35 AM, all the box lunches—which included 220 orders of potato salad, cold pop, and chips as well as the assembled sandwiches—converged on the movie set to the applause and delight of grateful crew members.

PERFORMANCE MAGIC

PERFORMANCE MAGIC
A surprisingly positive interaction between customer and organizational personnel experienced during the acquisition and delivery of a service or product.

MAGICAL PERFORMANCE
The manner that enables a service magician to take customers on an emotional journey so enchanting they cannot wait to tell the story.

"Each loves the play for what he brings to it."

GOETHE

THE KING OF HEARTS

The magician begins by calling for a volunteer from the audience. He then produces a sealed deck of cards, opens the pack, shuffles, and with the volunteer's help, counts out 25 cards. He sets the remainder of the deck aside.

He asks the volunteer to pick a card, memorize it, and return it to the deck. The magician shuffles the deck, and then deals the 25 cards into five facedown stacks of five cards. He asks the volunteer to pick two stacks and discards the three not chosen. Then the magician asks the volunteer to pick one stack and again discards the unselected stack. The magician spreads the five remaining cards—still face down—in a straight line across the table and asks the volunteer to choose two cards. The magician discards the three cards not chosen and asks the volunteer to pick one of the two remaining cards and discards it. The magician asks the volunteer to pick up the card that remains and look at it.

"Is that your original card?" he asks.
"Yes," the volunteer invariably answers.
"Is it the king of hearts?" he asks.
Again, the answer is always, "Yes."

Both audience and volunteer are awed and amazed. How did the magician do it?

The Trick

Technically, the *King of Hearts* works because the magician knows which card the volunteer will select before he selects it and into which pile of five cards the king will go when the 25 cards are dealt. Psychologically, the *King of Hearts* works because of the freedom the volunteer *seems* to have to select any card from the deck and any pile of cards on the table. The volunteer—not the magician—*seems* to be making all the important decisions.

In reality, the magician is deciding which pile to keep on the table and which to discard, and which individual cards to keep and which to discard. If the volunteer picks the pile with the king of hearts, the magician discards all the other piles. If the volunteer picks a pile without the king of hearts, the magician discards the pile the volunteer picked and asks the volunteer to select yet another pile. Because of the speed of the play and the verbal charm with which the magician presents the choices, neither the volunteer nor members of the audience notice these important subtleties. The action moves too quickly to focus on, think about, or comprehend each move.

Like the *King of Hearts,* Performance Magic depends on the service magician's skill in leading the customer to a positive outcome. But unlike the *King of Hearts,* which uses fast-paced, snappy banter and confusion—if not deception—to accomplish its end, service magicians use genuine rapport and personal connection with customers to create performances that are magical. Customers receive the product or service they want or need, but they also get that extra something that makes the experience unexpected, unpredictable, and memorable.

WHEN FISH FLY

Stroll through Seattle's Pike Place open-air waterfront market and you can see what has become a world famous example of Performance Magic. Pike Place Fish, a seller of fresh seafood, is renowned for its flying-fish act—it has been featured on *Good Morning America,* an episode of the TV sitcom *Frasier,* a corporate training film, a best-selling business book, and countless stories in newspapers and magazines.

The shouting fishmongers in white aprons and black rubber boots perform with gusto, tossing fish—large fish—through the air, while keeping up a rhythmic patter. A fishmonger shouts, "One salmon flying away to Montana," and flings it at a coworker 20 feet away. "One salmon flying away to Montana," all the fish guys repeat, as the designated receiver catches it. One fish guy juggles crabs, while another teases a youngster by moving the mouth of a large fish as if it were talking.[1]

The fishmongers' act draws a crowd, as they make strollers part of their flying-fish routines, entertaining them and pulling them into the show at the same time. Customers might try their hand at a bit of fish tossing or just learn some fishy facts while they make their purchase. Owner John Yokoyama explains: "We take the attention off ourselves (and look) for ways to serve them; to make their day. They experience being known and appreciated whether they buy fish or not."[2]

Service magicians deliver that kind of Performance Magic— whether they're selling fish or answering phones or cashing checks. Alert to customers' needs and moods, they read the often-subtle signals being sent. They know how to establish rapport with customers, sometimes mirroring their emotions and listening intently to ascertain the feelings behind the words—and respond in ways that acknowledge those feelings. They delight in taking customers on an emotional journey so enchanting they cannot wait to pass along the story of their magical experience.

THE SECRETS OF PERFORMANCE MAGIC

In the next three chapters, you'll learn the secrets to reading customers and meeting their spoken and unspoken desires. You'll find out how to create rapport with customers and build special—and profitable—relationships with them. You'll discover how to use customer-pleasing conversation to make the magical connections that will keep them coming back for more.

## CHAPTER ELEVEN

Reading Your Audience

Great stage magicians are masters of audience dissection. They spend countless hours learning what their audiences expect and what will create that "how'd-he-do-that" wonder. Service magicians exercise a similar skill when they observe customers, anticipate their needs, and match offerings to their sensitivities. The server who identifies at a glance the timorous and the high-roller, and adjusts his or her service style accordingly; the flight attendant who sees a passenger struggling to hoist a bag overhead and helps without being asked; the dental hygienist who recognizes a patient's unease and reassures without patronizing—all of these service magicians are performing feats of *read-and-match magic.*

They've learned to serve in a way that feels personal and spontaneous—performed "just for me"—to customers. But service magicians are, in fact, delivering studiously rehearsed acts. Service providers are more like street performers than stage actors, observe B. Joseph Pine II and James H. Gilmore in their book, *The Experience Economy: Work Is Theatre & Every Business a Stage.* The performances of street actors are elastic, shaped by the mood of the audience, random outside elements, even the mood of the performers themselves. Service magicians, like street-theater performers, "gauge the audience, identify those who will go along with their gags and those unlikely to (sometimes even delaying or postponing performances when the audience doesn't seem

'right'), and then turn every disruption into part of the act itself. . . ."[1]
Accomplished service magicians, like street actors and improvisational
club professionals, perform within some general parameters—they
have a set act, but with many options—and carefully choose which "bits"
from their repertoire to include for each customer.

How can you learn to pick and choose the right "bits" for the right
customer, matching your performance to the customer and situation?
That's where the trick behind the trick comes in. Just like mastering the
illusion of the vanishing coin, it's not hard once you've learned how to
do it. And you don't have to be Doug Henning or Lance Burton to pull
it off. You do have to cultivate your observation, listening, and interpre-
tation skills to recognize and understand what customers are telling you.

THE MAGIC OF OBSERVATION

As baseball great Yogi Berra wisely said, "You can see a lot by looking." Focused observation is the first step in learning to read customers.
The fact is, people reveal a lot about themselves without saying a
word—if you know where and how to look.

Part of the trick is simply paying close attention, taking yourself completely out of the picture for a moment, and focusing on the customer.
Does the customer seem happy, indifferent, annoyed, enthused, or sad?
Would you guess this person is an extravert or introvert? What seems to
catch his or her eye? You can't judge people by appearances, but you can
learn a lot about their wants and needs through observation—especially
when they don't realize you're watching them.

At Universal Orlando (which includes Universal Studios Florida and
Islands of Adventure), frontline team members are expected to use the
Look–Focus–Act service model to meet guests' needs, says Scot LaFerté,
senior director of training and development. "We want our team members to move beyond meeting to exceeding service expectations through
creating an emotional connection for our guests. Our team members
look, through scanning their environment, for opportunities to engage
our guests in conversation. This allows them to proactively anticipate
guests' needs, thus enhancing the overall experience."

One way Universal Studios Hollywood, Universal Studios Florida,
and Islands of Adventure folks reinforce the practice of this proactive
looking is by following the "10/5 Rule": Make eye contact with any
guest within ten feet and verbally greet or acknowledge any guest within
five feet or "Whassup?" range. Then they focus on scanning the situation for "service cues": Is the guest searching for a park guide? Or pos-

ing for pictures with the whole family? Or does the guest appear lost or distracted or disappointed? By practicing proactive looking, Universal team members appear to divine guest needs. They step up and offer to take that family picture or show that lost mom, dad, and kids the way to 'Toon Lagoon or Nickelodeon Blast Zone—and they do it *before* they're asked because their finely tuned "guest in need" detectors are always turned on.

Diligent observers of nonverbal cues—body language, clothing, eye contact, manner of speaking—can learn volumes about an individual by simply watching. It takes more than a chapter to cover the finer points of nonverbal communication. In fact, there's considerable literature that can help you develop people-reading skills. Here, we'll concentrate on passing on a few tricks of the trade service magicians use to read customers and adjust service-delivery performances accordingly.

Tricks of the Trade

What do service magicians watch for when they aggressively, proactively observe customers? Here are some of the nonverbal cues shrewd observers make it their business to note:

Clothing. How is this person dressed? Does his or her apparel serve a function or make a statement? A baseball cap once served a function—to keep sun out of the wearer's eyes. Now a cap flipped around and worn backward makes a statement.

What do people's clothes telegraph about their view of themselves and the world, and their mood or personality? An expensive custom suit says plenty about the wearer's self-image and how he or she expects to be treated, as does a faded T-shirt and raggedy blue jeans.

Eye contact. Does the customer meet your eyes? For how long and how frequently? People tend to make eye contact more when they listen than when they talk. If you ask a question that makes customers feel defensive, aggressive, or hostile, they often increase eye contact with you—in fact, you may see their pupils dilate.[2] Most people will avert their gaze when they are lying or prevaricating, or when they are asked questions that make them feel uncomfortable or guilty.

Kinesics or body language. What is the customer's body language? The way an individual holds him- or herself, gestures, facial expressions—all help you detect state of mind and personality. For example, arms crossed on chest may be communicating defensiveness or withdrawal from a conversation. Or it may be simply a position of comfort. Notice the hands: If they are in fists or gripping the bicep, defensiveness is a good guess.[3] Folded arms, turning the body slightly away while touching or rubbing the nose, may mean the customer is suspicious, uncertain, or doubtful about what you're saying.[4] A dental patient sitting with locked ankles and hands clenched on the arms of the chair is holding back strong emotions—apprehension about the coming procedure is a good guess.

Most people have no idea what their faces are expressing—that's why actors learn to control their facial expressions. From the customer's face, what would you guess he or she is thinking? Observe the customer's mouth. Is a mood etched there—or is one emerging?

Even smiles need interpreting: A smile that shows the upper teeth and includes eye contact is often used as a greeting; but the oblong smile that shows both upper and lower teeth and forms an oblong with the lips is more likely a forced grin, expressing the pretense of pleasure more than the genuine article.[5]

How does this person move? Observing the way a customer moves can reveal volumes about personality or mood. A customer who strides up to the counter is confident service will be immediately forthcoming; one who edges in the door and approaches slowly and hesitantly is more doubtful or anxious.

Voice characteristics. What can you glean—beyond the words—from this person's manner of speaking? What do the tone, inflection, volume, and speed communicate to you? Irritation may be an easy read when a customer is speaking loudly and emphatically. Is the volume turned up and words spoken so quickly that they're tumbling out? The speaker wants action or considers the request urgent. But what about a customer using the kind of measured and exasperated monotone you might use to order the dog off the sofa? This customer is probably impatient. Recognizing the embedded warning may help you avoid or defuse the anger that can't be far behind.

> **HINT:** Acknowledging obvious anger is a great defense: "Mr. Smith, you seem upset. Have I done something to anger you?"

The Magic of Listening

Of course, accurately reading customers also depends on listening—really listening—to them. The core skill for effective listening is getting focused and staying focused. When listening is your goal, make it *the* priority. Do not let *anything* distract. Pretend you just got a gift of five minutes with your greatest hero. If you could have five minutes—and only five minutes—with Moses, Mozart, Martin Luther King, or Mother Teresa, would you let anything or anyone interfere? You'd hang on every word and every nuance. You can cultivate that intensity through practice.

Try this the next time you want to listen intently to someone: Imagine you're a newspaper reporter from another culture. You've been sent here on assignment to get the story and report it. Your readers cannot see, hear, or feel this story except through your words. They also know nothing about the culture; you must convey every word, tiny clue, and miniscule shade of meaning to get the story right.

Your first interview is this customer. Now, in your role as a foreign correspondent, begin practicing your observation skills by describing every subtlety in the customer's tone, gesture, or expression. Especially notice the eyes—which have been called the "windows to the soul." Listen for the customer's words and expressions. Is there a deeper meaning behind the sentences you hear? Is there a message that is not initially obvious in the communication? If you ask a question or make a statement, how quick is the customer's response? What might be implied by silence? Is laughter polite, muted, or hearty?

Now that you've observed these cues, you can begin to draw some conclusions about this customer. Based on what you see and sense, how is this customer likely to respond to you? Remember, you're still in learning mode. Continue to check your read for accuracy, refining as you go, but now you're ready to listen—really listen—to the customer.

Listening—done well—is complete absorption. Ever watch Larry King on CNN? His success as an interviewer lies not in his questions but in his terrific listening skills. He zips right past his guest's words to get to the meaning. The mission of listening is to be so tuned-in to the other person's message that understanding becomes a true meeting of the minds.

Like all human connections, this dramatic listening requires constant effort and commitment. Service magicians who learn to do it can conjure all sorts of tricks for their customers.

Consider a businessman in a custom suit and Ferragamo shoes who enters a restaurant and walks right up to the reservation desk. He smiles, looks the host in the eye, and makes his presence known with a firm "hello." Contrast his entrance with this one: a middle-aged couple in khakis and comfort knits sneaks in the door, glances about them, and approaches the desk slowly and tentatively. The gentleman offers a small, hopeful smile and waits for a greeting.

The clothing and manner of the first individual make a statement about how he sees himself. His air of assurance and self-confidence announces an expectation of attention from the restaurant's staff—attention that's likely to be well-compensated. A skilled service magician will take a peek at the reservation book to put a name with the face and welcome the customer by name, if possible. The server will also assume a slightly deferential manner with this customer as he shows him to a table, confident of a tip commensurate with his customer-reading skill.

On the other hand, with a couple exhibiting uncertainty or timidity, the observant server may ask if this is their first visit to the restaurant and, if so, offer more help with the menu. The server also might watch carefully and listen to see if these never-here-before guests have some concern about cost and test the possibility that they do with suggestions such as, "Our hors d'oeuvres are quite ample. May I suggest you split the crab-stuffed mushroom caps? It's a wonderful starter for your meal." If the response is, "Oh, no, we want two appetizers," the server can revise his assumption about cost and smoothly adjust his approach. "Very good. Then may I suggest that if you are looking for something unusual, one of you might try the boudin blanc. We're one of the few places in town where you will find French veal sausage on the menu."

SERVICE MAGICIANS AT WORK

Universal Studios Hollywood, Universal Studios Florida, and Islands of Adventure team members who learn to accurately read guests' needs produce magical interludes that so impress park visitors they take time to stop by Universal's Guest Services to lodge compliments (instead of complaints!). Often small incidents, seeming trifles, so charm guests that they will go out of their way to report them: the Comic Strip Café employee who sees a young girl spill her basket of chicken strips on the floor, cleans up the mess, and delivers a new basket to the table—all without being asked; the attendant at the *Cat in the Hat* attraction who realizes that a small guest is afraid, takes time to explain the ride to the child, and then helps him get on. These service tricks are performed with seeming ease only because team members stop, look, and listen to guests, discern their needs, and deliver service that meets those needs.

Michael Morse, the flamboyant owner of Café Un Deux Trois, is another service magician skilled at reading customers. To Morse, the restaurant business *is* show business and he stages a performance every day at his French bistro in downtown Minneapolis. Although magicians are never to tell how a trick works, Morse doesn't hesitate to reveal the secret behind his: "I tell the staff, 'This is my house. These are my guests. We'll treat them like that every day.' The ones who come back (and 70 percent do) should be glad they did. The new ones should be glad they found us and be comfortable with the experience."[6]

Morse and his staff make sure they deliver that experience by observing carefully, listening closely, and anticipating customers' needs to an extent that appears—well—magic. Just ask the customer Morse heard raving about the egg rolls at the Chinese restaurant across the street. The next time Morse saw that customer's name in the reservation book, those egg rolls were served to him—gratis, of course. The customer is now a regular. Or talk to customers who visit the restaurant with children. Un Deux Trois doesn't leave it to parents to select something from the French menu for kids; instead, servers make a point of talking directly to children, serving them whatever they prefer—French fries or macaroni and cheese or a hamburger—as long as parents concur. And if Morse or one of his staff notices a restless young one amidst adult conversation, they quickly deliver a fresh box of crayons and coloring book.

A master at creating the illusion of serendipity, Morse exercises great care in matching wait staff to customer. For example, when four young women, obviously out for a night on the town, dined recently, his choice of server was a natural: "I put them with a young, hip waiter who is a lot of fun, a little assertive, and knows what's going on around town. They had a great time." Likewise, when he spots a new customer from out of state in the reservation book, he seats him or her with a friendly waiter or waitress who is a little lower key. These small touches add up to a dining experience that feels personalized to every customer. "I want everyone to go away feeling special and that they got value for their money," Morse says. "We don't worry about 'up selling' customers—we work to make the experience right."

Service magicians like Michael Morse don't possess a sixth sense. Nor do they have photographic memories. But they sometimes appear to because they note and use small details that put the perfect spin on every performance. Morse, for example, checks the reservation book for names he knows (and those he doesn't). If he sees an unfamiliar name, with an out-of-state phone number, he tucks the information away for future use. When a couple enters the restaurant at the appointed time, perhaps looking around a bit uncertainly—scanning the unfamiliar room to see just what kind of place it is—it's not a great leap to conclude these are the Nelsons from Fargo.

The trick? Morse greets them with: "Good evening, Mr. and Mrs. Nelson. Welcome to Un Deux Trois. Are you enjoying your stay in Minneapolis?" He has set the stage for a memorable evening for the Nelsons. It looks like magic to them, but it's simply the end result of preparation, observation, and practice.

Erroneous Reads

The taxi driver who decides in an instant that a fare isn't a "tipper" and not worth the effort of conversation, the retail sales clerk who ignores the shopper in his garage-cleaning clothes, the bank teller who moves in slow motion while cashing a check for a tattooed and pierced Gen Xer—for good or ill, all are reading customers. But is their read accurate?

Seinfeld, the '90s sitcom about a quartet of self-obsessed New Yorkers, often featured misadventures set in motion by errors in interpreting communication. One memorable episode featured a blink misconstrued as a wink. The hapless George Costanza, something in his eye making him blink, wandered through a day inadvertently "winking"—sending misunderstood messages to his boss, someone else's girlfriend, and virtually everyone else in his path. George's trail of disasters was entertaining hyperbole, but his experience is instructive: A wink says, "You and I have a secret," whereas a blink is simply a reflex to get a mote out of your eye—a gulf in meaning approximately as wide as the Grand Canyon.

Nonverbal cues can only take you so far. Failure to observe all the cues—body language, dress, and words—can contribute to erroneous reads and service disasters. Watch for congruence—a symmetry among all the communication signals you observe. If a customer's body language tells you she's relaxed, but her tone of voice tells you she's frantic, continue collecting information and be ready to revise your read of the customer and the situation.

Another caveat: Every customer deserves your best efforts, regardless of your read. Think of the scene from the movie *Pretty Woman,* when erstwhile call girl Julia Roberts attempts to shop at a Rodeo Drive boutique and is summarily dismissed by a haughty saleswoman. After hero and rich guy Richard Gere escorts her to another shop—and drops thousands on a new wardrobe for her—Roberts returns to the first shop to give the snooty saleswoman her comeuppance. Loaded down with bags stuffed with purchases from a pricey competitor, Roberts gloats: "Big mistake. Very big mistake."

Big mistakes aren't just played for last laughs in the movies. Take, for example, John Barrier's experience at a bank in Spokane, Washington. He asked a bank receptionist to validate his parking ticket after he'd cashed a check. With a glance at his dirty construction clothes, the receptionist informed him that he hadn't conducted a real transaction and suggested he make a deposit. The branch manager also refused to stamp the parking ticket (the value involved: 60 cents). Barrier called the bank's headquarters and vowed to withdraw all of his deposits unless the manager apologized. No call came. The next day, he came back—and withdrew $1 million. And the next day as well. That bank lost a customer with more than $2 million on deposit over a 60-cent parking voucher.[7]

Salespeople from car dealers to Realtors to contractors often ignore the signals that should help them read which half of a couple is the real decision maker. When the wife is making frequent eye contact with the seller, taking notes, asking most of the questions, while her husband repeatedly defers to her expertise in the matter at hand, it's a good bet that she has the final say in the buying decision. Sales and service people who fail to read the dynamics of such a transaction do so to their detriment.

Retail sales people are prone to similar errors in judgment. When a guy enters the jewelry store in his Saturday yard-work grubbies, he may be on a detour from a trip to the hardware store and be in desperate need of a diamond-studded anniversary gift for his wife who reminded him this morning of their 7:30 reservation at the most romantic restaurant in town—a dinner that won't be celebratory or romantic if he doesn't have a gift in hand, preferably an expensive bauble. The senior salesperson who looks askance at his clothes, and takes the opportunity for a restroom break, is misreading the situation—and losing a sizable sale to a junior associate. The lesson: Read customers carefully—then test your assumptions before you act on them.

A FINAL CAUTION

Regardless of read, all customers deserve to be treated with respect and in a way that makes them feel well served. Sure, "regulars" may rate some form of special treatment, but every customer is a walking advertisement for your organization, for good or ill. Treating even one person poorly goes way beyond losing a single customer. The salesperson or server who ignores a customer or dismisses a request with a perfunctory, "Sorry, I can't help you. That's our policy." may have positioned the organization to lose dozens—even hundreds—of potential customers.

Customers who feel ill-treated do not simply go away and stay away. They tell anyone who will listen about the rotten service they endured at the hands of your company. Several independent studies have confirmed that, although half of upset customers will complain to the organization's local outlets, as many as 96 percent of unhappy customers will not complain to the head office of the offending organization. Instead, the grapevine effect kicks in, and they tell, on average, nine to ten friends, acquaintances, or coworkers how bad your service is.[8]

Read-and-match Service Magic should have the opposite effect, leaving customers pleased with their experience and just a little puzzled at how you managed it. You don't have to reveal that the trick is no trick: You did it through careful observation, noting clothing, body language, gestures, facial expressions, and voice—and fanatical listening. Your disciplined practice of these reading arts enabled you to identify your customers' needs before they had a chance to voice them.

And that's a bit of magic that makes a lasting impression. Tricks that delight are often small deeds neatly executed—remembering a name or favorite dish, calming a fear, or unobtrusively appearing to make the experience just right. These acts, appearing improvised on the spot and matched to this customer's special need, never fail to charm and enchant. They are, indeed, magic.

## CHAPTER TWELVE

Magical Rapport

Matching Trick to Audience

Great service magicians match trick to customer, picking and choosing from their repertoire, changing their banter, style, and presentation to suit the situation and mood. They have learned to read the sometimes subtle communication cues we all display. They listen and observe carefully, picking up indicators from a customer's clothing, body language, facial expressions, eye contact, words, and voice characteristics.

The real trick for service magicians is sending as well as they receive; learning to nurture those connections with customers and build rapport with them. The pharmacist who suggests a customer shop for a birthday card or takes her blood pressure while she's waiting for a prescription, the waiter who responds to the standard query "What would you suggest?" by asking the diner's preferences in seafood or pasta, the airline ticket agent who expresses understanding when a family member's sudden hospitalization necessitates changing travel plans and waives the re-booking fee—all these service providers know how to establish rapport with customers by drawing them in, making them part of the service act, and encouraging them to feel they're sharing in the magic.

The goal of this rapport-building is to craft a special relationship that engages the customer's passion and interest. This is not magic as a spectator sport: It's not the appreciation of illusionist's skill you have watching David Copperfield make the Statue of Liberty disappear. It's the sense of being a part of the act you feel when a street magician pulls a coin from your ear. An audience that is involved, either directly or vicariously through other customer-participants, is more likely to be emotionally engaged in the experience and much more likely to be filled with wonder at the magic.

St. Paul Saints fans connect directly and vicariously with their team. They don't just sit and watch at a Saints game, but participate in the off-the-wall action. They might play "What's in the bag?" (a regular, between-innings contest that features a blindfolded fan groping his or her way to *something* hidden in a giant trash bag) or race a four-wheeler around the infield or don a huge sumo-wrestling costume to take on a fellow fan. Or they might enter into the spirit of the spectacle by having a Saints logo painted by the official face painter or by getting a massage from the masseuse in the stands or by joining the other hecklers throwing hotdogs at the mimes atop the dugouts doing (silent) instant replays of close calls. One way or another, nearly everyone in the stands becomes part of the magic.

Saints fans are never sure what brand of lunacy they'll experience, but they do know that Mike Veeck and his band of merry pranksters dreamed up these bits of theatre just for them—and the seemingly spontaneous, yet ever-changing entertainment will be repeated game after game, all season long. This is the magical and personal connection that makes the Saints more than a mediocre minor-league baseball team to their fans: "The Saints are part of [St. Paul, Minnesota's] culture, a spirited community citizen, a maverick organization with a heart, an organization whose top management greets fans as they enter the ballpark, a team that plays baseball in an outdoor stadium (unlike the Minnesota Twins who play in a domed stadium), a team with a blind radio announcer, a team that in 1997 signed the first female pitcher, Ila Borders, ever to pitch on a regular basis for a professional men's baseball team."[1]

Service providers from bus drivers to insurance companies can and do create that sense of magical connection with their customers. They use a variety of strategies to help them: They direct and focus customers' reactions during service encounters, they make personal bonds with customers, and they use communication techniques that help them establish and maintain person-to-person rapport.

SETTING THE STAGE

Service magicians take charge of customer encounters, setting the stage and the mood for the magical connection to come. Taking charge means assuming leadership of the situation, guiding the customer through the interaction with a sense of both confidence and deference. The stage magician says, "Ladies and gentleman, feast your eyes on . . ." to communicate that he is in charge of this encounter and is directing the focus of the audience. He telegraphs to the audience that something special is about to happen, and it is time to watch, listen, and be prepared to be amazed.

Likewise, the service magician guides the attention of the customer, albeit more subtly. The bellman who says, "Right this way," or the call center operator who says, "Take a look at the bottom right corner of your bill," is preparing the customer for the remainder of the transaction. These service providers are skilled at providing direction, while still deferring to customers and responding to their needs. Customers, after all, are the ultimate arbiters of service: They decide whether an interaction is magically memorable or forgettably mundane.

Consider a common service experience: Taking a shuttle bus from the off-airport car rental lot to the terminal. A quintessentially unremarkable event? Not in Atlanta, at least not when Archie Bostick is driving the Hertz bus.

After you turn in your car and go outside to catch the bus, the first thing you notice is Archie standing next to the doors. He's got a big, welcoming grin on his face, and he's having a great time taking charge of this service transaction. He greets and helps every customer onto the bus. Instead of a tip jar (baited with a handful of bucks to encourage reluctant tippers), Archie paper-clips dollar bills across the front of his shirt. Nothing subtle about that ploy—it's an attention-getter that announces this is going to be a unique experience.

Once on the bus, you realize Archie has mastered quite a trick: He delivers a stand-up comedy routine instead of the standard warning about the consequences of forgetting to turn in the keys to your rental car. He uses any excuse to break into song. ("The next time you're in Atlanta, maybe there'll be rain, and you'll be singin' in the rain, 'I'm singin' in the rain. . . .'") As Archie pulls up to the terminal, he announces, "Now that we're at your final destination, I may never see you again. I want us all to say together, 'I love Hertz.'" He convinces a crowd of strangers to holler, "I love Hertz" before they get off his bus!

Here's a service provider whose job is to get customers who are more than likely harried, distracted, and maybe even ill-humored, onto a shuttle bus and delivered to the airport. He could simply flip on a prerecorded message to pass on the necessary information and drive. Instead he creates rapport by delivering a wonderfully managed performance—and a memorably magical experience for his customers.

You don't have to be a moonlighting comedian to direct the service encounter. The server at the local designer coffee bar who welcomes the next customer in line with a smile, a cheery "Good Morning. What can we get for you?", and completes the transaction by telling the customer, "Sheila will have your grande half-caf-half-decaf latte with soy milk in a moment, right over here," gently moving the customer over to the adjoining counter, is directing the service transaction. The same encounter can be disjointed and uncomfortable for the customer when the server fails to provide these helpful stage directions.

THE MAGIC OF SYMMETRY

While organizations can develop the capacity for wonderfully personalized service offerings, it's people who make service truly magical. Practiced service magicians rely on communication techniques that help them build rapport—using certain words, tone of voice, pacing, inflection, volume, gestures, facial expressions, body language—even props—to create connections with their customers. At Children's Memorial Hospital in Chicago, for example, physicians and nurses often pick up a toy, a flower, or something that will be a conversation starter to help them connect with a patient. Restaurant servers who appear with pen and order pad in hand indicate readiness to take diners' orders. The auto mechanic who suggests customers change the timing belt at 60,000 miles—and shows them a piston with a valve forced through it—is making an impression with a graphic representation of how $300 worth of maintenance work can become a $1,200 engine rebuild.

While service magicians may use certain props to begin the rapport-building process, empathy is the crucial skill that solidifies the emotional connection with customers. Empathy, the ability to sense others' feelings and respond to their unspoken concerns or feelings, allows us to get in touch on a visceral level with customers' moods and concerns. Research by Robert Levenson at the University of California at Berkeley shows that couples adept at empathizing with each other actually respond physiologically: "Their own body mimics their partner's while they empathize. If the heart rate of [one partner] goes up, so does the heart rate of the partner who is empathizing; if the heart rate slows down, so does that of the empathic spouse. This mimicry involves a biological phenomenon called entrainment, a sort of intimate emotional tango."[4]

Customer and service provider also engage in an emotional tango—albeit a temporary one—that can be a pleasant and satisfying give-and-take or a toe-stubbing stumble. For any service organization, the latter can result in customers who disengage or who don't come back. For health care providers, the impact of empathic connections on customer's perceptions may have even higher stakes. In *Emotional Intelligence at Work,* Daniel Goleman reports: "Physicians who don't listen get sued more—at least in the United States. Among primary-care physicians, those who had never had a malpractice suit were shown to be far better communicators than their lawsuit-prone peers. They took time to tell their patients what to expect from a treatment, to laugh and joke, to ask the patients' opinion and check their understanding, and to encourage the patients to talk. And the time needed for a doctor to be successfully empathetic? Just three minutes."[5]

Aurora Health Care, which includes 11 hospitals, numerous clinics and pharmacies, and employs some 23,000 people, understands that emotional connections make a magical difference to patients. "We're in a competitive market," says Allen Stasiewski, director of service management. "People will come to a hospital the first time because their doctor told them to or because of the technology, but they'll come back the second time because of the service. If there's too much variability in the service, they'll choose another option. We want to provide a consistently high level of service—and provide it in personalized manner."

Aurora focuses on training people in "wisdom beyond competence," as Stasiewski phrases it. "We're judged not only by what we do, but how we do it," he explains. "In school, you learn certain ways to do the technical things you're being trained for. But you're probably not taught how to say 'Hello' or answer a phone or say 'I'm sorry,' in the right way."

Aurora Health Care employees learn to establish rapport with others by applying techniques rooted in NeuroLinguistic Programming (NLP). One technique is mirroring or matching patients' verbal and nonverbal behavior to put them at ease. That means using similar body language and word choices—for example, if a patient consistently uses visual words to express himself or herself ("I don't see what you mean."), it's likely to be most effective to address his or her concerns with a similar phrase ("Let me see if I can clear this up for you.").

Long used by therapists and often by salespeople, NLP techniques have not traditionally been part of training for health care providers. Matching or mirroring emotion is not what we have been trained to do in health care. We're trained to be calm," says Kari Schmidt, director of employee and organization development at Aurora Health Care. Yet that carefully cultivated manner can create disconnects with angry or distressed patients. If you initially stay calm when a patient is very upset, your demeanor sends the message, "This isn't very important to me."

The person assumes, "You clearly don't understood how upset I am." So the person increases intensity, uses profanity, or explains more graphically—and the situation escalates.

Yet, if you match, for at least 30 seconds, the level of intensity of this person's dissatisfaction—when a customer is upset and speaking very loudly and quickly, you increase your pace and volume—you communicate, "This is important to you *and* to me." (Of course, never match the volume of the person and never use inappropriate words with a customer. The simple act of increasing the rate at which you speak can be very powerful in sending the message, "I understand your concern.") Once the customer feels he or she has been heard, and begins to calm down, you can slow your pace and start solving the problem.

Stasiewski recently put this guidance into practice when a member of a patient's family contacted him, quite upset—even months after the fact—about her mother's care. "I raised the tone of my voice and speed. When she used 'upset,' I used 'upset,' so she knew I really heard her," he says. These simple mirroring techniques enabled him to show he cared about what happened, and that the hospital was serious about learning from these kinds of service breakdowns. As customers, especially customers with a problem, "We want someone to hear us," Stasiewski points out.

Next we want action. When something goes wrong, customers need to hear a simple, heartfelt apology as a prelude to problem solving. Take corrective steps quickly in a way that is visible, or their anger and frustration will increase. Show and tell the customer exactly what you have done and will do to address the situation, and promise actions—not outcomes (the outcome may be outside your control). You can control actions, on the other hand, and each action you take can show the customer you're working on his or her behalf.[6]

MAGICAL WORDS

In face-to-face encounters, service magicians learn to pay attention to body language, facial expressions, voice characteristics, and words—their own and those of their customers. All those verbal and nonverbal cues help us read situations and choose appropriate strategies for establishing a connection. In a call center, however, it's a different story: Words and voice are the only available cues, but service magicians can work wonders with them.

At MidAmerican Energy's call center, customer service associates (CSAs) learn to build personal relationships with callers—one customer at a time. "Our goal is to do the right thing for *this* customer," explains Claudia Neumann, the call center manager. Since they can't see their customers, call center associates are coached to listen: Are customers hurried, stressed, frustrated? They learn to pay attention to tone, pace, and the unspoken word, says Neumann. A customer may start a call by talking about a bill that's too high, but the real issue is that her meter has been estimated so many times she doesn't trust the bill. And her real frustration: She's watched that meter reader pass by her house for the past three months without stopping to read the meter. MidAmerican's associates learn to probe and get to the root of a customer's problem using a conversation model known as LIST:[7]

- *Listen.* If a call center operator interrupts a customer explaining a problem and jumps immediately into solving it, the customer doesn't feel heard—and the operator may not hear the whole problem. That means the customer will have to call back and one call turns into two or more. *Listen* is a reminder to slow down and hear the whole story.

- *Indicate.* Go over what the customer says: "OK, you have an issue with your bill. Is there anything else?" Feeding back information to the customer ensures accuracy, and asking for additional information may uncover a critical problem.

- *Solve.* Then begins the process of actually working to solve the customer's problem(s). "I'm looking at your account and I do see you made a payment on the 27th . . ."

- *Tell.* Recap what was accomplished: "Your issue was billing, and we found that you made a payment of $100. Is there anything else I can help you with today?"

MidAmerican CSAs are trained in soft skills ranging from conflict resolution to words and phrases to include in their conversational repertoires—and words to avoid. "Hot buttons" to steer clear of: "We can't . . ." "I can't." "You need to . . ." Savvy call center associates learn to say, "Is it OK with you if . . ." rather than "You have to . . ."; "Here are some options . . ." instead of "You can't . . ."; "Here's what I can do . . ." substitutes for "There's no way . . ."; "If you'd be willing to . . . we will be able . . ." will be more productive than "We can't do anything . . ." or "It's out of our control."[8]

Call center reps also learn to pay close attention to their own voice and body language—even though their customers can't see them—

since both help build rapport with callers. An alert, pleasant, expressive, strong, and clear voice tells customers you care about their issues. A flat, unexpressive monotone sends the opposite message. Maintaining an open, inviting posture (leaning forward slightly, avoiding crossed arms) helps keep your tone of voice positive.[9]

"Associates learn what gets them into trouble with customers," says Neumann. "We talk a lot about how to avoid being 'hooked' by customers—don't let a customer reel out the line and hook you. If a customer says, 'I don't like your tone' or is getting upset, that's the time to be calm and listen. Let them vent. Don't get angry, then you both lose."

When it comes to soothing the savage customer, here are 12 phrases that seasoned customer service representatives have shared with us— and they swear these lines are effective starting points with customers who have a problem, a complaint, or a disaster in the making.[10]

1. "I understand your concern. What do you think would be fair?"

2. "Mr. Customer, I'm so very sorry this has happened. How can we resolve this for you?"

3. "Sir, you deserve the very best and we seem unable to provide it. Because I want you to be well served, may I suggest . . . ?"

4. "Although you may not agree with my decision, I'd like to explain it so you will at least understand."

5. "Let me do some investigating on my end and call you back. Would you prefer me to call you this evening at home or tomorrow morning?"

6. "Have I done something personally to upset you? I'd like to be part of the solution."

7. "Thank you for bringing this matter to our attention. We will address it right away."

8. "We love to hear feedback from our customers, both positive and negative. It gives us a chance to be continually upgrading our service to you. Thank you for sharing your concerns with us."

9. "It is obvious that I have not been able to help you. If you don't object, I would like to let a colleague of mine attempt to meet your needs."

10. "Unfortunately, we are unable to give you a full-price refund without a receipt. I can, however, authorize a store credit for the current sale price."

11. "We see this differently, and I am going to have to put more thought into the perspective you have shared with me. It's helpful for me to understand how you see things. In the meantime, here is what I can do to solve the immediate problem."

12. "If I hear that language again, I won't be able to assist you. Unless we can find a different way to communicate, I'm going to have to hang up." (Then keep your promise.)

TIPS FOR KEEPING IT MAGICAL

We all know how to create rapport using body language and symmetry. Picture yourself at a family function where you see your shy six-year-old niece standing alone. How would you make a connection with her? You'd bend down to her level to talk to her, making eye contact and speaking softly. You'd take those actions to put her at ease, creating at least a temporary emotional connection that might encourage her to open up and become comfortable enough to talk to you.

Service magicians use similar approaches. They unobtrusively direct service encounters, setting the mood, and making customers comfortable with their role in the performance. They cultivate their empathy skills, using physical and verbal symmetry to demonstrate their concern. (A caution here: Use judiciously. Overly exact or obvious mirroring can be mistaken for parroting or mockery.)

They also listen closely to customers, paying attention to their spoken and unspoken words. They demonstrate that they are listening by using words that encourage customers to talk. ("Please continue." "What were you going to say?") They avoid words that can produce negative reactions. ("There's no way . . ." "I can't . . .") in favor of words and phrases that offer customers options ("Let's look at some possibilities . . .").[11]

Service magicians and organizations that routinely inspire a sense of wow and wonder in their customers use rapport to make every contact with their customers personal, memorable, and magical. You can do it, too!

CHAPTER THIRTEEN

Delivering Magical Dialogues

Stage magicians are expert at drawing in volunteers, mystifying them with coins that disappear and rabbits that pop out of hats, and holding them rapt until they applaud at the end of the act. Skillful service magicians perform similar feats: Customers find themselves caught up in the alchemy—whether they are simply checking out of a hotel or riding an attraction at a theme park or lunching at a local bistro. They become part of a performance that is both unexpected and unpredictable. But the real trick, for the magician and the organization, is delivering that magic routinely, shift after shift, day after day.

Magical dialogue is one of the tools that helps them do it. *Magical dialogue* choreographs the tone and feel of the interaction between service magician and customer. Though scripts can and do play an important role in Service Magic, as pointed out in Chapter 9, too much scripting can lead to interactions that feel preprogrammed and leave customers with a chill instead of an afterglow of delight. Yet, specifying a few well-chosen, critical words for service magicians to use—effective opening lines that set the right feel for the interaction, anticipate customers' needs, or gracefully end a transaction—helps them deliver a consistent level of service.

The best service magicians learn to balance the set patter—specific words or scripts—with the impromptu remark, the improvised rejoin-

der, or the authentic response to create personal connections with customers. The doormen at the Peabody Hotel in Little Rock, Arkansas
and the superbly renovated former Excelsior Hotel next to the Arkansas
state capitol, are masters of *magical dialogue*. Watch carefully to see if
you can spot the trick in a recently observed exchange between one of
the doormen and a departing guest:

>**Doorman:** *"Isn't this a magnificent place?"*
>
>**Guest:** *"Yes, it is."*
>
>**Doorman:** *"I hope you had a great time."* (The guest acknowledges that his
>weekend stay was terrific.) *"Can we expect you back?"*
>
>**Guest:** *"You sure can."*
>
>**Doorman:** *"Then we'll see you again."*

Seemingly simple—yet magical rather than humdrum. The trick
begins with the doorman's opener. It simultaneously reinforces the
guest's pleasure in a wonderful weekend in beautiful surroundings and
communicates the doorman's own pride in the place. He fits his responses to the guest's, and delivers a closing line that ends—rather than
simply stops—the dialogue: The customized goodbye deftly leaves the
guest feeling he's been engaged in an authentic conversation and, at
the same time, lightly plants a suggestion that a return to the Peabody
would be a positive experience.

Quite a bit of magic packed into a few moments of dialogue!

ESTABLISHING A VISION: BEDROCK FOR THE MAGICAL DIALOGUE

A service philosophy or mission is one of the most important behind-
the-scenes supports for customer-pleasing conversations. The Peabody
Hotel prides itself on service excellence and impeccable attention to
detail. Universal Orlando urges its frontline staff to "take every opportunity to make every Universal guest feel like a guest in your home."
The organizational vision of a positive customer experience sets the
tone and tenor for the sort of conversation and dialogue that will add
to that desired experience.

A simple philosophy guides the 160 customer service associates (CSAs) who answer some 140,000 calls each month at MidAmerican Energy's busy call center: "Doing the right thing for customers." That core value touches every facet of the utility's operations, from the care and training of CSAs to the care, they, in turn, lavish on customers.

The magical difference is clear as soon as a call is answered: MidAmerican's customers don't receive the standard name-rank-phone number grilling that has become standard operating procedure in phone centers everywhere. Instead, customer service associates begin dialogues by listening: They make sure they understand the problem before they jump into solving it. They take notes in longhand on a pad next to their computers and move into entering data as seamlessly as possible. A conversation might proceed: "I see. I see. You have a problem with your bill. . . . Let me pull up your account on screen. . . ."

MidAmerican gives CSAs little in the way of scripted dialogue, but one line it does prescribe is this prelude to a conversation ender: "Is there anything else I can help you with?" The question begins the closure process and effectively prompts customers to remember any other possible problem or concern they might have forgotten. But for the most part, says call center manager Claudia Neumann, CSAs are encouraged to personalize their conversations with customers, forming dialogue with five specific "Customer Care Practices" in mind: (1) Use the MidAmerican name in opening and closing, (2) use the customer's name at least once during the conversation, (3) apologize for long silences, (4) use the mute button when appropriate, (5) and—above all—treat customers with dignity and respect.

For example, a customer calls in about late fees she's been charged. She explains that her payment is late because she was divorced two months ago and has never been responsible for paying utility bills before. A CSA might respond, "I'm so sorry to hear that. That can be very difficult." Not, "What is your account number?" That's where the commitment to conveying empathy and compassion and the training in "doing the right thing for customers" comes in. "If a customer is pouring her heart out and the CSA is all business, that does not create the warm feelings we want that customer to have," says Neumann.

If you do the right thing—try your best to solve every customer's problem, and treat every customer with dignity and respect—your customer satisfaction scores fall into place, observes Neumann. "It's what makes us different, and highly rated by customers in the best and the worst of times. When we ask our customers how we're doing, they rate us good to excellent in customer satisfaction."

PERFECTING THE MAGIC

Though service magicians make connecting with customers look effortless, an adept stage manner doesn't just appear with the wave of a wand—it's painstakingly built by rehearsing the magic makers until their delivery is all but flawless. At Ritz-Carlton Hotels, employees begin every shift with a ten-minute stand-up meeting (called a line-up meeting), a portion of which is devoted to reviewing one of the 20 Ritz-Carlton Basics. Any wonder every employee knows them by heart?

Likewise, every new CSA at MidAmerican Energy receives a minimum of seven weeks of classroom training that covers both technical and customer care skills such as listening and conflict resolution. Since MidAmerican serves consumers in four states, CSAs must become knowledgeable about each area's regulations and credit laws. Just-in-time training is also at their fingertips: Online access to news updates about price increases or power outages ensures they won't be caught flatfooted by an onslaught of calls about an event they know nothing about in one of those service areas. "We constantly chat about the news of the day so that CSAs will know how to address a concern being expressed by a customer," says call center manager Neumann.

When initial formal training ends, informal training continues. Novices are paired with mentors to continue learning the ropes. First, they simply listen in to customer calls, then they add talking, and—finally—they progress to talking and typing. Many service magicians develop their stagecraft by practicing their most common moves to perfection before ever facing customers. The approach is similar to one long used in sports, explains Carl Binder of Binder-Rhea Associates, a Santa Rosa, California consultant who specializes in conducting FluencyBuilding™ workshops for sales and service practitioners. "In golf, you get good at driving not just by playing holes of golf; you get good by standing in one place and hitting a whole bucket of golf balls," he points out.

You get good at serving hotel guests or answering customer questions in a call center by intensively practicing the parts of the job you're required to perform most frequently. The 80-20 rule applies: Initially, employees need to be able to perform 20 percent of the job to perfection says Binder. It's often a small portion of what the entire job entails, but it pays to practice those parts until the service magicians become fluent—proficient, fast, and accurate.

Stroll the Minnesota Renaissance Festival any weekend between mid-August and the end of September, and you'll witness the transforming magic of fluent performances. Costumed minstrels, jugglers, comedians, and artisans of every stripe range the grounds from dawn to dusk. Hawkers verbally battle for your attention with tasty popovers, pico potatoes, Florentine ice, and—that universal symbol of Renaissance largess—the giant roasted turkey leg. A king and queen in full regalia, along with the royal court, preside over daily festivities including entertainment on 12 stages and a full-contact armored jousting match.

Every performer—whether jouster or seller of turkey legs—practices the art of staying in character, and contributes to the illusion that this 22-acre theme park 30 minutes south of downtown Minneapolis is a 16th-century European village at harvest time. "Staying in character is the Renaissance Festival," says Karen Walne, director of marketing and administration for the parent company, Mid-America Festivals. Everyone who has contact with customers wears a costume and attends a one-day orientation that includes a back story (see *Man-Made Place Magic*, Chapter 5), a language guide, character sketches, and sample scripts. "For example, we encourage food workers to use 16th-century English and try hawking their wares," said Walne. "There are competitions between booths, and we give prizes to people who make up songs and rhymes that engage our customers."

Those aspiring to advance beyond the "peasant class," such as entertainers and any other employee who wants to brush up on character skills, are required to attend a six-week academy. There, the finer points of the European enlightenment are taught by Renaissance veterans and members of Minneapolis's vibrant theater community. The academy curriculum is a blueprint for the rollicking atmosphere of the Renaissance Festival: history of the village, period language and dialects, character development, improvisation, costuming, music and dance, and protocol—"How to properly interact with royalty, each other, and guests."

Festival patrons expect to interact with employees and be part of the magic says Walne. The illusion is so complete that customers sometimes don period clothing, affect an old English accent, and sprinkle their speech with thee's and thou's. "Sometimes it's really hard to tell the employees from the customers," laughs Walne. "Really, the festival becomes a large theatre with a living play staged over 16 days and performed by a cast of 300,000 customers and 800-plus employees!"

The key to this Performance Magic is practice—all service magicians practice until the mechanics become automatic. Then, with the confidence to perform, the right staging, and the right props, they're ready for customers.

THAT MAGICAL FEELING

Service magicians learn to look for opportunities to show their stuff—that's how they consistently deliver unexpected and unpredictable, yet replicable and repeatable, Service Magic. The magical rapport they create communicates a generosity of spirit when they talk to customers. They are saying, in essence, "I acknowledge your individuality. You're special." They speak to the person and look for ways to treat him or her as the unique individual he or she is.

Does that seem too—well—sentimental? That is exactly the feeling Universal Studios Orlando committed to with its 2002 goal: "Delivering world-class entertainment and unforgettable experiences that create a deep, lasting, and emotional connection with our guests."

Though guests come to Universal for the rides and attractions, the emotional connection Universal wants guests to experience is more than just the delicious thrill of the *Jurassic Park*™ riverboat plunging 80-some feet into blackness to escape the gaping jaws of T-rex on a rampage. Or the poignant tug an aging baby boomer gets dancing to Smokey Robinson tunes at oldies night in the Motown™ Café in Universal's CityWalk entertainment complex. It's also the connection that a pair of Universal team members created when they noticed a family becoming increasingly agitated waiting in a 60-minute line to get into *The Amazing Adventures of Spiderman*™. The two approached the guests and asked if they had already experienced the attraction. Discovering they had not they took them in through the VIP entrance—an interaction that made this family's Universal experience a little more memorable and magical.

The dialogues that create such memorable experiences begin with a service model that directs employees to "Look–Focus–Act." This model defines explicit standards that guide behavior and opening lines for *magical dialogues*. "Look," includes the "10/5 Rule" that requires Universal team members to "nonverbally acknowledge guests when they are ten feet away with eye contact, a head nod, and a smile. Verbally greet or acknowledge guests within five feet." When a team member sees a guest in need, sample conversation openers included in the "Focus" step portion of the service model are: "How can I assist . . . ?" "I see . . ." or "I understand. . . ."

Everyone is encouraged and expected to take these baseline requirements and fashion them to the needs of the moment and the customer—simply to be as thoughtful and gracious as you would be to a guest in your own home. Adherence to that underlying principle leads to employees who take the time to observe a customer's real needs and do what they can to meet them—whether it's procuring dry clothes for a guest who got caught in a sudden downpour or stopping to chat up a family of five from Kansas to ask if they're enjoying their visit to Orlando and Universal Studios.

It's all a matter of responding to customers' real needs—not always the specific question they ask or the help they first request. By carefully listening to customers, service magicians learn to decode the question behind the question and answer *it*. That's a skill that appears a mystifying, but welcome, bit of mind reading to a confused, uncertain, angry—or soaking wet—customer.

Consider, for example, a customer who asks, "What time is the 3 o'clock show?" The service magician does not respond with the obvious and smart-alecky, "Oh, I don't know. Would 3 o'clock be a good guess?" Instead he or she answers the real question the customer is attempting to ask: "What time should I arrive for the 3 o'clock show?" Or when the customer of a trust company complains, "Now look here. My pension checks are due the first and the fifteenth. I know that you purposely hold them over the weekends just so you can make money on the float." The service Houdini astounds by ignoring the insult and insinuation by addressing the real problem: "Why aren't my checks arriving on the dates I expect them?" [1]

TIPS FOR CREATING MAGICAL DIALOGUE

How can you create *magical dialogues* with customers? These steps will help you leave customers astounded by your feats—or at least with that pleasurable feeling that comes from experiencing a wee bit of magic:

- *Establish—and publicize—a clear service philosophy.* Universal Studios, Orlando, committed to "delivering world-class entertainment and unforgettable experiences that create a deep, lasting, and emotional connection with our guests." Scripted openings and behavioral standards help employees spin dialogues with that goal in mind. A statement of purpose as simple as "doing the right thing for customers" encourages dialogues that seem so personal and serendipitous that customers will swear you're performing just for them.

- *Build proficiency through practice.* Stage magicians rehearse their acts until every part of the performance appears effortless—that easy stage manner, the casual banter with members of the audience, the entertaining onstage repartee with helpers, and, of course, the flawless execution of the tricks themselves. Likewise, service magicians build performance proficiency by training and practicing until the mechanics become automatic. Practice is what gives you the confidence to perform magical, memorable dialogues with customers.

- *Magical openers.* These words set the tone and character of the dialogue to come. Scripted starters can be helpful: "How can I assist?" "Good evening, madam." "Don't miss your chance to soar with the dinosaurs." With experience, many service magicians—like the Peabody doorman who expressed pride in his workplace by asking a departing guest, "Isn't this a magnificent place?"—learn to customize great openers that fit their personality and their customer's mood.

- *Listen, listen, listen.* Service magicians shine at the deceptively simple art of listening. And that's true whether they are hotel doormen or theme-park maintenance workers or ICU nurses. It's axiomatic: Only when you take the time and make the effort to hear what a customer is *really* saying can you create the magic that makes a dialogue special.

- *Magical enders.* A dialogue that simply stops doesn't leave a customer with the satisfying feeling that the circle is complete. Certain lines are helpful signals: "Is there anything more I can help you with?" begins the closure process and helps ensure that nothing is left unfinished. The final step in the service recovery process is the follow up that double-checks the faux pas fix and asks the customer to give the outcome a thumbs up or down. Similarly, an effective ender defers to the customer. Remember: You may be directing the encounter, but the dialogue isn't over until the customer says it is.

CHAPTER FOURTEEN

The Tenants of
Performance Magic

In the hills above Hollywood stands a spookily elegant Victorian mansion, complete with intricate gingerbread trim and towering turrets. Tour guides point it out with great reverence, but it's not a movie star's home or elegant hotel. It's the Magic Castle, home of the Academy of Magical Arts Inc., a private club for magicians and lovers of magic.

Open only to members or guests of members, the Magic Castle sets the stage from the moment you step in the door. The garish foyer has the look of the bookcase-lined library from the board game Clue®. You gain entrance to the club proper by uttering a secret phrase, and—voila!—the bookcases separate, and you enter a bar and dining room gleaming with fine old woods and crystal. From the dining room, you pass through a corridor covered with photographs and playbills of some of the world's greatest magicians.

And, finally, the main attraction. The three performance stages: the Palace of Mystery, the largest space, host to grand illusions and stage performers; the Parlor of Prestidigitation, which re-creates the Victorian experience of the "parlour" (living room) magician; and the Close-up Gallery, which presents masters of the art of close-up magic in the smallest of the theaters and seats only 22 guests.

On a typical evening, magicians dine and watch "the best of the best" of their colleagues on one of the three stages. Eavesdrop in the bar or dining area and you hear chatter that might be hallway conversation at a magician's convention. Ask a few questions, and—as long as you don't try to get the secret behind a sleight-of-hand trick—they are delighted to speak of their art and craft. Magicians themselves thrill to the mystery when they are on stage. "It is the most amazing theatrical rush," says one magician. "You feel like you're so full of power and energy that you must appear like you are glowing to the audience."

Seasoned magicians speak of feeling incredible joy when they are performing, as if they have a special gift to give to the audience. The connection between magician and audience creates an enchantment that affects the magician as much as the spectators. "I feel like a real magician—like I am really doing magic," says professional magician Howard Hale. "If I make something appear to disappear during a performance, I believe it does. I know the difference between magic and miracle, but when I'm doing magic, I truly believe a miracle will happen."

Magic Castle General Manager James Williams explains the mindset: "Magicians create awe because they are awed. They cause people to feel captivated because they, too, are the captives of the world of magic. Bottom line, we believe in magic."

Service magicians believe in magic, too—that's how they make believers out of customers. When server and served share a delightful service moment—one delivered with skill and charm and received with pleasure and just a bit of awe—the interaction is just as magical as an on-stage phenomenon. The service magician who combines technical know-how with the magical properties of Place, Process, and Performance can succeed in making a believer out of even the most skeptical of customers. Suddenly, the mundane turns into magic: the lunch at the chain restaurant is memorable instead of forgettable, the shopping trip is delightful instead of wearing, and the wait in the dentist's office is entertaining instead of boring.

Key to service magicians' masterful orchestration of customer experiences are these fundamental tenants of the magician's art and craft: Believe in—and enjoy—the magic, respect your audience, practice and perfect your craft, and master the art of performance.

BELIEVE IN—AND ENJOY—THE MAGIC

"You must believe you are a real magician, not just a huckster with a fast hand," as one magician puts it. Service providers who deliver magic maintain a similar mind-set: They believe in creating a special experience for every customer—no matter what the job.

If you want evidence that attitude can transform even the most mo-notonous of tasks, you can find it in a tollbooth on a busy interstate in Pennsylvania. Every driver recalls this particular tollbooth attendant be-cause of his seemingly endless enthusiasm. What's his secret? He con-fided it to a curious driver one day: He sees his job as an opportunity to perform. "One day," he said, "I won't be in this tollbooth. I'll be danc-ing on Broadway. Until then, I get to rehearse all day dancing on this stage. Passengers are my audience; the toll is my tip. I'm not working a tollbooth. I'm practicing giving you a really great performance."

Performers who become immersed in their delivery are said to be "in the zone." A stage magician is "in the zone" when his skill and artistry combine in perfect proportion to dazzle spectators. Every rou-tine goes off without a hitch and his performance sparkles with energy, wit, and precision. He's so in tune with his craft that he *cannot* make a mistake—believing is effortless and enjoyment . . . spontaneous.

This feeling goes by many labels. Writers say they've been touched by "the muse," singers talk of "being in the groove," athletes call it "play-ing over your head," dancers refer to it as being "hot" or "on," and artists speak of "flow." Whatever you call it, it's characterized by a com-plete lack of self-consciousness and a sense of losing track of time.

Service magicians have similar moments. Customers know they have been part of an "in the zone" service experience, just as a theatre audience knows when actors have that special chemistry. Service providers who work in the zone focus their mental energies on the in-tersection of process and performance—where the procedure meets the customer's needs. If they focus solely on the mechanics of the per-formance, the customer becomes a witness; if they focus solely on the customer, performance falters from lack of steering.

Service Magic providers deliver such delicately balanced "in the zone" experiences to customers every day. The emergency room doctor who "knocks" on a curtain to preserve a patient's dignity and privacy; the Ritz-Carlton doorman who arranges a personalized welcome for a guest's weary spouse; the Un Deux Trois server who makes a meal un-forgettable by divining a diner's needs and meeting them—all have achieved that special and joyful magic.

RESPECT YOUR AUDIENCE

Great magicians demonstrate respect for their audience in many ways. Yes, they relish confounding them with illusions, but the practice of conjuring allows for certain deceptions and not others. Magician and author Henning Nelms compares the magician's code to the poker player's: "No one expects a poker player to tell the truth about the cards he holds. However, if you try to deceive by dealing from the bottom of the deck, you may get shot and you will certainly be shunned."[1]

Similarly, he points out, magicians are allowed to keep their methods secret, but not to leave the audience believing they possess supernatural powers.

The same type of respect for customers is necessary for service magicians. They treat customers as individuals worthy of dignity and consideration, not as adversaries or dupes. They observe customers closely and listen fanatically so they can respond to their real needs—not always the ones voiced in the heat of the moment by an angry or confused individual.

Service magicians believe customers are honest and trustworthy—even if the occasional bad apple may prove otherwise—and treat them that way. They meet complaints or requests for special, policy-busting treatment by responding with, "I'm sorry" or "Tell me more . . ." or "Walk me through exactly what happened." They never argue with customers, but search for ways to make them right—"If I were you, I'd feel that way, too."

Demonstrating respect for customers doesn't mean throwing out policies willy-nilly; it means walking the fine line between bending a rule and becoming a doormat. A retail salesperson might take back a dress without its original tags intact, but enforce the store's tags-on policy when it comes to taking back an obviously worn prom dress. Service magicians can make calls that require that kind of balancing act—because they respect customers, they will always tilt decisions in their favor.

PRACTICE AND PERFECT YOUR CRAFT

Great magicians rehearse, rehearse, rehearse until their stage magic looks effortless. They master the mechanics of their craft: They know how to use sleight, patter, stage presence, and persona to direct—or misdirect—the audience's attention. They spend countless hours studying the steps to a trick and practicing the required moves so that the audience will be baffled when the volunteer's king of hearts reappears.

Service magicians are equally well prepared. Some, like those customer service reps (CSRs) at AT&T Wireless Services, practice the tasks they need to perform from their first day on the job. Timed practice and drills are key to helping them build fluency—just like baseball players who improve their hitting by concentrated batting practice, these CSRs master core skills and build up speed through practice before they ever talk to a real customer. When they go live, when "the curtain goes up," they exhibit and inspire confidence.[2]

Mastery of their craft enables service magicians to make their performances look spontaneous—and indeed sometimes they are—but seemingly serendipitous moments often occur because the service magician knows how to spot an opportunity. As a stage magician says, "It all looks natural and unexpected to the audience, but truly unplanned magic is rare."

A first-time guest at the Rihga Royal Hotel in New York was amazed that on the second day of her stay, wherever she went in the hotel, every employee seemed to know her name. Cornering a bellman in a hallway, she begged for the secret. "Knowing your name is very important to us, so we've worked out little ways to pass it along to each other," he explained. "Sometimes we mouth your name to another associate when you're not looking." Hotel employees plan and practice this bit of magic so that they can make guests feel recognized and special.

MASTER THE ART OF PERFORMING

Watch a great magician interact with the audience, and you see a great performer. In theatrical terms, he "owns the stage." He takes possession of the performance, pulling the strings and controlling the factors that make it all work. He establishes his authority on stage, directing the audience's attention by telling it "I need a volunteer,"—not "Can I have a volunteer?"—and skillfully handling hecklers.

Service magicians also maintain control of customer encounters—they never let someone or something interfere with the experience. They are attentive to potential invaders. The waiter who eyes the glare of the setting sun and closes the blinds, the clerk who monitors the volume of the background music, the call center employee who chastises her noisy colleagues engaged in a background conversation—all are guarding the customers' experience and demonstrating unshakable commitment to making the service encounter magical.

Like all memorable performers, great magicians create a stage persona—the distinctive character that delivers the words, gestures, facial expressions, and movements that contribute the dramatic reality that draws in audiences. Magicians use the same tools actors do to reinforce their illusions—costumes, props, voice, words, gestures, expression, movement, body language. The magician in tuxedo or spangles and dashing black cape presents a character that primes the audience to be amazed and impressed by his act. His props—playing cards, coins, rope, silks, hats, doves, rabbits, tigers—are devices that help him create memorable illusions and focus the audience's attention where he wants.

Service magicians also use costumes and props to help them stay in character. Call center reps decorate their spaces, sometimes including a mirror that allows them to see themselves, their expressions, and body language as they talk to customers. Limo drivers polish their cars and wear dark suits and starched shirts to present passengers with the spiffy formality they expect. Home Depot employees wear orange aprons that reinforce their "here's a guy who knows his plumbing supplies" image. The performers of the Renaissance Festival, from strolling minstrels to food hawkers, have raised this illusion to a fine art.

A performer's signature style contributes to his stage persona. Style distinguishes the Amazing Creskin, the fast-talking mentalist, from Siegfried and Roy—who barely speak while they create the illusion of a tiger vanishing in a puff of smoke—and from Julianna Chen, who can flood the air above an audience with flying playing cards. These performers have forged a brand that makes them immediately recognizable and distinctive.

Service magicians develop a similar kind of brand or trademark. They can make a unique imprint on customers, consistent with the organization's vision and appropriate to the situation, of course. Southwest Airlines developed a signature style based on the wacky spin it puts on the dreariest of announcements—only on Southwest will a flight attendant announce "Welcome to Acapulco" when you land in Houston. Macaroni Grill servers cheerfully introduce themselves, and then perform one of the restaurant's signature routines: Signing their name on the paper tablecloth with a flourish, using a crayon to write upside down (right side up to the customer).

The stage magician closes his act with a flourish, saving a marvelous illusion to leave the audience impressed and wanting more. But he's not done yet: He takes a bow, acknowledging his fans' applause, and expressing appreciation for their attention to the show. Service magicians leave customers on a similar note: A "thank you for your custom," a sincere thanks for the business, is a graceful and necessary ending to every service transaction.

A DIFFERENT KIND OF MAGIC: THE VIRTUAL REALM

VIRTUAL MAGIC
Internet operations that live up to the broken promises of the past.

VIRTUAL MAGIC
Internet operations that make the customer's life simpler and more interesting—not more complicated and burdensome.

"Customer service is the online experience. Online, no transaction is tangible. A customer is in a self-service environment. So retailers must know what the customer wants before she tells them. From start to finish, the experience is the only thing that matters."

ANNA MUOIO
NET COMPANY

"Technology doesn't try harder, people do."

AVIS ADVERTISEMENT

Experiencing the awe and wonder of Service Magic requires a certain willingness to suspend disbelief: enjoy the moment, accept sometimes novel, and unlikely premises. Many of the well-funded e-commerce experiments of the late '90s proved to be based on the novel premise—indeed, the belief—that value, profits, and performance were not connected. We went along with the illusion until the New Economy hocus-pocus evaporated at the dawn of the new decade.

Organizations that had diligently applied "old economy" lessons to new economy ventures, emerged from the collapse with well-positioned and profitable virtual operations. Many traditional retailers who kept their sights on the fundamentals avoided the trap of overfocusing on technology and underfocusing on customer needs. E-service ventures with staying power are skillful practitioners of "virtual" Service Magic, masters of the same Place, Performance, and Process magics as their brick-and-mortar brethren.

CHAPTER FIFTEEN

Virtual Place Magic

The *magic of place* is unmistakable in the opulent shopping shrines of Rodeo Drive or the luxurious environs of a Four Seasons Hotel. Place Magic is more than a physical attribute: Look, feel, and usability are equally important in virtual places. Magical Web sites promise more than pedestrian e-shopping experiences. They beckon customers with textures and tones that lift their spirits and assure them that their every need has been considered.

Walk into REI's flagship store in Seattle, Washington and its giant climbing wall and vast display of adventure equipment immediately excite you with the prospect of climbing, canoeing, or camping with REI gear. Visit the company's online arm, REI.com, and you enter an equally alluring environment. The Web site offers more than 78,000 individual REI items, but e-shoppers never feel overwhelmed with choices or suffocated by clutter. The design and organization of the site makes it easy to find whatever you need—whether it is in-depth product information, expert gear advice, online clinics, or forums to swap adventure tips and experiences with other REI customers.

Click to the Web site of Chipotle, the restaurant chain featuring gourmet burritos and tacos, and you experience the same fun, interactive, fast-moving environment found in its physical stores. The design of each brick-and-mortar Chipotle mirrors the idea behind the food: Simple ingredients put together in creative new ways to elevate them to a

145

higher level. While each Chipotle restaurant uses the same basic components—polished steel tables, blonde wood chairs, Mayan glyphs, Gothic trash cans, red concrete floors—no two ever look the same.

So, too, at Chipotle.com, where clever use of Flash animation engages and entertains users with interchangeable graphics without overpowering the Chipotle story. Click on "Eat" and a huge burrito drops from the top of the screen (accompanied by the caption "They beep when they back up") with text explaining Chipotle's obsession with only the finest, freshest ingredients, and cooking techniques similar to gourmet restaurants. Click on "Speak" and you're asked to tell "Virtual Joe" about your latest Chipotle experience, memorable or forgettable, with the promise of a fast, personalized response (one option for unhappy customers is "Crush Joe with a massive burrito"). Move to "Find" and there's a virtual magnifying glass to help you quickly locate your nearest Chipotle restaurant.

Design is only one part of the formula for creating distinctive virtual place. Ease of navigation, one-click access to customers' vital information needs, and a way for e-shoppers to get help and advice from a human when they need it are also requirements. Dime-a-dozen Web sites that do little more than offer a list of items for sale dominate the Internet. Memorable sites—the ones that shoppers bookmark and recommend—maintain their distinctive magic by applying certain principles. To set your site apart from the masses, apply these magical concepts.[1]

Brand every touch point. Branding elevates a site from garden-variety to memorable and buzz generating, and is the first step toward capturing customer loyalty. Brand-name recognition will bring shoppers to your site once, but only a site designed with customer and brand in mind keeps customers coming back.

Many well-known brick-and-mortar names build click-and-order sites that are pedestrian—worse still, some are so frustrating and annoying they damage existing brand loyalty. Better to stay out of cyberspace than to go there and do badly. If you are a pure dot-com, your Web site *is* your brand identity. Consumers judge you at first click. Their experience at your site—and your follow-through—is all you've got to secure their loyalty. If your site doesn't inspire confidence and demonstrate your competence and personality, you lose. There is no room for error.

A memorable and magical e-commerce site brands every touch point. A touch point is anywhere a customer comes in contact with your company: ads, titles, links, click-through approach, search capabilities, FAQs, order process, and e-mail contacts. Think of customer touch points as opportunities to enthrall or enrage. Each one is a chance for the customer to make a positive or negative judgment about your organization. Every step a customer takes through your site must be both foolproof and effortless, sending the message, "We obsessed about meeting your needs."

Evoke emotion in the online experience. A well-branded site is remembered, enjoyed, and talked about—in part because it evokes emotion. Every graphic and link is well thought out and works to create a consistent mood. Illuminations.com, for example, is a site that sells candles and bath oils. It works its magic by calming visitors and lulling them into a state of relaxed awareness with pictures of candlelit patios and silky bubble baths. Curiosity and interest are present almost by definition.

Visitors thus enticed are ready to surrender to the allure of *e-magic,* to be delighted by easy-to-find information that gives them what they need in as short a time as possible. They are already predisposed to buy something, or at the very least, to click to see if you have anything that piques their interest and merits bookmarking for future visits. At the same time, they know they aren't stuck in your site. Irritate them and they quickly click away. Enchant them and they are yours.

The emotions you choose to evoke depend on your goals and products. REI.com gets visitors jazzed about the prospect of visiting a natural wonder and climbing and biking with REI gear. So, too, with All-Outdoors Whitewater Rafting (www.aorafting.com), where visitors can experience the thrill of guided California river trips through 360-degree photographic simulations. In both cases, the sites elicit emotional connections with visitors to make the visit a magical and memorable virtual place experience.

Engender trust with design quality. Trust continues to be a big concern for online shoppers, especially at a site without an established brand name. If consumers trust your site and believe in your company, they'll shop there and tell their colleagues and friends to do likewise. The look and feel of your site shapes customers' perceptions.

All of the facets of distinctive design—branding, ease of navigation, uncluttered presentation, current and clear information, and up-to-date technology—contribute to those perceptions. As a shopper in one of our e-commerce focus groups said, "If a Web site is designed well, then it's more probable that other shopping details such as delivery and correct billing have received proper attention." In other words, if you look good, more customers will give you a chance to be good.[2]

Each time someone clicks on your site, she looks for evidence of your trustworthiness. A link that says "women's jeans" had best lead to women's jeans, not to an error message, outdated or incomplete product descriptions without prices, or to women's swimsuits. Such problems set off alarms for customers—alarms that become foghorns for first-time visitors.

CHAPTER SIXTEEN

Virtual Performance Magic

Just as a virtual place can surprise and delight the customer, the performance of an e-commerce site also can deliver a magical experience. Performance is critical because customer impressions of e-service are formed with a click of a button.

No matter how aesthetically alluring your site or how well it visually manifests your goals—if it crashes, downloads content at a glacial pace, doesn't answer customers' key shopping questions, or frustrates them with confusing or clumsy design—you will fail. You will, in effect, be reverse branded and become known for being all style and little substance. Indeed, if there isn't much behind the "curtain" of flashing icons or other high-tech glitz on your site, most of your customers will be one-hit wonders.

A triad of factors is key to e-Performance Magic: security, ease of navigation, and speed. Master all three and you're sure to turn online shoppers into loyal customers.[1]

Assured minds. Even novice e-shoppers look for the padlock icon and security guarantee before offering up personal information. Online shopping requires consumers to supply considerable personal information—name, address, credit card number, and the like. People aren't comfortable sharing this confidential data with just anyone, and are still—a decade into the Web-shopping phenomenon—wary of being scammed by shady online dealers and imagined hackers who can lift their credit card information from any Web site. The challenge is even greater for pure-plays and other Internet start-ups without the brick-and-mortar brand name of a Wal Mart, REI, or Federal Express on which to build trust.

Practice "easy-to-do-business-with" design. Skilled virtual service magicians practice easy-to-do-business-with (ETDBW) thinking. This ETDBW mind-set requires everyone involved in site design to think first like a customer and last like a technical wizard. Everything is seen through the lens of an impatient and skeptical customer sitting at the keyboard, who wants nothing more than a fast, effortless, and fruitful shopping experience.

Critical to ETDBW is ease of navigation. Shoppers tell us time and again that if they know what they want from a site, they should be able to arrive at the home page, type a search, and click directly to that product, choose it, and checkout—and they want access to checkout on every page. Even if customers don't know precisely what they want, they want to be able to locate it within a few clicks, not after a 20-minute goose chase.

Since the ability to comparison shop is a big draw for online customers, your product prices should be up front—and omnipresent. List them next to every initial product link and again with the product description. When you make customers drill down to a product description to find a price, the frustration quotient ratchets up. Likewise, discerning online shoppers want to know shipping costs long before they get to checkout, since it's the variable that often makes the choice between shopping online or in physical stores. The customer who finds the perfect product, loads up her cart, and then discovers shipping costs to be out of line with her expectations is looking for heads to roll. An easily spotted link to shipping information on the home page solves the problem.

Speed wins in e-service. Most customers shop online to avoid the time-sucking hassles of shopping in the physical world: the need to look presentable, stress-producing traffic jams, filled parking lots, pesky salespeople, or long, fruitless hunts for the right product at the right price. When your Web site makes them jump through too many hoops or is painfully slow, that advantage disappears.

The single biggest complaint heard about Web sites is that they don't get to the point. E-customers have very little patience for waiting; pages must load quickly and then provide easy access to information the shopper wants. The checkout process also must be fast and painless, with less than three screens to check out. Each time a site makes it impossible to complete an order (especially if significant time has been spent shopping there), consumers will leave, implore others not to go there, and mark it off their list of return-to sites.

Requiring customers to fill out registration forms with names, addresses, and shipping information is a necessary process, and customers will do it once—if it guarantees faster checkout in subsequent visits. But companies adept at Performance Magic streamline this process to make it less painful for impatient shoppers.

A great example of grasping this need for speed is Clinique.com. The company knows its customers are loyal to certain product lines, and it accommodates them with easy-to-find links on a home page to every product Clinique sells. It's the kind of rapid-fire shopping process today's consumers have come to demand from Web sites.

## CHAPTER SEVENTEEN

Virtual Process Magic

Having a memorably designed and technically adept e-commerce site sets you squarely on the road to success, yet those factors represent only two-thirds of a winning virtual service formula. E-shoppers quickly forget the virtues of aesthetics or easy navigation when they have product or service questions that can't be answered promptly and accurately by live human help, good search engines, or well-constructed frequently asked questions (FAQ) lists. Likewise, world-class Place or Performance becomes less than magical to customers, and can even appear as diversionary tactics, when product shipments arrive far beyond promised delivery dates or if shoppers are forced to jump through hoops to return products. The processes, policies, and service standards in place to make the online shopping experience as responsive, personalized, and hassle-free as possible are crucial to creating e-Service Magic. We believe those processes should contain these core elements and features.

Personalize the shopper's buying and service support experience. Shopping on the Web can be a solitary and soulless experience. When nothing makes that experience personal or memorable, it's easier for a shopper to abandon a site or look to the competition. But just as sales reps in physical stores engage shoppers by reinforcing their selections or helping them choose appropriate items for their styles, personalized Web experiences are little bits of magic that help tie buyers to a site and push them to make that critical initial purchase.

Clinique.com's "Personal Consultation" tools help customers figure out their "look" and directs them to colors and product lines suited to their features. Once a Clinique.com customer fills out her color profile, it's permanently stored at the site. Whenever she clicks on a product category, the page automatically suggests shades and product lines that complement her coloring and skin type.

Amazon.com is another pioneer in e-personalization, noted for offering recommended reading or music lists for customers based on their history of past purchases.

The need for personalization extends to e-mail contact as well. Customers judge online customer service not only by the speed of response to their e-mailed questions, but how those responses are crafted to address their idiosyncratic needs. Electronic service encounters allow no chance to charm customers with sparkling smiles or enthusiastic delivery. E-service can still delight customers, but e-mail replies and solicitations created by artificial intelligence tools make online operations easy prey for the tortured version of "personalized" scripts made familiar by direct-mail marketers. You know the kind: *"Dear John Smith: We're offering you, John Smith, our valued customer, a special discount for a limited time only. John Smith, we know that quality and price are important to you. . . ."* Ugh. The Department of Motor Vehicles seems warm and fuzzy by comparison.

Many e-commerce sites use auto response systems to answer high volumes of e-mail and control the costs of product support, but such systems can backfire if used as one-size-fits-all solutions. Consider this Dell Computer reply to a plea for help troubleshooting the erratic clock in a new Dell computer:

> "Thank you for contacting Dell U.S. eSupport. An artificial intelligence tool designed to interpret your message and respond quickly will conduct this first reply to your message. The first paragraph of the response should tell you whether the document accurately addresses your question.
>
> If this response does not address your question, you can reach the next available e-mail technician by replying to this e-mail. Before you reply, please go to the very bottom of this e-mail. You will find useful information there on how to use alternate Dell support resources and what to include in your reply."

There followed 11 pages—"a collection of specific solutions," according to Dell—of directions for diagnosing and fixing a host of computer time-keeping problems. This reply, received after clicking through 10 pages to finally access a screen that allowed a question to be typed in, was enough to cause one customer to throw up her hands in disgust. The lengthy reply failed to include a phone number or a specific e-mail address for a support technician that would allow a customer to seek help from an actual human. Dell, reputed to deliver some of the best online service, blew its chance in this encounter to deliver a magical service moment.

In contrast, some Internet companies use their technological prowess to awe and delight customers with sleight-of-hand personalization. They excel at the art of combining response templates with personalized answers to e-mail inquiries. Many use personal messages with names of customer service representatives (CSRs), deliver custom responses to questions, and include a personal, thoughtful sign-off. All too often when customers click on a "contact us" button on a Web site, it simply launches an anonymous, preaddressed e-mail screen with no information about who the message is going to or when the sender might expect a response. Customer-sensitive companies sidestep this bland practice by placing e-mail contacts into specific categories, with many using personal e-mail addresses of specific employees.

When we sent an e-mail to Godiva.com, a CSR responded in less than ten minutes with a pleasant personal note that answered all the questions we asked, included the CSR's name, e-mail, phone and fax, and encouraged us to "have a sweet day" (playing on the site's signature chocolates). And when customers contact Amazon.com, as hordes do each day, CSRs have some 1,400 prewritten responses to draw on—and to personalize as the situation dictates.

LillianVernon.com, the online presence of the home furnishings catalog retailer, is another that understands the power of personalization. After searching for a shower curtain with a seashore or ocean theme and coming up empty, our e-mail question resulted in the following response in less than 15 minutes:

Dear Ms. Miller,

Thank you for your inquiry regarding the ocean theme shower curtain. After researching our products database, we are sorry to inform you this item is not found in our current inventory.

Should you need to search further, you may try contacting these individuals at other catalog companies or check their Web sites:

- Harriet Carter   800-377-7878

- Miles Kimball   800-546-2255

- Walter Drake   800-525-9291

- Taylor Gifts   800-829-1133

- Just For Kids   800-654-6963

Customer service is our number one priority. If we can be of further assistance, please contact our Customer Service Representatives at 800-505-2250, or custserv@lillianvernon.com, 24 hours a day, 7 days a week. Or visit our Web site at www.lillianvernon.com.

Thank you for shopping with Lillian Vernon Online.

Now that's magic!

Offer multiple ways to access live human help. Even though online shopping is largely a do-it-yourself venture, the opportunity to link to a live human and get help, if even for a moment, has great appeal for many. At times, there's no substitute for the wisdom and grace of the human touch.

That starts with making an 800 number easy to find on your Web site, and working to reduce customer hold times. But today's e-customers expect more ways to access human help: Multichannel customer response systems combined with automated answer capabilities have become table stakes in the e-service game.

To speed up the response process, many e-commerce sites have implemented a live CSR option, making available living, breathing humans who can talk to customers through one-on-one chat boxes while they shop a site. On a technology level, live text chat is fairly easy to implement. The real magic comes in hiring and training CSRs who can communicate effectively in writing with customers in this free-form style. If consumers actually link to live chat, chances are their questions will be more complicated than, "What's your return policy?" They'll expect answers to questions about product quality, technical specs, repair records, or advice on what to buy. CSRs manning this channel must be well prepped and carefully chosen for the duty, or the personal exchange can leave customers disappointed and skeptical of the organization's professionalism.

Multichannel response systems require CSRs who can perform as effectively in writing as in speaking on the telephone—a selection and training challenge for service centers. Good phone skill doesn't always translate to good writing skill. It's dangerous to assume that service staff trained to speak with cheery voices, interpret spoken clues, and master phone technologies will be equally adept at crafting clear and customer-sensitive e-mail, or will seamlessly pick up the new technology skill that goes with it.

Deliver soup-to-nuts service. The reality is most e-customers don't hand out service report cards until their ordered product arrives on schedule, unharmed, and without fulfillment error. If there is a problem midstream in a fulfillment or delivery chain—especially for business-to-business customers—they want rapid notification or online access to check inventory or shipping status. And if problems prove so daunting as to warrant a product return, online shoppers want return and exchange policies that are synchronized between online and off-line channels, and that don't give them migraines with endless conditions or convoluted machinations.

If it's *magical e-service* you're after, it's important you give as much attention to the last half of this service race as the first. While plenty of Web sites have licked front-end design and transactional challenges, building the back-end infrastructure and mastering the logistics to move product efficiently from manufacturer to warehouse to e-customer has proved far more vexing.

Create e-service standards pegged to customer expectations. Surveying online shoppers as they complete interactions with your call center or self-service functions, or capturing impressions of Web site design, checkout process efficiency, inventory selection, or other factors helps you stay on top of ever-shifting perceptions and experiences on your site.

Done right, online surveys—including Web-based surveys delivered in real time—can reduce surveying costs and improve response rates compared to conventional mail or phone survey tactics.

Organizations that understand how Service Magic drives customer retention and profit take such measurement and standard setting seriously, often linking management incentives to achieving key service goals. They also ensure standards for elements like response time to customer e-mail are pegged to "Internet time" and not to the rhythms of their own company systems.

THE VIRTUAL MAGIC CHECKLIST

Here are six characteristics of e-commerce sites that consistently deliver Service Magic. Take them to heart and you'll create more satisfied e-shoppers who will stick to your site like Velcro. These magical sites:

1. **Understand the overt trumps the implicit.** Good Web site design makes everything obvious. The best way to do that is to make every vital link and tool accessible on every page, and to err on the side of redundancy. Web shopping is about simplifying the experience, not impressing customers with graphical prowess or high-tech stunt flying. It should be easy to search, check out, return, get help, or find any information relevant to making buying decisions. Remember this rule of thumb, and you'll stand apart as an e-service magician: If there are hoops to be jumped through or races to be run, make sure they happen outside the customer's field of vision.

2. **Respect e-shoppers' time.** Shoppers are drawn online by the promise of an experience faster and easier than fighting the hordes on the roadways or at the local mall. If desired products aren't easy to find, if prices are missing or out of date, if the site keeps crashing, or if tracking down shipping costs and other key decision-making information becomes a *Where's Waldo?*, like exercise, the incentive to shop online goes out the window.

   And remember, e-customers measure product-delivery time from the moment they complete the online transaction—not hours later when it actually gets processed or when the item comes into stock.

3. **Think of customers as adults.** Many e-commerce sites still seem to think whirling, rotating, moonwalking, or flashing features are critical to grabbing the attention of jaded or distracted online customers. These sites forget they're appealing primarily to adults—not adolescents enthralled by effects that might be at home in the hottest new video game. Nothing says, "We're more concerned about showing off our latest animation skills than expediting your shopping experience" than a Web site splash that

does nothing but lengthen a customer's time online. E-service magicians know the difference between design features that are extraneous and ego-driven—and those integral to enhancing the purchase process.

4. **Give customers multiple contact options.** Nothing turns online shoppers off faster than a site that doesn't have easy-to-find contact information or forces them into a non-human contact option. Creating an e-commerce site doesn't mean you'll see a reduction in customer service contacts. Sites that understand this put an 800 number on every page, and increasingly offer multi-channel contact options like real-time text chat or other Web-enabled tools (and provide specialized training for the reps who work those channels). Service Magic sites also understand the power of listing names of employees, along with categorized job functions and e-mail addresses, under their "contact us" options, so customers aren't frustrated by generic "info@company.com" addresses when making inquiries.

5. **Offer recurring access to shopping carts.** Providing continuous access to the shopping cart gives e-customers a sense of security; it lets them know what they've chosen and that nothing has been accidentally purchased or lost. At Web sites like Clinique.com, every product chosen is listed at the top of every page under "items in the bag," so consumers can always keep tabs on their purchases. The next best option is one-click access to the shopping basket on each page.

6. **Streamline the product-return process.** If you've ever ordered a product from an e-commerce site, needed to return it, but discovered company policy forbids you from dropping it at the site's brick-and-mortar sister store *ten minutes from your house,* you've probably made a mental note to never again shop that virtual merchant—and maybe the brick-and-mortar store as well.

   If you have online as well as offline sales channels, make sure customers can return merchandise at any one of your locations. If you are a dot-com only, include a return label and return shipping instructions with the package so if something is wrong with the order, the customer can simply retape the shipping box and leave it for the postal carrier. Make your process for returning products as easy as your process for buying them, and you're sure to stand apart in the "we-still-don't-get-it" world of e-commerce.

WHERE THE THREE Ps COME TOGETHER

"One of the secrets of selling is knowing how to stage a great show."

CARL SEWELL
SEWELL MOTOR CO.

"The dollar bills the customer gets from the teller in four banks are the same. What is different are the tellers."

STANLEY MARCUS
FOUNDER, NIEMAN-MARCUS

"All that we do is done with an eye to something else."

ARISTOTLE

In Sections Two, Three, and Four we purposely focused on the Magic of Place, Process, and Performance in isolation. Along the way we explored organizations that excel in one or even two of these elements. Organizations that have mastered all three of the magics are few and far between.

In this section we present five organizations that seem to have definitely mastered all three magics—to their great benefit.

Some of these magical service companies have never known any other driving force. They were literally imbued with a strong service focus by the founder or founders on Day One. They were born great. Others have come to the service obsession and Service Magic later in their histories. The difference between starting out as a service-conscious organization and learning the trick after the fact can be considerable. Conversion, it seems, is always a more difficult accomplishment than simply having *a priori* knowledge and faith. Ignatius Loyola's insight into twigs and trees is as apt for organizations as it is for individuals. Companies that have made that difficult transition have achieved greatness for themselves the hardest way possible. But the fact of their conversion is an important testimony to the doability of change for the better. Old dogs can learn new tricks—and magical ones at that.

Last, but not least, are the companies that have had their Service Magic commitment thrust upon them. These include organizations that because of the nature of their business or the strong and obvious demands of their marketplace have learned to scramble—consciously or not—to serve, serve well, and serve a little magically. There are lessons to be learned from all these organizations, regardless of the route that has them distinguished from the rest of the pack by their success in running service-focused organizations.

Whatever the motivation behind their *magical service*, the fact remains that they have succeeded where many others have failed. As you read their profiles, we think you'll be enchanted by the ways they dazzle their customers—we hope you'll also be inspired to go out and discover where you can sprinkle some magic on your own organization.

CHAPTER EIGHTEEN

Romano's Macaroni Grill

Where Life Is Delicious—and a Little Magical

Walk into a Romano's Macaroni Grill and you get the feeling this isn't just another chain restaurant. It's a feast for the senses: Gold-clothed tables covered with white butcher paper and spread across a giant dining room, fresh flowers and gleaming glassware shine from spotlit center islands. From the open kitchen along one wall wafts the aroma of red sauce simmering and garlic sizzling. Servers in crisp white and splashes of red hustle from tables to kitchen, bursting into song now and then to add voice to the Italian classics playing in the background.

Romano's Macaroni Grill	
President:	John Miller
Headquarters:	Dallas, TX
# of employees:	14,000
Sales (2002)	$600+ million

All is by design. In addition to pasta and pizza, Macaroni Grill serves up Service Magic that is artfully choreographed and reliably delivered, day after day, in 200 locations from Orlando to Omaha. The organization's motto—"Making Life Delicious!"—testifies to its exuberant personality. The look, the music, the smell, the action, the sensory on-slaught—all contribute to Macaroni Grill's theatrical flair. Customers feel it as soon as they walk in the door and stand at the top of an entrance ramp that offers a precisely planned sightline: The seating stand takes center stage, the open exhibition kitchen sits stage left, the wine wall on the right, and the whirl of high-energy performers. The host steps down-stage to welcome customers to the Tuscan farmhouse set and leads them to a table. The server hurries over to introduce himself by writing his name on the papered tabletop. And the show begins.

The magic of Place, Process, and Performance is embedded in a dis-tinctive culture that unifies the chain of restaurants now owned by Dallas-based Brinker International. It's a magical combination that pays off handsomely: The casual eatery with fine dining touches is a perennial winner of the annual Choice in Chains Award, based on thousands of customer surveys and sponsored by *Restaurants and Institutions* maga-zine. Macaroni Grill captured the platinum award in 2003 for the fifth year running, winning for best food, menu variety, service, atmosphere, and cleanliness in the Dinner House division.[1] The moderately priced restaurant has also won kudos in *Consumer Reports* polls, earning ratings equal to such premium-priced places as Morton's of Chicago.[2]

How did Macaroni Grill conjure up *that* trick? Service Magic has a lot to do with it. Whether customers visit for a quick lunch or a celebratory dinner, they get a taste of the Italian magic—the old country welcome, the warm atmosphere, the good value, and the entertainment—that is part of every meal.

THE BACK STORY

In 1988 Phil Romano launched Romano's Macaroni Grill in Leon Springs, a town in the Texas hill country outside of San Antonio. The first-generation Italian restaurateur started with an old dance hall and re-created, with authentic nostalgic flavors, the Northern Italian home of his childhood. The golden-hued stone and stucco inside and out, dis-plays of fresh food, jugs of wine on the table, strings of bare light bulbs like oversized Christmas decorations hanging from the ceiling—homey touches that remain in the restaurants to this day—are reminiscent of the Romano family kitchen in Italy.

This Place Magic has been composed with an artist's eye—literally. Romano, a painter of abstract impressionist canvases as well as a suc-cessful entrepreneur, is considered one of the top restaurant concept creators in the country. In addition to Macaroni Grill, his credits include

Fuddrucker's, Cozymel's Coastal Grill, EatZi's (a gourmet to-go store and produce market), and 25 other restaurant concepts. A profile of Romano in *Texas Monthly* magazine observes that his colleagues in the industry compare him to Steven Spielberg, another master of Place and Performance Magic, and describe him "as a wizard who can imbue an idea with the sizzle and magic that make it a megahit."[3]

Part of the original sizzle was a wily bit of pure expectation magic that put Macaroni Grill on the map in the early days. On random Monday and Tuesday evenings, every customer in the restaurant received a letter in place of a bill. The letter explained that Macaroni Grill intended to make customers feel like guests, so it seemed awkward to charge them for their good time. Once each month on a Monday or Tuesday, always unannounced, everyone would eat free. "Tonight is your lucky night," the letter announced, adding, almost as an aside, "Tell your friends about Macaroni Grill."[4]

The free-meal twist was discontinued long ago, but part of the mystique remains: Macaroni Grill welcomes diners into the restaurant, striving to make them feel at home in the house Romano built. He may be the wizard behind the concept, but his able apprentices continue the magic. Part of every general manager's role is to greet and talk with customers to ensure they enjoy their visit.

That's a role no one plays with more gracious warmth than Vic Pisano, the original general manager of the original Macaroni Grill in Leon Springs. A gray-haired, Italian ambassador of good will, whose look and manner evoke old country hospitality, he's been delivering Performance Magic since the doors opened. Yet to Pisano, there's nothing magic about what he does—it's just caring, he says. "You welcome everyone who comes in the door, you make sure the food is good, and you make sure the people you serve are happy." The only way to do that, he says, is by visiting tables and talking to customers—a job he relishes, and a task he emphasizes to new servers and managers alike.

Pisano was at his post at the front of the restaurant, shaking hands and greeting customers with a friendly "ciao, belle" until the summer of 2002, when torrential rains flooded the original Leon Springs building (for the third time) and the restaurant moved to Sonterra Park, another suburb of San Antonio. "I hated to leave the old lady," he says sadly of the 1930s vintage building. "I built a family there, a huge family. I've got customers who met there, got married, and now bring their children in—they call me Papa Vic. But we hope to duplicate it. That's what I tell our customers—it's a new building, but we'll make a home out of it."

The signature Tuscan farmhouse ambiance of the chain, with a few unexpected twists, remains the Macaroni Grill look. Part of the magic involves a certain juxtaposition of elements—intriguing contrasts that are pleasing to the senses and to the pocketbook. Thus, the gold table cloths covered with white butcher's paper; the fresh flowers and the strings of bare light bulbs; the elegantly clad servers who introduce themselves by using the crayons at each table to write their first names—upside down to them—on the table papers; some patrons dressed for a night on the town and others in jeans and shorts; a menu featuring traditional Italian favorites and chef-prepared features often seen at much costlier places; and an average check of $14 per person.[5] The upshot is "the best of both worlds, where you can be casual and not stuffy," says Keith Rodenberg, Macaroni Grill's Midwest regional director of operations.

THE PERFORMANCE

Performing is part of the job at Macaroni Grill: Waiters spontaneously break into song, usually an Italian opera. When one breaks a dish, all of them applaud. Chefs prepare food in exhibition kitchens, sautéing and grilling away in full view of customers at tables or waiting to be seated. "We're inviting you into our house, like you are part of the family. We want to get an interaction going between the guests at a table and the people serving them and cooking behind the lines," Rodenberg says.

The restaurant prefers to hire experienced servers who want to deliver entertainment along with dinner. "Our managers look for that person with a gregarious personality, that person who is so full of energy, he's fidgeting, about ready to explode," Rodenberg says. Vic Pisano adds another criterion: "You've got to really like your job—taking care of customers." Macaroni Grill wants servers who believe in Performance Magic, and who know how to draw customers in and conjure quick fixes for whatever challenge might occur. The rest it teaches them in a combination of classroom and one-on-one training in the restaurant's dining room.

New hires learn both technical skills (how to identify ingredients such as mussels, clams, penne and fettuccine pasta, as well as complete dishes) and soft skills that help them build rapport with customers and read their needs. These "steps to service," in the company's parlance, include learning how to greet a table, lead customers through the menu, explain features, suggest the appropriate wine for the meal, propose drinks or desserts, and answer questions. More advanced training teaches the finer points of wine, helping servers understand that a dish like "Scampi alla Romano" with garlic butter and shrimp in pasta goes better with a nice Pinot Grigio than a heavy Cabernet.

Training continues on the job and is provided by "employee-developers" —experienced employees who act as trainers. These are key people who teach newbies to wait tables, work other stations, or take on pantry, prep, or sauté cook positions. Brinker has a strong commitment to promoting from within, and "developer" is often the first rung on the ladder for future managers and executives.

Macaroni Grill developers are distinguished by the green towel (rather than the standard red) they wear over their shoulders. "That's a status symbol that says you have a leadership position in the restaurant," Rodenberg explains. Developers take that mark of distinction quite seriously he says. When a restaurant runs out of green linen on occasion, "I've had people almost refuse to work with a red towel."

Memorable Performances

Because the folks at Macaroni Grill make a habit of talking to and listening to customers, the magic continues to evolve. Customers' suggestions create continuous changes and refinements. Booths were added in some of its new facilities because people said they would like them, and the feature "Create Your Own Pasta" that allows customers to choose among a variety of ingredients. Macaroni Grill goes the extra step for customers. Employees know that tradition and follow it without hesitation.

There was the time a gentleman stopped by the Austin Macaroni Grill in midafternoon to ask for help staging a little drama of his own. He was planning to propose to his girlfriend that night at the restaurant and wondered if the staff would deliver the engagement ring at an opportune moment. Of course they would!

That evening, after the couple finished dinner, the server appeared with a tray of freshly made desserts. Nestled in the center of the tray was the jewelry case. The server lowered the tray to say, "Are you folks interested in dessert tonight?" whereupon the gentleman picked up the case and flipped it open. "She burst into tears, everyone in the place started clapping, and we sang for them," says Rodenberg.

When the occasional service breakdown occurs, Macaroni Grill prides itself on its ability to stage a magical recovery. Rodenberg's favorite example: A customer brought her daughter in for a birthday dinner. Standard procedure at Macaroni Grill is for the singer on duty to sing "Happy Birthday" in Italian to the birthday girl and to give her a free dessert. But on this evening in this restaurant, no singer was on duty. So when the mother signaled the server that it was time to bring in the dessert, there was no singing accompaniment. The customer wrote to the general manager of the restaurant to tell him that she and her daughter had been disappointed.

His response? He bought a cake and balloons, and called the customer to ask if he could come to her house. He and several staff members from the restaurant drove over and knocked on the door. When the mother and her daughter came to the door, he handed the girl the balloons, presented the birthday cake, and everyone sang "Happy Birthday." In the end, both mother and daughter were moved to tears.

"It was a memorable situation, where we admitted we dropped the ball," says Rodenberg. "We had to go the extra mile and really take care of that guest." The fitting epilog to the story: The mother wrote another letter saying she was a customer for life.

That's *service recovery* that makes right the misstep for everyone involved, and creates a memory as magical for the employees who delivered it as for the customers who received it.

CHAPTER NINETEEN

Von Maur

Midwestern Magic Spreads Across the Prairie

Step into Von Maur and you know immediately you're in an upscale department store. A sense of luxurious space, the wide aisles and unobstructed wall-less views on each floor, reinforces the impression. People sense the well-executed Place Magic as soon as they walk in the door. Comment from several customers, overheard by spending a few moments in the entranceway: "Isn't this a beautiful store?" Indeed it is.

Von Maur	
President:	James D. von Maur
Headquarters:	Davenport, IA
# of Employees:	3,000
Sales:	$300 million

Antique furniture, lovely artwork, fireplaces, and white porcelain tile floors harmonize with jewel-toned carpets in peacock blues and rosy maroons. A pianist plays tasteful background music on a grand piano flanked by sofas and chairs for weary shoppers or their spouses. Shining wares and artful displays greet you from every department. Luxuriously tasteful. Quietly lavish.

Suddenly, a sure tip-off that this is a magical place: A sign, nestled in among the Kosta Boda crystal, reads, "Please touch the merchandise. You'll love it."

THE BACK STORY

That's the kind of unexpected and delightful twist that defines Von Maur, the last family-owned and operated department store in the country. Since 1872, the von Maurs have guided this small gem from their home base in Davenport, Iowa. The company has grown into an 18-store chain, with locations in Nebraska, Illinois, Minnesota, Kansas, and Indiana, in addition to its home state. Current expansion plans will add stores in Chicago, Ann Arbor, Detroit, and Louisville.

The "Nordstrom of the prairie," as the store is sometimes called, remains relatively unknown outside the Midwest. But don't think corn and cattle—try Ralph Lauren and DKNY. Von Maur specializes in high-quality fashions for men, women, teens, and children, boasts a shoe department nearly the equal of Nordstrom's, and sells fine accessories and gifts. The growing retailer employs approximately 3,000 people, and Hoover's Online estimates 2001 sales at $300 million (the private company releases no figures).

Von Maur is proud of its solid midwestern roots and history of succeeding by serving customers well. Originally a dry goods store established in Davenport by C.J. von Maur and partners R. H. Harned and E.C. Purcel, the business prospered in the early years of the 20th century. The company bought out its largest competitor in 1916, and earned a reputation as the finest department store west of Chicago. In 1937, the von Maur family acquired sole ownership of what was then called Petersen Harned Von Maur, and it has been a private, family-owned operation ever since.

Brothers Charles R. and Richard B. von Maur, grandsons of the founder, guided the organization for several decades. In 1988, they realized that to survive in an era of retailing giants they had to differentiate themselves from the competition. They set out on the physical and strategic transformation that would come to distinguish them. From a traditional department store with home goods and bedding, the company became a fashion department store. Existing locations were remodeled into the distinctive open spaces of today.

At the same time, the company made sweeping changes in its retailing approach. It all but eliminated advertising, devised an alternative to the continuous "sale" marketing strategy of most retailers, and introduced distinctive service amenities to build loyalty among customers. The store was renamed Von Maur—a name more appropriate for a fashion store than the law-firm sound of the old name, notes James von Maur, president and the fourth generation of the family to lead the company.

Even as it evolved from a 19th-century downtown dry goods store into a chain of 21st-century mall-based specialty department stores, Von Maur kept sight of the original values of founder C.J. von Maur. His customer service philosophy isn't especially remarkable: Treat every customer like family; commit to quality and service; Rule No. 1 is the customer is always right; and Rule No. 2 is if you think the customer is wrong, refer back to Rule No. 1. What is remarkable are the ways in which C.J.'s descendants have put those principles into practice.

THE WOW

Even the most jaded shopper will feel pampered by Von Maur's magical policies. Try these on for size: an interest-free credit card (there's no catch—no interest, no annual fee, 20 percent of the balance due each month), a straightforward no-questions-asked return policy, free gift wrap, and free shipping (all year round) to anywhere in the United States.

Such Service Magic draws attention in an era when department stores generally make their profits by charging interest rather than selling goods. All too many have implemented draconian return policies that telegraph mistrust to customers, while cost cutting has made gratis amenities rare. In contrast, Von Maur follows a philosophy perhaps best summed up as an abiding respect for customers.

That respect begins with the design of the stores themselves, magical places all. Stores are carefully laid out to make shopping at Von Maur easy, quick, and comfortable. Each floor is open—no interior walls divide up the space. You can find your way among departments without getting caught in a confusing maze of racks, counters, and walls. Vertical transportation is in plain view—escalators and elevators are as easy to spot as they are in a hotel lobby. Wide aisles are free of merchandise, designed to make navigating easy.

"Customers tell us their most precious commodity is time," says von Maur. "When you make a store confusing, you frustrate them. We make it easier—you can get in and get out. You can see where you are at all times."

You won't see signage with advertising messages and images. Nor will you see Von Maur advertising sales in newspapers or television commercials. Jim von Maur doesn't believe in discounting merchandise for weeklong or weekend-long or daylong sales, and then marking it back up. "We don't play games with customers," he says. "Why reward people for shopping on weekends? Why should the customer who shops on Friday pay more?"

Instead of sales, Von Maur uses aggressive markdowns, practicing an idiosyncratically defined "first in/first out" merchandising strategy—"first to spot new trends and the first to mark them down after they've peaked."[1] That way, the store is fresh and full of merchandise customers want, says von Maur. Merchandise marked down up to 75 percent is displayed on racks topped with discreet "sale" signs.

Von Maur advertises only vendor promotions—a trunk show or a free gift with purchase of certain cosmetics, for example. The store prefers to rely on word of mouth from pleased customers to generate buzz. The considerable sum it does not spend on advertising is sunk into the customer amenities (interest-free credit, gift wrap, and delivery), and on hiring plenty of salespeople and training them to deliver magical service—all with an eye to amazing customers.

No wonder Von Maur reminds people of their hometown department stores, now mostly long gone or gobbled up by big chains and corporate conglomerates. First-time Von Maur shoppers often reminisce about the stores they remember from the good old days.

Jim von Maur is familiar with the sentiment. "Whenever we go into a new market," he says, "we hear it from customers: 'This store reminds me of the old family department store that used to be in our town.'"

A CULTURE OF HEROES

Von Maur's clear vision and respect for customers guides its hiring and developing of the people who deliver its distinctive Service Magic. Behavior-based interviewing techniques help select candidates who know what it means to go above and beyond for customers, says Amy Davis, Von Maur's training manager. "We want people who can demonstrate through their past experiences that they have the qualities we're looking for."

But Von Maur's secret is really simpler than that: "We look for friendly people," says Davis. Jim von Maur explains: "My dad had a theory: We can train them to sell. We can't train them to be nice—that was their parent's job."

Those nice, friendly people are then given the tools they need to provide outstanding service. They learn the policies that help them deliver

Von Maur's special brand of enchantment, and how to develop Performance Magic that will earn them a loyal clientele. Von Maur maintains high staffing levels on the sales floor so that salespeople can devote sufficient time to customers and concentrate on delighting them, one customer at a time.

New associates are inculcated with Von Maur's commitment to fine service. "Our first mission in training is to ensure they establish a connection with the company and a sense of pride in its traditions," explains Davis. "We really communicate that message: 'We're counting on you to help us continue to build on our tradition of service.'"

New employees begin absorbing the company's customer service philosophy while they draw on their own experiences as customers—good and bad—and observe veteran Von Maur employees delivering great service. Then they are paired with a manager on the sales floor to solidify their learning.

As sales associates develop their own relationships with customers, they build a follow-up book that includes name, contact information, sizes, brand and style preferences, and so on. A salesperson can provide the kind of service that wows when he or she knows the customers and understands their likes and dislikes.

And customers love it. Here's an example from one loyal customer of the SouthPark store in Moline, Illinois: "One of your associates in the shoe department, Dee Dee, makes me feel like Cinderella. (This is no small feat as I wear size 11 shoes.) It's fun to get phone messages from Dee Dee: 'The new Franco Sartos are in,' or 'That pair of sandals you like has gone on sale.' I have probably bought 20 pairs of shoes from her this year and will continue to be a loyal Von Maur customer because of her help. . . ."

In another instance, Von Maur magic saved the day in a bridesmaids' dress emergency. The dresses—bought elsewhere and delivered just a day before the wedding party was to leave for the out-of-town ceremony—were disasters. A coordinated effort by Von Maur employees in the women's dress, children's, and shoe departments decked out the bridesmaids in just a few hours. The grateful bride wrote: "The dresses turned out to be exactly what I wanted and more. Your store, and the exceptional service of your employees, saved the appearance of my wedding. That means so much to me."

One more: Herb and Pat, employees of the stock department, noticed a car spewing steam from an overheated radiator pull into Von Maur's parking lot. Pat filled a gallon jug with water and filled the radiator. Herb noticed a leak in one of the hoses, cut, and reclamped it. The man and his daughter continued on their way with the leak fixed.

Von Maur encourages such attentive service with a recognition program it calls "Heroics." Customer raves and compliments for outstanding service from coworkers earn employees kudos and cash awards at Heroics meetings held each Saturday morning. When these tales of service above and beyond are read aloud at storewide gatherings, says Davis, "it reinforces what employees already know, gives them new ideas, and encourages them to set the bar even higher."

Promotion from within is an important value at Von Maur—all managers have spent time working on the sales floor so they understand the challenges of the job. They model the kind of magical performance expected from associates whenever they have contact with a customer. It's a culture of service that builds on itself, explains Jim von Maur. "When new employees see managers and executives going above and beyond for customers, it makes them want to do it, too," he says.

And, of course, the magic ultimately begins at the top. "When employees see me, the president of the company, helping customers, holding the door for them, taking packages to their car—that sets the pace."

## CHAPTER TWENTY

Children's Memorial Hospital

We're Not in a Hospital Anymore, Toto

As you are ushered into the Brown Family Life Center at Children's Memorial Hospital in Chicago, Dorothy's memorable words from the *Wizard of Oz* leap to mind: "Toto, I've a feeling we're not in Kansas anymore." Behold a magical oasis of curving walls inlaid with bright mosaic tile, sun streaming through an arching skylight, and a very unhospital-like atmosphere of laughter and music located smack dab in the middle of a major metropolitan pediatric medical center. There's a parent business center whirring with computers and fax machines, a family living room rocking with a big-screen television, and a central play area that looks like FAO Schwartz.

Children's Memorial Hospital	
President/CEO:	Patrick Magoon
Headquarters:	Chicago, IL
# of Employees:	5,000
Net Patient Care Rev:	$240.2 million

The Brown Family Life Center—dubbed a "medical free zone" for patients and their families—is the gleaming jewel in the customer service crown that shines from every nook and cranny at the 265-bed Children's Memorial. Just entering the hospital is a delight. Little visitors are immediately drawn to a huge Dr. Seuss-like contraption surrounded by several interactive displays created in tandem with the Chicago Children's Museum. Receptionists are replaced by a blue-jacketed concierge staff (hired based on their smile quotient) who serve up information and directions with a delicious cup of coffee. Painted train tracks guide you to your destination on any of several floors (which are designed around a different nature theme including sea, earth, flowers, and forest).

Children's Memorial Hospital is the *Emerald City* of pediatric care in Chicago's fiercely competitive health care market, exemplifying the successful combination of Place, Process, and Performance Magic. Each year, Children's 1,000 pediatric specialists and 2,000-plus health care professionals care for more than 80,000 kids and their families. Nearly 13,500 surgical procedures are performed annually, and 43,500 emergency room visits are recorded. Its prowess in clinical services, education, and research has earned Children's Memorial a ranking among the top ten pediatric hospitals by *U.S. News & World Report* for nine years running. And recently it earned prestigious *Magnet* status from the American Nurses Association as one of the 55 best hospitals in the nation to work for nurses.

CYCLONE OF ADVERSITY STARTS SERVICE JOURNEY

The yellow brick road in this tale of magical customer service starts much like that in the mythical land of Oz . . . from a cyclone of adversity. "The mid-90s were very challenging for Children's," said Gordon B. Bass, chief operating officer. "In 1997, satisfaction levels among patients, families, physicians, and employees were below national norms. At one point, the hospital was losing more than $1 million a month along with patient volume and market share," he said. There was also a concerted effort under way by some staff to unionize Children's workforce.

It was during this dark hour that the Board of Directors turned to Patrick M. Magoon, naming him president and chief executive officer. A 20-year veteran of the hospital management team, Magoon convened a strategic planning committee to reexamine all operations from the ground up. The committee instituted five strategic initiatives based on renewing growth, strengthening brand, improving financial performance, demonstrating superior clinical quality, and improving customer satisfaction for patients, families, physicians, and employees. Such lofty goals look great on paper, of course, but according to Children's COO Bass, there was a difference this time out. "We set goals that were measurable," he said. "We stuck to them without losing focus, and the resources were there to make good ideas and dreams a reality."

Children's leadership further strengthened the turnaround equation by asking for feedback and, better yet, listening to it. Patient satisfaction is gauged through weekly Press Ganey surveys, a constant stream of internal data from patient relations, patient and family focus groups, and heightened reliance on an unusually proactive Family Advisory Board. Employees were surveyed for the first time in hospital history and are re-polled every 18 months. Magoon also launched "leadership rounds," routine visits by the executive team to all hospital units to ask employees, patients, and families how service could be improved.

LIONS AND TIGERS AND ROLLING CAFÉS ... OH, MY!

It might seem that Service Magic would be automatic when caring for sick children. The story of Julia O'Malley, a staff nurse in the hospital's ambulatory stem cell unit, certainly qualifies. At age 15, Julia came to Children's for help battling non-Hodgkins lymphoma. She was so inspired by the work of her caregivers that she vowed to enter the health care profession and return some day to help other young people struggling with cancer. Now a radiant 28-year-old, Julia's dream has come true as she serves as a role model for cancer survivors and their families. "If I can do it," she reasons to a child nauseous from meds or bloated from steroids, "so can you."

One of those special kids is Russell Witek, a seven-year-old who was treated at Children's Memorial for ALL (Acute Lymphocytic Leukemia). Julia and Russell recently marched together in the Cancer Survivor's Celebration and Walk with Russell hitching a ride on Julia's back for the last mile. Not surprisingly, Julia has had a tremendous impact on Russell and his family as they have fought through his illness. "You want to know the really great thing?" says Karen Witek, Russell's mom, "as exceptional as Julia is, at Children's Memorial she's the norm."

Words of such magical performance are music to the ears of Maureen Mahoney, corporate manager for service excellence at Children's. Nevertheless, Mahoney will tell you that customer service breakdowns do occur even in the rarified atmosphere of a children's hospital. Pressures from a competitive business environment collide with highly charged emotions to put tremendous strain on employees at all levels. Mahoney cites the newly created position of service excellence manager as a clear signal that hospital leadership is serious about improving satisfaction.

To start the patient/family satisfaction ball rolling, a task force was formed to brainstorm a list of "quick hit, high-impact" initiatives that laser in on key drivers of satisfaction. The magic they created now permeates the hospital. Pop your head into any patient room and you'll note two medical charts, one traditional and one titled *All About Me* for kids to fill out in crayon on what they like and don't like, what soothes them, and what "bugs them the most about being sick." Twice a day an amenities cart will roll in with free toiletries and other personal care items for parents who haven't had a chance to freshen up. Another favorite is the "big blue café on wheels," fully stocked with a variety of food for anyone who wants to buy a snack without trooping down to the hospital cafeteria.

The changes generated immediate positive feedback from patients and buy-in from staff. The next challenge, as hospital leadership saw it, was to develop a vertically integrated customer service initiative that would push Service Magic deeper into the routine of hospital life.

JOURNEY TO SERVICE MAGIC

"We realized we needed universal service expectations as a foundation for truly wowing our families," said Mahoney about the service excellence initiative. Mahoney and her colleagues crafted a set of seven service principles that now serve as the touchstone for hospital staff and management as they strive to transform the customer experience. They read:

1. Treat the people we serve with respect and courtesy at all times.

2. Demonstrate pride in our personal appearance and the appearance of our facility.

3. Respect the privacy and confidentiality needs of the people we serve.

4. Anticipate the wants and needs of those we serve, and respond promptly.

5. Act to reverse negative service situations, using "acknowledge, accept, and amend."

6. Work to actively listen to and communicate with the people we serve.

7. Demonstrate a sense of ownership and pride toward our work, recognizing that it is a reflection of Children's Memorial and ourselves.

The new strategy was unveiled in a two-phase rollout plan. Phase One introduced the leadership staff to the theories behind exceptional customer service, a review of the hospital's core strengths and weaknesses, and highlights from the research on which the plan was based. A service culture is created when people, systems, and processes align around the service principles, the management team said. In practice, this means pushing the principles out through a wide range of actions: hiring, orientation, coaching, staff empowerment, reward and recognition, communication, accountability, performance appraisal and measurement. Phase Two introduced the same concepts to the staff. Within nine weeks, the service excellence initiative had been showcased for more than 80 percent of hospital and physician leaders and nearly half of the staff.

Posters were developed from the Press Ganey survey findings for display throughout the organization. And scripting was introduced to employees in a presentation built around the seven service principles. Statements like, "May I come in?" before entering a room, or "I am pulling this curtain because I am concerned about your child's privacy," promoted the third principle of privacy. Under principle four, "anticipating needs," employees are asked to end every patient encounter with "Is there anything else I can do for you?" (See Chapter 10.)

There's No Place Like Home ...
Except Maybe Children's

Children's headlong dive into Service Magic is working. Press Ganey scores have shown significant improvement. Annual employee turnover has been reduced from 30 percent in 1997 to 14 percent in 2001. Plus, the hospital posted a $26.5 million revenue turnaround from 1997 to 2001, with net operating income for 2002 estimated at $9.5 million. Board members are delighted, hospital executives are encouraged, and employees are approaching work with renewed energy. "I want us to be an organization that truly creates the best possible experience for our patients and families," said Mahoney.

Click your heels together three times, swoosh back to the Brown Family Life Center, and you'll see that wishes like Mahoney's really do come true. The "Bingo Guy" is cracking kids up in one of several game shows produced by the staff of Skylight TV, Children's own interactive television station. Next up is the guitar-playing, joke-telling hospital chaplain to lead a rousing sing-a-long. And later there will be Story Time with Dot, today reading *The Wizard of Oz* (of course). The smiling, giggling, clapping, dancing kids here would still say that there's no place like home. But if you have to be sick, Children's Memorial Hospital in Chicago comes in a close second.

21

All-Outdoors Whitewater Rafting

Where Magical Rides Start on Virtual Rivers

It's a breathtaking day as you paddle the long, bending curves of the Merced River in central California. Despite the bright sky, stunning canyon scenery, and easy current, you feel the tension building in your raft. Suddenly, you sight the renowned "Three Bears" rapids, part of a long straight alleyway filled with truck-sized boulders and stomach-churning drops.

All-Outdoors Whitewater Rafting	
President:	Gregg Armstrong
Headquarters:	Walnut Creek, CA
# of Employees:	175
Sales (2000):	$760,000

You push away from the computer keyboard to catch your breath. After all, you aren't really feeling the spray of whitewater or undulations of the raft. You're on a simulated river tour on the Web site of All-Outdoors Whitewater Rafting (aorafting.com), a Walnut Creek, California–based adventure company, enjoying a little virtual Place Magic.

These virtual river runs, which give prospective customers a 360-degree taste of 12 rivers on which All-Outdoors (AO) offers guided trips, are but one reason the family-run company's Web site has become the gold standard for the adventure-travel business. Designers knew such glitzy features would draw many to the site, but the key to winning their trip business—and keeping them coming back—was user-friendly design, clear answers to rafters' most pressing questions, and superior online service. It was that service magician's toolkit—the combination of Virtual Place, Process, and Performance—that helped AO win *Inc* magazine's prestigious award for General Excellence in its 2001 Web Awards competition, besting 800 other applicants.

GLITZ DRAWS, SERVICE MAGIC RETAINS

While the virtual river tours are the site's signature, AO management knew prospects weren't coming to the site merely to play with the technology. That's why it crafted a site that exemplifies the "ETDW" virtual magic principle—Easy To Do Business With.

The site's 250-plus pages are organized in a simple, clutter-free architecture that tells the company's story with compelling photographs and concise blocks of text. The *Inc* award judges lauded AO for creating a site with "streamlined good looks." Instead of superfluous visual adornment or verbiage, there is a reliance on good search engines. The site flaunts redundancy like a badge of honor, providing one-click access to any page and making sure those links are omnipresent—users aren't forced to hop, skip, and jump to find a page they need. It's obvious this Webmaster spent some time in his e-customers' rafting sandals. Main navigation buttons aren't located on the bottom of the home page where they're hard to find, but stacked neatly on the left side of the page, easily spotted upon opening. The buttons represent categories including About All-Outdoors, California Rivers, Plan a Trip, and Contact Us. The Rivers link contains the shoppers' page, which has maps of each river where AO provides guided trips. Clicking on a "river" button reveals trip descriptions and costs, as well as the 360-degree virtual tours that feature iPIX three-dimensional photo technology. The simulations require no troublesome plug-ins for users, only a Java-enabled browser. Using their cursor and a mouse, viewers have the power to "step inside" the picture to look up, down, and all around—from earth to sky—immersing themselves in the virtual waterways. Each simulation has a mile-by-mile tour of several scenic highlights on each river, including rapids, campsites, and side hikes.

Visitors have no shortage of alluring waterways to choose from. Because of AO's long and safe guiding history, it has acquired an elite set of permits that give customers access to some of the most spectacular canyons and rivers in California and Oregon. And more permits equate to more river choices, more dates, and more availability for customers.

Clicking on the "Plan a Trip" button allows users to Pick a River, Pick Your Friends (organize a group trip), Pick a Day, and Make a Reservation. In addition, a "Quick Reference" section provides real-time data on river conditions, trip availability, price lists, and trip discounts, as well as access to a list of frequently asked questions.

Visitors also can send photos or postcards directly from the Web site to promote an upcoming trip or simply say hello to a friend with an electronic postcard featuring action shots from a river they're about to run. All they need to do is pick a river photo, add a personal message, review it, and send it off. AO also encourages rafters to volunteer reactions, reflections, or insights about their own trips for others to read on a feedback page.

PERFORMING MAGIC—ON-RIVER AND ONLINE

Although the small company that began with founder George Armstrong running weekend trips for his family has grown into one of the larger outfitters in the industry, it still treats most of its customers like family. AO takes pains to hire guides who not only possess the proper certification and on-river experience, but also have exceptional people skills and caring attitudes—along with the ability to whip up scrumptious riverside meals for even the most discerning palette. Letters from satisfied customers routinely compliment the warm and friendly personalities of AO's 175-plus river guides.

While the company's primary goal is to create magic in the form of thrilling, memorable, and safe river trips, AO guides also take time to educate rafters about the river environment during the journey. A healthy river system provides clean drinking water, stable fisheries, and irrigation water—and guides remind customers that the water they drink at home may be the same water that carried them downstream on their rafting trip. AO regularly conducts interpretive workshops for its guides that focus on the natural, cultural—and even political—history of a river.

That on-river attention to detail and personal care carries over to the Web site, as well, where visitors can make tentative reservations, get maps, check river and weather conditions, arrange accommodations at local campgrounds or hotels, and much more. In fact, there's a "trip details and maps" Web page for each river AO runs. The idea is to answer most—or all—of a prospective customer's questions or concerns with one trip to the site, with little need for follow-up phone calls to AO staff.

Although customers can choose a river trip and pay for a reservation online via credit card, they must send in a form that requires an AO's employee to respond. That's partly because reservations are made far ahead of time before river conditions are known. But AO also believes a well-trained, experienced human is far better at gauging a prospective customer's true rafting skill level than any Web-based Q&A, so the follow-up phone call is mandatory. To comfort the rafting-wary—typically parents or chaperones of teenage groups, but also skittish first-time rafters—there are testimonials on the site from the likes of a top U.S. risk manager about AO's proven safety record, as well as information about the training and experience levels of the company's river guides, all of whom are certified in first aid and other river safety skills. AO has long operated guide schools that allow beginner guides to learn at the shoulders of more senior guides and prepare to work their navigation magic on increasingly challenging Class IV and V runs.

The Magician's Flair Drives Profit

This focus on creating Service Magic, both online and during the river trips, has paid off handsomely on AO's bottom line. In addition to capturing *Inc* magazine's top award for general excellence, the AO Web site was also a second-place finisher in the magazine's return-on-investment category. According to the *Inc* awards' profile, AO's revenues from the Web site alone grew from $55,000 in 1997 to $760,000 in 2000.

Much of what the traditional marketing the company once did— Yellow Page ads, glossy print catalogs, and direct mail—has been shifted to the Web site, although hard-copy advertising still plays an important role in drawing customers. Because AO knew many of its computer-savvy customers would seek it out on the Web, it sought prime placement early on with the established search engines, and persuaded numerous other sites to funnel traffic its way. Not only did the Web site enable AO to consolidate marketing efforts, it allowed for faster and more cost-efficient updating of marketing campaigns—and the ability to better track outcomes of marketing efforts. Now, AO management can easily determine how much of its revenue is coming through the site, and where those customers are coming from.

Putting more service features online also has helped AO limit call center expenses, since customers can answer more of their questions about rafting trips by visiting the site, creating a "virtual" call center effect.

22

QVC

Real People Creating Virtual Magic

Spend time with top leaders at QVC Inc., and you'll quickly under-stand how the company became the world's top televised shopping ser-vice and an e-commerce leader. It's not simply because of the company's unique selling venue and strong price/value proposition—it's also QVC's passion for performing service and magic for its customers.

QVC	
President:	Doug Briggs
Headquarters:	West Chester, PA
# of Employees:	14,000
Sales (2001)	$3.9 billion

BUILDING RAPPORT WITH CUSTOMERS

QVC's most obvious hallmark is the vast array of quality merchan-dise—beauty products, home furnishings, electronics, and fine jewelry—

it makes available around the clock via its "virtual mall" on TV or on its Web site, QVC.com. Hundreds of QVC buyers comb the world to introduce some 300 new products to these venues each week.

Equally impressive, however, is the shopping experience QVC creates for customers once they flip on the TV, log onto the Web site, or pick up a phone to order. From day one, customer service representatives in QVC's global "care centers" are taught to advocate for customers; they are *not* to search for ways to nickel and dime them, maintain an all-business manner at all costs, or assume bad intentions on the part of complaining customers. While intimate knowledge of QVC's diverse product line and efficiency are vital parts of the reps' jobs, so too is adding a magical, personal touch to their interactions with customers.

"Although we're a big company, we need to take time to have conversations with customers," says John Hunter, QVC's senior vice president of customer service. "We present product on TV with what we call the neighbor-across-the-back-fence approach, and we want the same feel to carry through to our call centers." That means if a chatty customer asks where a rep hails from or "what the weather's like there today," the rep takes time to chit chat and doesn't push callers directly on to business. When Hunter stresses the value of such rapport building to his staff, he often refers to the personal, old-fashioned care his family received from a corner grocer during his childhood in Brooklyn. "I'm old enough and corny enough to think these things still matter to customers," he says.

To learn the interpersonal and technical sides of their jobs, QVC customer service employees spend three weeks in training—one week of orientation and classroom training heavy on call simulations, and two weeks in the "incubator," where they take live calls in the presence of a supervisor or trainer. Once released to work teams, they're usually assigned a "buddy" or on-the-job mentor. To root out QVC policies or practices that get in the way of providing magical service, general managers in each call center hold "round tables" with their center's 1,000-plus employees every year. The idea is to ask those who know best whether the company is enchanting customers—or delivering the kind of ham-handed service that might hurt repeat business. "We tell our people that if we're doing something that's not to the benefit of our customers, we want to hear about it right away," says Hunter. Dedicated "customer focus" teams are charged with capturing and categorizing that rep feedback to identify patterns or recurring trouble spots—often following up with the reps by phone for more detail—and then filing reports to management.

CEMENTING LOYALTY THROUGH
MAGICAL RECOVERY

Central to QVC's service philosophy is a commitment to fixing any product or service problems quickly, without finger pointing or diversionary tactics. When it mistakenly shipped some exercise equipment without an accompanying videotape, for example, QVC moved fast, calling a vendor and requesting additional tapes ASAP—and then rushing out those tapes along with an apology letter to customers before most even had a chance to call and complain about the tape's absence. Service Magic, says Hunter, is about being proactive where others might write off such snafus as the cost of operating a high-volume business, or who might not take action until complaint calls reached a critical mass.

Customers know that if a problem results from an error by QVC, there will be quick, magical recovery and some atonement. Take the year QVC was selling NFL team rings at a record pace—wives were buying them for husbands as Christmas gifts—and guaranteeing pre-Christmas delivery. But when that delivery promise fizzled, QVC knew it had to go beyond simply crediting customers for their purchases, as many other companies might have done. "You just hate to be late with any Christmas delivery," says Hunter. Enterprising employees remembered there were some quality NFL team jackets in the QVC warehouse, so the company matched them against the ordered team rings and mailed them before Christmas at no cost to customers, who (by most accounts) were delighted with the "save."

Says Hunter: "This kind of recovery is always the right thing to do ethically, but we've also proven it has big financial payback in terms of customer retention. We've documented that people buy at a higher rate from QVC when they've been part of a service recovery situation that wowed them or exceeded expectations. To us it's not throwing money away, but building long-term relationships with customers."

THE POWER OF CHOICE

Of the 130-million-plus customer calls QVC receives in a given year, some 75 percent are pure order-entry transactions—customers who've made up their minds about purchases and have no clarifying questions or concerns. Given that statistic, most companies might funnel as many of those callers as possible into automated ordering options to reduce labor costs. But QVC understands that customers don't like being painted into corners, and limiting their options dulls enthusiasm for repeat visits. Those calling QVC's 800 number do have an automated buying option, but customers who want to order through a live human can do so. Callers might get a message saying, "All of our phone representatives are currently busy, but if you would like to reserve your product and wait for a rep to speak to, please push 1." Clearly, many shoppers prefer the human contact. Operators assist with 54 percent of QVC orders; the remaining 46 percent is handled by automated ordering.

Hunter is particularly wary of the effect automated-only buying options can have on new QVC customers. "We want people to be able to choose voice response ordering, not be forced into it," he says.

QVC also strives to deliver the same consistent, exceptional level of service to customers whether they call the 800 number, send an e-mail query, or use a live text chat option on the Web site. "These lines have blurred in our business, and we have to deliver a seamless, high-quality service experience across all contact channels," says Hunter.

Service reps who handle live chat functions on QVC.com, for instance, receive the same intensive service training as phone reps, but with additional education in categories like electronics or beauty products that require more specialized knowledge, as well as training in delivering good advice in written, rather than spoken, form.

MEASURES THAT MATTER

Companies that deliver Service Magic are fanatical about assessing and continually upgrading employee performance, and QVC is no exception. "We measure everything that moves around here," says Hunter. Among the most important service quality metrics is the number of repeat calls to call centers. "The last thing we want is for customers to have to call our centers back about the same issue," Hunter says. "Our goal is 100 percent first-call resolution." While some repeat calls represent customers calling back simply to confirm product delivery information, others call again because a problem or concern wasn't fixed right the first time. The good news for QVC is that over the past ten years, such repeat calls have dropped from 17 percent of all customer calls to an impressive 3 percent.

Call transfers are equally discouraged in the QVC culture—the mantra is "one call, one person." Unlike other organizations where that objective may get lip service but little follow through, reps at QVC receive the training and technology support to make it happen.

In addition, every 18 months QVC conducts a global customer satisfaction survey (through an outside vendor) tailored to assess customer loyalty. A shorter, modified version of that survey is sent each month to 200 customers who have had recent contact with QVC call centers.

Recognizing Service Magicians

The frontline magic performed by service magicians is, by definition, transparent and performed with a consistent level of grace, competency, and effort. The danger is that great performances become easy to take for granted. Even the most experienced, self-assured magicians need affirmation of their value to the company, best delivered through a combination of informal and formal recognition.

Hunter makes it a priority of regularly celebrating acts of Service Magic performed on QVC's front lines. When customers write a letter, e-mail, or phone supervisors about some memorable service they received, Hunter asks that all such kudos be forwarded to his desk. He jots short congratulatory notes to the employees responsible—writing up to 50 such thank-you's monthly—and posts them on public bulletin boards for all to see. While he feared the practice might grow stale over time, Hunter says employees continue to seek him out when he visits call centers to thank him for the recognition, often telling of notes posted proudly on home refrigerators or saved as keepsakes.

QVC also has formal recognition plans that reward hourly workers for consistent levels of service excellence as well as managers who provide top-notch service coaching. A peer-nominated award culminates in a splashy annual banquet where employees receive plaques, monetary awards, and more public recognition. Hunter believes the peer-nominated component is what gives the recognition impact. "Your coworkers see you every day and they know who's doing the job and who's not, and they can be pretty tough critics," he says.

The Closing Act: Rapid Delivery and Hassle-Free Returns

QVC management knows all the personal warmth and transactional expertise on the front end does little good if customers don't receive product in a timely and error-free fashion. "With televised selling, everything from phone call to doorstep delivery has to be smooth," says Hunter. "When customers have to wait a week for product, their enthusiasm for us can start to wane."

To that end, QVC's goal is to ship 95 percent of product within 48 hours of phone or Web site orders measuring its performance against that objective daily. QVC customers know which specific day their products will arrive and are rarely let down. They also know that any fragile merchandise will arrive in good shape. QVC even created special packaging for shipping its fine jewelry.

The company takes its shipping promise so seriously it often resorts to "zone jumping" to get product into customers' hands faster. QVC shipments can be delayed at the primary sort locations of outside carrier. To get around those bottlenecks, QVC will itself often truck product deeper into certain zones and zip codes—known as a zone jump—especially if there's high volume headed to particular hubs. "It allows us to bypass several stages of the sorting process and, as a result, pick up a day or two on delivery transit time," says John Hare, QVC's senior vice president of distribution and logistics.

Should customers need to return product, QVC strives to make that process as hassle-free and magical as ordering. One goal is to credit customers' accounts within 72 hours or less of a product return. "Some might say we could live longer off the float, but that's the customers' money, not ours, and the faster we credit them, the more enthused we think they'll be about buying from us again," says Hunter.

THE SERVICE MAGICIAN'S POCKET TOOLKIT

Something Old, Something New, Many Things Borrowed, Nothing Blue

"What we need are more people who specialize in the impossible."

THEODORE ROETHKE

"Find a happy medium between knowing your business and knowing how to make your customers happy. If they trust you, then the hardest work is done, and you can focus on the real work: making magic happen."

STEVE MACLAUGHLIN

Magic comes in all shapes and sizes. Some magic requires a large stage, sets, accomplices, and a space shuttle full of high technology to invoke its illusions. But most magic comes in smaller, pocket-sized packages: card and coin tricks, ropes and dice; intimate little tabletop illusions; mysteries and sleights of hand. Pocket magic is the stuff of living room performances, the stuff of beginner's delight; the skill-builder's drama and the professional's warm-up exercise. Tricks and effects that make us smile and—sometimes—laugh. And always make us ask, "How did you do that?" and "How did you know?"

The four chapters that follow serve up 75 pieces of Service Magic: little amazers that we've seen, tried, read about, and heard others describe in glowing terms. They are organized as you would expect, as Place Pocket Magic, Process Pocket Magic, Performance Pocket Magic, as well as Service Recovery Pocket Magic. If you go through our list and realize your favorite Service Magic pocket trick isn't mentioned, send it to us at <www.service-magic.com>—and we'll send you a pocket magic trick you can use to amuse and amaze your friends, colleagues, and—of course—your customers.

23

Place Pocket Service Magic

In addition to the earlier discussion in Chapter 6 on decorating and amenities, there are many little place enhancers that bring a smile and add to the experience: ways of dressing the set—even gilding the lily a little—that are worthy of your consideration. We share them with you as they were shared with—or experienced by—us.

- At the Hotel Monaco Chicago, the pillow mint has been replaced with a "treat of the day." Sometimes the maids leave a Bit-o-Honey or candy necklaces—or even a yo-yo or kazoo—on the guest pillow at turn-down time. And on the rare occasion, guests are surprised with a genuine, absolutely for real Illinois lottery ticket. Zowie!

- Several hospitals around the country are celebrating the arrival of newborns with a quiet lullaby. First Tune, a program developed by Mark Maxwell, a classical guitarist from Athens, Georgia, allows parents in the labor and delivery unit of a hospital to press a doorbell-like button and play a 20-second lullaby over the hospital's public address system. The tune boosts the morale of patients, staff, and visitors as they share in the good news. Debra McKell, of Brandon Regional Medical Center in Brandon, Florida, says "We are expecting to hear more than 3,000 lullabies at Brandon Regional Medical Center this year."

- At Bloomington, Minnesota's Mall of America, the largest mall in the United States, there are more than 520 stores plus a dental office, health clinic, post office, high school, university, aquarium, theme park, and wedding chapel—something for everyone! Realizing the convenient access they could offer their potential students, the National American University jumped at the opportunity to move into the mall. After being in the mall for several months, it realized there was an additional service it could be providing to the "mall-walkers" cruising the long corridors of the mall (more than four miles on all four levels). NAU began offering computer courses in the early morning hours so the walkers—many retired—could learn how to e-mail their grandchildren.[1]

- The Howard Johnson's motel in Council Bluffs, Iowa caters to the needs female travelers in simple but thoughtful ways that make staying in the hotel surprisingly memorable. It begins with the shuttle driver offering a step stool to help women get into and out of the airport van without "sharing their undies with the world," notes Camille Price, a pleased patron. Upon arrival, their bags are delivered directly to their rooms, and the desk clerk makes a point of offering transportation to anywhere in the city during their stay. "They drove me to my work site each morning, and shuttled me to restaurants and shopping in the evening eliminating the need for cabs," she adds. By the second day of her stay, the staff was greeting her by name when she left and returned. "It was comforting to think that if I didn't return one night someone might notice," she says. "It helped me feel safe."

   In the lobby there is a vending machine stocked with the kind of sundries—pantyhose, nail files, hair spray—the female traveler dearly appreciates but rarely finds. "The thing that amazes me about that experience was that none of what they did was particularly expensive or flashy," Price says. "It was a series of small things designed to make me personally more comfortable."

- McKenna Family Dentistry has a novel way to help avoid the stress of dental work: They distract their patients with movies. Every office in the Palo Alto, California clinic features a VCR, wireless headsets, and a selection of kids' videos, popular movies, and TV comedies (without the commercials). More than 85 percent of customers use the VCR during fillings or other dental procedures, says Judi McKenna-Edwards, hygienist and office manager.[2]

- If you pull into Harry's Marathon Service station in Saline, Wisconsin, you can pump your own gas or have it pumped for you. But Charlie will take your money or credit card and return with change and receipt. What makes this cashier unusual, however, is that Charlie is a golden retriever! Patrons of Harry's love Charlie's service, and even started a 401K-9 retirement plan for him.

- Seattle, Washington's Seatac International Airport has equipped its water fountains with speakers. When travelers stop at a fountain for a drink, they are treated to the sound of a peaceful, cascading waterfall.

- The Garden Patch in Excelsior, Minnesota lacks the orderly, antiseptic look of the modern suburban nursery. Its curb appeal is minimal. From the road it looks like a jumble of lean-tos, weathered pot benches, corrugated steel and fiber glass roofing. And it is. Once inside the front gate, the low ceilings (signs warn visitors to watch their heads), slanty beams, and a maze of rooms give a feel of Winnie the Pooh's under tree house or a cozy earthen Hobbit hole. The back lot, shaded by ancient yews and bordering a cat-tailed pond, completes the mood of Garden Patch as a place for the magical nurturing of plants, flowers, vegetables, and herbs.

  Rough gravel paths and floors add to the "not-your-antiseptic-garden-store" feeling. The crowning accent—the Garden Patch shopping carts—a fleet of Radio Flyer® wagons customers pull along as they prowl the nooks and crannies of the place ducking low beams, chuckling with other gardeners as their bright red Flyers rattle and bounce behind them. First time visitors are obvious. All share the same wide-eyed, taken aback look. Not quite sure what to do or how to breach this obvious anti-shopping experience. As the buzz and low level discomfort of the unfamiliar abates and they see other customers—wagons in tow, plying the rows, dodging hanging baskets, and evaluating plants—they relax and let their barefoot inner kids come play in the garden.

- To create an earth-friendly and nourishing atmosphere, a Marriott Hotel in Miami offers environmentally correct "green rooms" that include special air and water filtration, water conserving faucets, and energy-efficient light bulbs. It's also installed a $12,000 machine that releases natural floral and citrus plant extracts into the lobby through the central air conditioner. The desired effect of this aromatherapy is to reduce stress, and was tailored to the hotel's predominantly Central and South American guests.[3]

- Byerly's, the Minnesota-based grocery chain, has created a grocery shopping experience so elegant and luxurious that it's not uncommon for out-of-town guests to put the shop at the top of their sightseeing. The experience begins and ends in the parking lot where extra large spaces accommodate even the biggest SUVs. The store itself is low-lit with wide carpeted aisles and an array of delectable samples offered throughout.

  Jazz trios play in the chandeliered foyer during the winter holidays and every child is given a sombrero on Cinco de Mayo. If a loader loses a bag of your groceries, for example, a manager will "reshop" them and have them delivered to your house within an hour with a complimentary pie or box of chocolates.

- The Old Northwoods Lodge, located in Minnesota's boundary waters canoe area, is a place where visitors go to enjoy one of the last bastions of unspoiled wilderness on Minnesota's Canadian border. Even though the lodge is deep in the north woods, the staff goes out of its way to add personal touches, to make the customer's experience a memorable blend of rustic and elegant.

  When a recent guest went to the lodge for a birthday dinner with her husband and son after a day of canoeing, she was amazed at the extra effort put into her birthday celebration. Her mother had called ahead to order a bottle of champagne for the occasion. When the group arrived they were seated at a window table with a beautiful floral arrangement. The server immediately arrived with the bottle of champagne, and a greeting card that read "Love, Mom and Dad."

  The guest observed the server had set three champagne flutes on the table. One for the birthday girl, one for her husband, and a third for her nine-year-old son (to make sure he was included in the occasion). "The owners of the lodge and our server cooked this all up because my parents had called to order the champagne," the guest says. "It was the best birthday I can remember."

CHAPTER TWENTY-FOUR

Process Pocket Service Magic

It's hard to imbue a policy or performance of a procedure with magic. After all, consistency and predictability are the hallmarks of process that give customers that warm, secure "I'm doing business with the right people" feeling. Just the same, a few have trod where others fear—and succeeded:

- Valleyfair Theme Park, located in Shakopee, Minnesota, has recently introduced a new program to assist parents in reuniting with their lost children. Guests with children can register for the program "KidTrack" at Guest Services or Berenstain Bear Country, where a special KidTrack wristband with the parent's cell phone number is placed on the child's wrist. The lost child is instructed to go to any uniformed Valleyfair employee, who will contact Valleyfair's Operations office with the child's contact information and the parents are immediately called.

- Universal Studios Hollywood has recently implemented the world's first-ever theme park guaranteed rain check. All guests visiting on a day when the park receives over $\frac{1}{8}''$ of rainfall will be offered a rain check good any time in the following 30 days.

- The Walt Disney World staff is well-known for giving children a magical experience. When a friend took her seven-year-old son there, they were both delighted, but not just with the rides and attractions. "What thrilled me was the way the Disney employees treated my son," she says. It was apparent to her that her child was their primary customer: He was addressed first in restaurants, and greeted at the rides and attractions. The looking at him and speaking to him made him feel important. "At Disney," she says, "they treated my son as though he was as special to them as he is to his mother."

- Progressive Insurance of Cleveland, recognizing that clients who have just been in a car accident have specific physical and emotional needs, tailors its customer service to that experience. The company gives every adjuster a van outfitted with a personal computer, satellite uplink, and everything else needed for the singular purpose of efficiently resolving a claim from an accident site. Progressive claimants not only receive checks on the spot, but they are also offered a cup of coffee and, if need be, a few minutes to relax on the couch in the van and the chance to call family members from the adjuster's cell phone.[1]

- Regular customers of Superquinn, the supermarket chain based in Dublin, Ireland, often have the feeling that store management is reading their minds. Customers wondered why, for instance, they had to pay for broccoli stalks and carrot tops they never used—and PRESTO—their wish was granted. Superquinn now provides scissors at displays so customers can cut off those portions they don't want.[2]

- Some shoppers found it difficult to decipher their grocery receipts, so Superquinn now provides a running total on checkout screens directly facing customers, and organizes the receipt by product category rather than by the order that products come through the scanner.[3]

- Most grocery shoppers dread the idea of simultaneously looking through the fruits and veggies and keeping track of one or more rambunctious aisle acrobats. To lighten the load, Pittsburgh, Pennsylvania–based Giant Eagle food stores created the "Eagle's Nest," a secure playtime area for children ages three to nine. Kids love the activities, computer and video games, and other play areas provided by the trained, qualified professional staff. Women, who still comprise 70 percent of grocery shoppers in the United States, love the break from child chasing even more.

- Stratis Morfogen, CEO of FultonStreet.com, takes the round-the-clock nature of online shopping to heart. Although his online fish market is a small company, he assigns at least one of his five service reps to respond to customers' requests and man the live chat room at all hours of the night and day. He fills in himself on occasional nights and weekends. "E-tailing is 24 hours, so customer service should be 24 hours. Otherwise, it's like having a 7-Eleven store with no one at the counter from midnight to 7 AM," he says.[5]

- Bob's Stores, a New England retailer specializing in casual clothing and shoes for the Gap-set, offers hard-to-fit men and women (in other words, just about everybody) the option of ordering affordable custom-fit chinos. Once the exclusive domain of major brands like Lands' End and Levi's, Bob's entered into the custom-fit market offering $39.99 pants that ship 21 days after the order is placed. Thanks to a straightforward Web page design and an astute question tree, the whole process won't take more than ten minutes, unless you're overcome by all the options. As the site says "Give us your details, we'll make your pants. Yes, it's that easy!" Go to <www.bobsstores.com> and check it out.

- Customization and personal guidance make the service experience at General Nutrition Centers special. Associates are trained to guide buyers through the selection process and deliver goods in convenient specialized packages for easy use. For example, when purchasing a custom vitamin package at GNC, a service associate first helps the consumer choose one of nine basic lifestyle packages, each of which has a set of suggested vitamins. Using the lifestyle guide, buyers are encouraged to alter the selection or start from scratch until the package provides exactly what they desire. Once the associate verifies that no supplement exceeds recommended levels, the selected vitamins automatically flow out of bulk bins into a long plastic strip that is sealed and perforated into a set of 30 daily packages, each printed with the buyer's name and selection information. GNC records all of this information on the customer's profile, giving them the option to have the supplements automatically refilled once a month and delivered by UPS.[6]

- The John Akridge Companies, a real-estate business in Washington, D.C., sends potted plants to *former* tenants who relocate to other commercial office developments. "Exit interviews indicate that customers are pleased with our services but choose new facilities to meet their expansion needs," says Amy McBroom, director of communication. "Our gift is a token of our appreciation for their business and serves as a permanent reminder of our high level of service." And that attention to detail pays off. They've had several customers return to their properties because they didn't receive the same level of service elsewhere.[7]

- It is a point of pride at ScriptSave that a human being answers every 800 call and there is no limit on how long a conversation with a customer can last, says Charlie Horn, CEO of the Tucson-based company that manages prescription drug benefit programs. The primary job of ScriptSave's service staff is to explain prescription benefits to customers of health insurance companies. Most of those callers are elderly and require individual attention. When a woman had to interrupt a call to ScriptSave because her husband had suddenly taken a fall, the phone rep insisted on keeping track of how the couple was faring. Later, the woman e-mailed her thanks to the company for the extra service. "We don't do it for publicity. That's the way we want to be," says Horn.[8]

- When the CEO of Green Hills Farms, an independent grocer based in Syracuse, New York, noticed that a number of valuable customers hadn't been coming around, he instituted a lapsed-customer communications effort to find out why these customers had "defected." It turned out that the "defectors" started shopping elsewhere—they were "snow birds" who regularly spent several weeks of the winter in Florida. To meet the needs of this segment, Green Hills began shipping products hard to find in the Sunshine State right to the customers' Florida doorsteps.[9]

- The Apple Computer Store at the Mall of America in Bloomington, Minnesota understands that customers don't want to lug heavy delicate packages through the long hallways of the enormous complex, so the staff delivers all large purchases directly to a mall exit. Customers are given two-way radios that they use to signal the delivery person as they pull up for loading.

- For the team at Edwin Stipe Inc., customer service doesn't end when the service call is over—it's just beginning. Customer service reps, from the Easton, Pennsylvania plumbing company, call each and every customer a couple of days after the work has been done with a list of questions about the service provided. While chatting with customers they make notes about items of a personal nature. "When a customer opens up to one of our employees and tells them about a birthday, an operation they just had, an anniversary, we make note of it," says owner Henry Scherer. "We send out a get well, birthday, or congratulations card. Everything is handwritten, the note, the signature, and the address on the envelope—it's even got a regular postage stamp."

- It's the special touches at the Marriott Rivercenter in San Antonio that customers love. Take the business traveler awaiting the arrival of her husband and son for a weekend getaway after a long business conference. She mentioned to a hotel staffer that they were delayed by severe weather in Dallas. To her surprise, he had milk and cookies sent to her room when the two weary travelers finally arrived at 10 PM. "The simple, unexpected gesture of milk and cookies was a welcome surprise," she says.[10]

- Privacy is a big issue for patients at the Assisted Reproductive Technology Program, a Birmingham, Alabama fertility clinic. To address concerns, the company expanded its voice-mail system to create 10,000 individual voice-mail boxes for clients. Patients can dial an 800 number to retrieve messages at their convenience, day or night. A confidential PIN ensures security. Patients can use another 800 number to leave questions for a nurse, who supplies the answer with a phone call or by leaving a message in the patient's voice-mail box. "We need to be in constant communication with our customers about the timing of appointments and the results of routine procedures," says Margaret Cook, executive director.[11]

- Year end and year out, Kansas City–based H&R Block has been completing tax returns equaling approximately 10 percent of all returns filed in the United States. Many tax services charge their customers a percentage of total income or a commission based on the size of refund. Since 1955, regardless of size of income or amount of refund, H&R Block has based its fee on the number of forms that need to be completed. Small wonder that 75 percent of its customer base returns year after year.[12]

- Don Beyer Volvo in Falls Church, Virginia believes in forcing outstanding service to happen for customers. The company has a "goodwill" budget of $100,000 a year. The only requirement for the fund is that it *must* be spent—and it is—on everything from complimentary car washes to free or reduced repairs when a complaint is decided in a customer's favor.[13]

- Every quarter for the first four and a half years after a car is sold, Don Beyer Volvo customers can expect a call from their sales representative. They'll be queried about how the car is running, about any service problems, and they'll be invited to drop by some-day soon to see the new Volvos in stock. Their answers are re-viewed for valuable market intelligence and clues to developing problems that can be nipped in the bud.[14]

- An elderly patient at Aurora Health Care's St. Luke's Medical Center in Milwaukee, Wisconsin was being released to the care of her son for a week in bed following surgery. She was only to get up to go to the bathroom. On the day she was to be released, her son had to go out of town for two days. She insisted the hospital let her remain since she had no way to get out of bed without help. A creative nurse allowed her to take home a hospital step-down with rails if she would sign a hand written contract for its return. To the patient, she must have looked like an extraordinarily em-powered nurse with an "I trust you" attitude. In actuality, the hos-pital allows frontline employees to negotiate hand written contracts with patients under unique circumstances.

- SuperShuttle, the Los Angeles-based airport transportation ser-vice, makes magic by utilizing good systems and good people. SuperShuttle's well-scrubbed vans carry no more than three pas-sengers. By computer-matching customers with similar arrival or departure times and nearby points of origination or destination, the system reduces the time any individual traveler spends waiting or in transit. Computer terminals in each van tell the driver who to pick up and where, where each passenger is going, drop-off order, even what route to take to avoid traffic slowdowns or wasted time and motion.[15]

- The Four Seasons in Palm Beach, Florida ensures every guest feels like the most important person in the hotel. A couple on their honeymoon at the hotel were amazed by the level of personal ser-vice. The day of arrival the front desk staff had their flight infor-mation and was expecting them. Addressing them by name as they walked in the door, they were escorted immediately to their room where flowers and champagne were waiting. Throughout the week, everyone, from the cleaning staff to the bungalow rental agents, addressed them by name and anticipated their needs. Every time they left that room, whether it was for the day or the hour, the dedicated floor steward tidied it up and was gone before they returned. Prior to their arrival, the front desk made reserva-tions at different restaurants for every evening of their stay, and presented the couple with a calendar, restaurant write-ups and directions. "It was the best customer service I've ever experienced," says the happy bride.

- Riverside Methodist Hospital in Columbus, Ohio, is near one of American Honda's large automobile and motorcycle manufacturing plants. To better accommodate Japanese-speaking patients and their visitors, the hospital has provided a card for all employees that gives Japanese translations for common phrases like "When can I see my doctor" and "Please call my family." For more extensive conversations, Japanese interpreters are on call 24 hours a day. Preadmission and patient-education materials also have been translated and reprinted in Japanese, and special menus are available.[16]

- At Fields Infiniti in Glenview, Illinois, customer service doesn't stop when buyers drive their new cars off the lot. Every Saturday, for as long as they own the cars, buyers can come back to the dealership for a free carwash. While they wait, they can dine on bagels, lox, and coffee in the mornings, or a gourmet lunch buffet in the afternoons.

- SweetWater Tavern in Falls Church, Virginia, knows magic. No matter how small your group, you are served by at least six people. Everyone in the house is alerted to your drink preferences. Any server in the place can take care of you and never needs to ask you what your refill is.

## CHAPTER TWENTY-FIVE

Performance Pocket
Service Magic

"Come a little closer. Watch carefully. Nothing up this sleeve, nothing up the other sleeve. Watch closely. Watch closely. At no time will my fingers leave my hands."

Performance pocket magic is a very up close and personal art. It requires naturalness and composure, timing and salesmanship. And a high level of cool. The simplest trick, done with style and conviction, can make a terrific impression on a customer. And the most wonderful pocket full of surprises can fall flat—when presented in a bumbling, unsure, insecure, or self-conscious manner. As you look over this list of little wonders, remember: At the core of Performance Magic is the desire to please your customer and the confidence that you can.

- The guest checking into the Anaheim Marriott was stunned when the desk clerk looked up, smiled and said, "Good Evening, sir. Welcome back." How did she know? The bellman told her—sort of—when he tugged his right earlobe in sight of the clerk as he deposited the guest's luggage in the check-in queue. How did *he* know? He asked. In the driveway. As the guest stepped out of the cab. "Welcome to the Marriott," he said. "Have you stayed with us before?" He continued. The guest said "yes," and forgot about it.[1]

- A similar situation was observed at Walt Disney's Magic Kingdom Resort. Mary was walking through the turnstile at the beginning of her day. The friendly attendant greeted her with a hearty, "Hi, Mary! Welcome Back." Mary was startled! How in the world did this woman know her name? Disney gets 45 million visitors each year. Her spouse looked at her and said, "Uh, your earrings say 'Mary' on them." Mary giggled as she realized how easy it was, then she said, "Yeah, but how did she know I'd been here before?" Answer? More than 70 percent of Disney's guests are return visitors. The ticket attendant just made a calculated assumption—and it paid off in Mary's eyes.

- A patient moved out of state and received a bill from Aurora Health Care in Milwaukee, Wisconsin that exceeded the amount it should have been. A call to the billing department confirmed she had been overcharged. Remembering that the woman complained about having to call long distance to correct "their" mistake, the billing department included a complimentary phone card along with her refund check.

- World Famous Pike Place Fish attracts hordes of visitors every year to its corner of Seattle's open-air, waterfront marketplace. People come from all over the world to watch the company's fish-flinging and seafood-juggling crew perform. The act is more than a "shtick" for these multitalented fishmongers. Fifteen years ago, employees themselves decided on the "world famous" appellation as their vision for the company and it became a reality without one dime of advertising. They did it by being great with people—entertaining shoppers, bantering with kibitzers, and performing their fishy antics for passersby.

    Occasionally, they add an extra little pinch of pixie dust—like the time an elderly couple from New York wanted to haggle over the price of fish. When the two learned prices aren't negotiable, they got upset—until Sammy, one of the fishmongers, went into action. He jumped into the conversation with, "Hey are you from New York?" I grew up in New York, where do you live?"

    Owner John Yokoyama describes the rest of the performance: "By the time they left, Sammy knew their names and the kind of work they had done as well as stories about their children, their life in New York, their trip to Seattle, and how many people they were having over for dinner when they got back home. He also knew what kind of fish they were serving because he helped them pick it and even gave them recipes for cooking it. Their order was for more than $500. A week later, Sammy received a letter telling him all about the great party and thanking him for making a difference for them.[2]

- A friend raves about Shirley, the housekeeper she met during a recent vacation to Walt Disney World. "The first day, when we checked in, I saw the 'Your room was cleaned by Shirley. Have a great stay' note. I noticed the "i" in Shirley was dotted with a little Mickey. That was cute, but we were at Disney. The third day Shirley really amazed me. I'd left a note asking for more towels. When we returned to the room, there was a 'Do Not Disturb' sign on our bathroom door. Inside, Shirley had taken our morning paper and the eye glasses I'd left by the sink and arranged the extra towels in the form of a man sitting on the toilet reading the daily paper. I laughed so loud—I don't think I'll ever forget that."

- Sewell Village Cadillac in Dallas has a strict policy: "If the customer asks, the answer is always yes." That was a great answer for one of the dealership's favored customers, who lives half the year in Dallas and half in France. At the end of one of her annual trips to Paris, she called the company and said she planned to spend some time in New York before returning home but didn't want to rent a car there. She said all New York rental cars were dirty and smelled of cigarette smoke. She asked if the dealership would rent her a car in Dallas and have someone drive it to New York for her. They could, and they did.[3]

- Sue Cook was late for a flight and had to check out of the Ritz-Carlton Buckhead quickly. The desk clerk went to another counter, completed the transaction, and returned. Only then did Cook realize she was standing at the concierge desk rather than the front desk. When Cook apologized for the mistake, the desk clerk said, "Don't be silly, Ms. Cook, you can check out anywhere you like."

- Phase II, a chain of eight personal-training centers based in Raleigh, North Carolina, pumps up customers with one-on-one attention. The job of Phase II's trainers extends way beyond the gym. If a customer is on the way to an appointment and has a flat tire, a trainer is expected to rush to his aid. One 68-year-old woman (who doesn't drive) regularly gets a lift home from Phase II with a gym employee. At monthly staff meetings, CEO Wade Harris salutes his trainers for their acts of service. "Once new trainers see what the other trainers are doing, they look for opportunities so that they're not left out," he says.[4]

- At Iams Pet Food, a subsidiary of Procter and Gamble, they recount the story of Ms. C., a 30-year-old woman who wished to prove to her parents that she could successfully care for a cat—despite the challenge of being blind. She called Iams to inquire about their magazine *Your Cat.* Lori, a consumer relations specialist for Iams, could tell that Ms. C. was sincere in her wish to learn about cats, and promptly read her two articles she believed would be beneficial. Ms. C. was very pleased with Lori's help, but really wanted to be able to read the magazine independently. She was receiving an automatic reading device in a few weeks and thought this would help her. Lori offered to personally mail her each issue and suggested placing a raised star shaped sticker on the envelope to identify the magazine. After purchasing a supply of stickers, Lori placed an electronic reminder in her calendar to send the magazine each quarter. Nearly three years later, Ms. C. is still happily reading her magazine and learning about cat care.

- Home Depot, the do-it-yourself home improvement store, can turn anyone into a handyman, says David Yang, a husband and homeowner who lives in Deerfield, Illinois. Over the past five years, thanks to the staff at the Home Depot near his home, he has completely gutted and remodeled his hall bathroom and kitchen, re-wired electrical, sweated pipes, made new venting systems, hung drywall, and refinished cabinets. "My wife is astonished at the skills and the knowledge I possess," he says. "But the truth is, whenever I can't figure something out, I go to Home Depot. In any department I can find an expert staffer in that trade." Whatever his problem, someone at the store takes the time to explain to him how to get things done, shares the tricks of the trade, and makes recommendations on what he needs and how to use it. Furthermore, whatever he doesn't end up using, from unnecessary tools to custom-mixed paint, Home Depot takes back with no hassles (even if he doesn't have a receipt).

- At Lowe's Home Improvement store in Pasco, Washington, employees go out of their way to help customers find what they need—even if it is not in the store. Recently, a customer shopping for a miter saw found the only model left was in a box that appeared to have been rummaged through. A helpful associate offered to check the inventory and returned in a few minutes with a new saw in a box that had not been opened. Later, as they searched together for a suitable dust bag attachment, a backroom employee came over and asked if he could help. Realizing they were out of the size needed, the employee suggested a competing store that might have more bags in stock.

Already delighted with the service he'd received, the customer was further wowed when the associate rushed up to him at the check out counter carrying the right dust bag (that he'd found in back). "Now you can start using your saw right away," the associate said with a smile.[5]

- On a recent trip to Washington, D.C., a colleague stayed at the Morrison-Clark Inn, a moderately priced hotel with a European atmosphere. While checking in, he realized his credit card had expired a day earlier and was no longer usable. He called his bank for help but was told there was nothing that could be done before his return home. What could have been an awkward situation was remedied immediately by Milan, a hotel employee, who took initiative and guaranteed the room personally—an impressive display of empowerment and customer concern. But that was only the beginning of his memorable customer experience.

  Milan then discovered that the room that had been reserved was unavailable due to water damage and there were no other rooms available. Instead of sending him on his way, Milan took his bags and sent him to the hotel bar with several drink coupons and a promise to find a solution within the hour. In 30 minutes, Milan returned to the bar with a room key and an apology. The only accommodation available was a small but clean employee suite. The next day, Milan greeted our friend (returning from his business meetings) at the door with the news that a new room— one much nicer than the original reservation—was available. Milan had also taken the liberty of moving all of his things to the new room, had hung up his clothing, and placed his toiletries in the bathroom.

  Upon checkout a couple of days later, Milan was not on duty, but had communicated the entire story to the manager. The manager restated the hotel's apologies, gave the first night's room gratis, and offered to send the remaining bill to accommodate the problem of the expired card.

- Nordstrom is legendary for unusual service. Betsy Sanders, former VP and general manager, recalls a story from her days managing a moderate dress department. "I looked up one afternoon to find five Nordstrom family members walking through one of my departments—my quick review of the department revealed no obvious flaws. They seemed to be merely using my department as a throughway to the store manager's office, so I began to relax.

Then Bruce Nordstrom became visibly distressed. Sighting me, he peeled off from the group. 'Betsy, how did we fail those two women?' he asked, pointing to customers heading for the exit. I had not even noticed the pair, so had no answer. 'Well,' he continued, 'they were just saying they have never been so disappointed in their whole lives. Please go find out what happened.' Already chagrined, I raced after our departing guests, not sure how to stop their determined retreat. Failing to come up with anything couth, I blurted out that Mr. Nordstrom was concerned because he had overhead them expressing disappointment with the store. Their surprise at being accosted turned to pleasure at his thoughtfulness. They explained it was not the store that had disappointed them, but life. They coveted a dress they could not begin to afford. After encouraging them to show me the object that had upset their equilibrium, I invited them into my fitting rooms and kept them busy trying on beautiful things they could afford. This time when they headed for the exit, they each had two dresses in their possession and smiles on their faces."[6]

- Eddy Garza, doorman extraordinaire at the Westin Riverwalk in San Antonio, Texas, recently went on a hotel tour to learn from the best of the best hotel doormen. Garza is never bored with his job—he is ambassador, traffic cop, security guard, and mediator. "You're a maestro," Garza says. "I'm making beautiful music with my coworkers." Garza's top tips: (1) People don't want to feel like tourists—even if they are. (2) They all want to feel like a VIP— even if they aren't. (3) Everyone wants to be treated with respect.[7]

- At The Ritz-Carlton San Francisco, Door Captain Scot Smith reads nametags on bags as he lifts them from the trunk so he can greet guests by name. To get even more personal, he takes note of the fare on the cab's meter—if it's about $40, he figures they're coming from the airport and asks how the flight was.[8]

- Doorman George Vera has been wowing conventioneers and high rollers for 28 years at Las Vegas's Caesars Palace. He's learned to read people's body language along with what they have to say. "A guest might say, 'Yes, I've been here before,' when it's obvious that it's his first time." Vera responds by saying, "Well, some things might have changed since your last visit, let me share with you those changes." Vera also dispenses complimentary bottled water to cab drivers on days when it's warmer than 100 degrees. It's a clever nicety that gives him an edge in what can be a love-hate relationship between doormen and cabbies.[9]

- Airline companies are rarely known for their generosity of spirit, but American Airlines bent the rules to accommodate the needs of a grieving daughter. When she didn't have enough frequent flyer miles to fly home to Florida for her mother's funeral, an AA ticket agent honored her request and kicked in 300 miles to get her there.[10]

- Remember the ad campaign "Hey, Culligan man"? It may have originated as a catchy commercial gimmick, but Culligan man Michael Vet makes sure every one of his customers values the service he delivers. Unlike most water delivery service reps who dump the 40-pound five-gallon jugs on customers' doorsteps, Michael rings each bell, then carries all of the new bottles into the customers' homes. He stacks the jugs in their designated storage area, replaces the bottle on the machine—making sure to turn the Culligan logo face out—and carries away the empties. It takes Michael at least twice the amount of time to complete his service calls, but he feels that being friendly and helpful is all part of his job.

- A Northwest Airlines pilot recently took service matters into his own hands to appease a group of delayed customers. A mechanical problem necessitated the travelers get off one plane, trot across the terminal, and get onto another plane. The pilot knew he was facing angry and frustrated passengers. The new plane was only partially stocked as they settled in for another 30 minutes to finish loading the food and supplies. The pilot made an executive decision: He stopped the dinner victuals from being boarded and readied the plane for take off. Then, as they were taxiing down the runway, he told the passengers about his decision, saying he figured they'd rather get to their destination on time than have airplane food. To make it up to them, he gave every passenger three free drink coupons to use on the plane or anywhere in the Orlando airport. The flight arrived within 20 minutes of schedule, and no one complained about the lack of dinner.

- When eight-year-old Ruby Ford went to get her first pair of glasses, the associate at LensCrafters understood the significance of the occasion for the nervous little girl. She immediately engaged Ruby, taking her by the hand over to the childrens glasses section, all the while asking her questions about her favorite colors and what kinds of glasses she liked. As she helped Ruby try on different frames, the sales rep told her about getting her own first pair of glasses when she was eight, and how the frames now were much lighter and cuter. "All your friends will be envious of you," the associate confided, making her giggle. An hour later, Ruby proudly walked out of the store with the perfect pair of purple frames—along with a special purple case that the rep had remembered seeing on a storage shelf.

- When a boy in Menlo Park, California did a cannonball on a trampoline and split his tongue open, his parents raced him to the nearest hospital—only to be told that the hospital needed permission from the boy's pediatrician for admission. The boy's frantic mother called Urgent Care at the Palo Alto Medical Clinic. They also said they wouldn't take the boy without a pediatrician's referral. But when she explained that she had a little boy bleeding in a parking lot and couldn't wait that long, the gentleman on the phone said to bring him right in. When they arrived, the boy was seen immediately and got four stitches in his tongue. They were in and out in a half hour. "The guy on the phone had clearly bent the rules," says the mother, "and we were very grateful."

- A Massachusetts woman, a frequent traveler to Austin, Texas, rents a Chevrolet Malibu (the model she prefers) from her local Enterprise Rent-A-Car. Employee Susan Davis always picks her up in a Malibu and takes her to the branch to fill out the waiting paperwork.

  On a recent trip, the woman was due to arrive after 6 PM—when the Enterprise office was closed. Susan told her, "No problem," offered her personal cell phone number, and told the customer to call when she arrived. Susan would drive back to the branch to deliver the car—no matter the time. The customer managed to catch an earlier flight and arrived at the branch before closing, but after Susan had left. Another employee quickly provided her with her waiting Malibu. The next day—the Fourth of July—Susan called the customer at home to check that she had received her car.

  "I was astounded that someone would take time out of their holiday day off to call to check up on a customer," she wrote in note to the company.

- Columbus, Ohio's Riverside Methodist Hospital has added a volunteer to the front-desk staff to personally escort patients and visitors who need assistance or aren't sure they can find the right department or room. Patients from outside Columbus are given the name and phone number of a member of the patient-relations staff who will be available during their treatment to provide information and assistance.[11]

CHAPTER TWENTY-SIX

Magical Recovery

Fixing bent and broken customers, and returning them to a state of grace with the organization, is a special art form not many accomplish on a regular basis. The few who have mastered it are doted on by their customers:

- Stanley Marcus of Neiman Marcus department stores identifies the importance of keeping customers as the most important retailing lesson he ever learned. A woman once returned a damaged lace gown she had obviously mistreated. Stanley's father instructed his son to give the woman a full refund and to "do it with a smile." Over the years that woman spent $500,000 at Neiman Marcus.[1]

- Even if product quality is sub par, excellent customer service can make the experience memorable. Last spring, Bill and Nancy decided to remodel their bathroom adding a very expensive antique-style tub and shower hardware that they purchased from Frank's Plumbing. When the installation was complete, either the contractor's work was less than perfect, or the fixture itself was faulty, but the fancy new bathroom set didn't work properly. They called Frank's Plumbing to return the fixtures to the manufacturer for repair or replacement. "The associate didn't even ask to see a receipt," says the homeowner. "He advised us over the phone of all of our options, took back the fixture, gave us a "loaner" faucet, and promptly sent the fixture back to the manufacturer—all at no extra charge and with no hassle." The error added a month to their remodeling process, but the couple has only great things to say about Frank's Plumbing.

- Oakley Sunglasses, rated by *Forbes* among the top luxury brands in the world, are high-end, high-quality expensive sportswear. Every pair comes with a one-year warranty—which is why a long-time client didn't expect the company to do much for his broken five-year-old glasses. He e-mailed the service department letting them know his frames had cracked and asking if there was anything they could do. They said no, but he mailed the glasses back to the company anyway, so they could study the break for future design changes, he says. He did not expect a response, but the company was so appreciative that ten days later it sent him a brand-new pair of glasses, free of charge.

- When six-year-old Gretchen Olesen failed to received her Jetson's cup—the free prize in her kids' meal, Gretchen's mom decided to call Wendy's to see if they would send it to her. Wendy's said they would put the cup in the mail; ten days later it still hadn't arrived. Because Gretchen was so disappointed that she didn't receive her cup, Mrs. Olesen wrote a letter to Wendy's then-CEO, Robert Barney, explaining the incident. About ten days later, Wendy's customer service department delivered not just one Jetson's cup—but a set of them—with a letter of apology and coupons for two free meals. That same evening, Frank Kline, Wendy's local director of area operations stopped by the Olesen's house to personally apologize and deliver two more Jetson's cups. But it was the final letter, personally addressed to Gretchen, that really did the trick. George Jetson himself and his dog Astro wrote to reassure her that Wendy's wasn't trying to cheat her, and that they were sorry she hadn't gotten her cup right away. Astro even included his pawprint for a signature.[2]

- On a winter vacation in Tucson, Arizona, a family purchased two pairs of shorts for their son at a Wal-Mart. After the trip, the shorts were not worn again until late May. In early June, both pairs had zipper problems. They went with the original receipt to their local Pennsylvania Wal-Mart to see if they would replace the shorts, since their son had worn them only four or five times. Even though they had missed the 90-day return limit, the customer service rep gave them a full store credit for the amount of the shorts. They responded by buying several more pairs, along with $80-worth of other items. Sam Walton would be proud![3]

- Mattel Toy's service staff understands that even the sturdiest toys can break in the hands of their young customers, and they respond accordingly. When a six-year-old's little brother broke off a piece of his prized Matchbox Jetz Launcher, mom called the company to try and order a replacement part. She shared her story with the "pleasant, knowledgeable, and articulate customer service representative," and together they tried to figure out what the broken piece was called. When they determined that the "runaway" piece was not available by itself, the service rep sent an entire new Jetz Launcher, free of charge, within 7–10 days. "I expected to be charged between $5–$10 for the part plus shipping and, instead, I got a replacement toy free! What great customer service," mom says.[4]

- Li'l Tikes Toys, a division of Ohio Art, offers such phenomenal service that one grandmother still raves about her experiences with the company 22 years ago. As a young mother in the '70s, she bought her three-year-old son a Li'l Tikes ride-on car—which he played with for hours. Three weeks after he got it, he stood on it to reach for something and the plastic body cracked. She called their customer service department, told the representative what had happened, and asked if she could buy a new body part—to save herself the cost of replacing the whole toy. When the rep learned that the boy was three, she said, "Those cars were built to withstand anything a three-year-old could dish out," and she sent a new body at no charge. When the woman argued that she wasn't trying to get something for free, the rep insisted that Li'l Tikes' reputation was one of high quality and good service, and she wanted to make sure it stayed that way.[5]

- On a sizzling 100-degree afternoon in Charleston, South Carolina, the car carrying a Maryland couple and their nine-year-old daughter broke down. By the time the car was towed to a repair shop, it was after 6 PM, the family was stranded far from their Isle of Palms hotel and, they were told, the nearby Enterprise Rent-A-Car office was closed.

  Desperate for a vehicle, the family headed for the Enterprise branch anyway. The door was locked and employees inside were obviously finishing up the day's paperwork. Josh, one of the employees, came to the door, heard their dilemma, and immediately brought them inside. Ten minutes later—just as rain began falling—they had the keys to a rental.

The next day, their car's dead battery was replaced and they were back at Enterprise—a half hour after the weekend closing time of noon. Once again, Josh unlocked the door, closed out their car rental, then loaded their luggage into their car for their trip home.

- Biaggi's restaurant in Madison, Wisconsin turned a major service blunder into a memorable, positive experience. After receiving sub-par treatment by the new restaurant's staff on what was meant to be a special occasion, a customer e-mailed the manager to complain. Shortly after, she received this response:

> Dear Marilyn,
>
> Thank you for the honest and critical feedback on your experience at our restaurant on Oct. 27th. As a newer business to the community, we can only continue to grow and improve if we receive both praise and criticism from our valued guests. We strive to provide only the most pleasurable of dining experiences, however, in this case, we have most certainly failed to deliver on our commitment to you and your party. For that, you have my most sincere of apologies.
>
> The treatment of your guests from my host staff and bar staff is most certainly not the standard we have set. The situation was mishandled by us, and as a result your party shouldered the inconvenience. I have taken the last two days to share your experience with my staff and fellow managers to ensure we do not have this matter arise in the future. Of course, this does nothing to fix the problems you encountered. To that end, I would like to extend an invitation to you and your party to dine with us again. I would also like to send you some complimentary certificates for you and your guests to use if you decide to come in again. All I would need is an address to send them to. If you would care for my help in setting up your next party or if there is anything else that I can do for you, please do not hesitate to contact me. I remain . . . at your service.
>
> Steve Hable
> Managing Partner
> Biaggi's Madison

- Loyalty to Ben & Jerry's is "built one euphoric transaction at a time," says Gary Henderson, special consumer services manager. Henderson himself was recently reviewing closed-out customer letters and came across one from a woman who had written about her dissatisfaction with "icy and crunchy" ice cream. The woman had been sent an apology letter and a free coupon, but to Henderson that response seemed "lame" and he thought the company could do better. Noticing the woman lived in a town where he regularly vacationed, Henderson grabbed 18 pints of ice cream and personally delivered them to her door.

  "I held up our response letter and told her I didn't think she'd tasted the product like it was supposed to be sold," he says. "I opened up the cooler, her eyes bugged out, and she asked, 'Are you guys always this aggressive with customer service?' Every year when I go back now, I run into her. She tells me that she shares this story with everyone and nobody gets her ice cream business but Ben & Jerry's."[6]

- Customers at Midnightpass.com, a specialty online retailer, are pleasantly surprised to receive personal calls and e-mails from the company's CEO Brad White, checking to see if they are happy with their purchases. His commitment has won the company Yahoo's Top Service award and floods of "happy letters" glowing about customer service experiences. One example comes from a woman who purchased a Kittywalk Pet System (an enclosed outdoor cat walk). When the door of her Kittywalk split apart two months after purchase, she called MidnightPass. White not only agreed to replace the door, but suggested sending her a recently returned Kittywalk—in perfect condition—that could be added to her existing system giving her cats an additional ten feet of walkway and an extra door, at no cost.

- Used to having low expectations of airline personnel, a delayed traveler was delighted with the service he received from America West and United Airlines ticket agents, *who worked together to help him get home*. While in Indianapolis, road construction forced him to miss his flight. The America West agent went out of his way not only to find another carrier to get him home, but to be sure that it would accept the America West ticket, and that he would not be charged any additional fees. To do this, he had to go to the United Airlines service counter and talk with one of their agents. Together, they brought the boarding pass for United over to the customer, and he was ready to board United's next flight to Phoenix in 20 minutes. "Their exceptional customer service turned a really bad situation into a good one," he says.[7]

- Some of the most magical recovery experiences come from employees who handle service screw ups with grace and concern. Case in point: the manager of the Wildfire Grill restaurant, in Oak Brook, Illinois. A family was given a 45-minute wait-estimate for a table, but in fact was not seated for two hours. Although they had easily passed the time having drinks at the bar and didn't complain about the delay, the manager came to their table and explained that the entire meal would be on the house because they had seriously underestimated the wait. He apologized and encouraged them to have a great meal. What was most surprising was that they had not complained to anyone about the wait. The waiter urged them to order whatever they wanted and to have a great time without considering cost, going so far as to suggest a mid- to high-priced bottle of wine.

- No purchase is more memorable—or nerve wracking—than that of an engagement ring. S.A. Peck Jewelers, a family-run jewelry shop in Chicago, takes excellent care of all of its clients, regardless of the size of their purchase. Two years ago, a friend bought his fiancé a beautiful but modest ring over the phone from the company's catalog. This past spring, three tiny diamonds fell out of the band and were lost. His wife called the company and spoke to the same woman who sold her husband the ring.

  "She knew the ring from my description," his wife says. The associate she spoke to instructed her to package and send the ring, insured, back to the store. As soon as she received the ring, the associate called to let her know it was safe, and called again shortly after with an estimate for the stone replacement and repair. When it was returned to the woman—two weeks after her initial phone call—the total cost, including shipping, was under $25. The ring was sent back to her in a small enamel box, with a note that read "Please accept this little gift."

- Michael Graze had been looking forward to his birthday party. He and his mom had planned it in great detail, inviting many of his school pals. So when the six-year-old's Power Rangers birthday cake from the local H-E-B grocery store arrived with Michael spelled "M-I-C-H-E-L-E," he was distraught. The great centerpiece of the party had turned to an object of derision through a spelling error! He swore he could never show his face in school again. When H-E-Ber Julie McCoy heard of Michael's plight from his mother, she didn't hesitate. Apologies and refunds, she knew, would be small solace for a little boy's crushed spirit. So she arranged for a new cake and a new party—at a local children's amusement park, with Michael as host and H-E-B as benefactor.[8]

The Service Magic
Impact Audit™

Customers experience and interact with your organization in countless ways. In-person visits to your stores or e-commerce sites, your advertising, observing others using your products, on the streets or in friends' homes, word of mouth, even community-event sponsorship, temper the way customers evaluate your company—and your service quality.

Identifying and understanding all these touch points is critical to making the most of the Service Magic technology. Each of these evaluative points of contact or "moments of truth"—whether they be functions of Place, Process, or Performance—offers opportunities to add a little magic that can make a big impact on customer perception and loyalty.

We've developed an opportunity assessment system called the *Service Magic Impact Audit* to help you blueprint these customer encounters with your organization. The audit identifies areas where an infusion of Service Magic can have a high return in terms of enhanced customer satisfaction and buyer commitment to the organization.

THE SERVICE MAGIC IMPACT AUDIT

The Service Magic Impact Audit draws a comprehensive map of the customer's experience with the organization, helping you discover what is done well and shining a light on any Place, Process, or Performance issues that need fixing. The audit identifies and captures the most important events in a customer's service experience, and divides those events into their component parts.

The audit has three phases: experience chunking, Cycle of Service Mapping™, and Moment of Truth Impact Assessment™.

Phase 1: Experience Chunking

Experience chunking takes a particular customer need and divides the total experience of meeting that need into a manageable "chunk." The customer need for a hotel, for example, is a group of complex experiences—or chunks—such as reservations, check-in, baggage transport, room quality, restaurants, and the like. The chunks for an airline customer could be reservations, ticket counter, flight, baggage claim, and more.

Experience chunking examines customer need and determines if the component experiences the customer goes through to meet that need are overly cumbersome, grating, or tedious.

If the customer's need is simple—getting a car washed, for example—there may be no need for experience chunking. The experience is, basically, one "chunk." But if the customer need is more complex and involves multiple sites or several departments and employee interactions, chunking is essential to the audit process. Assume, for example, that a customer has a service need from a local phone company. The experience chunks in this case are signing up for the service, getting a phone installed, problem-free use of the phone, bill paying, and getting the phone repaired. For illustrative purposes, we've selected "getting the phone repaired" as the experience chunk to be studied.

Now, we are ready to move to the next Service Magic Audit step: developing and analyzing a full cycle of service.

Phase 2: Cycle of Service

A *cycle of service* identifies the sequence of experiences a customer has with your organization from the time the customer identifies a need until that need has (or has not) been met. In the customer's mind, this cycle is a single event (even though there may well be "sub-events" and smaller encounters along the way). Think of it as the customer's diary of his or her journey through your organization.

In any cycle of service, there are various forms of customer contact. Sometimes the contact is repetitive and institutional, but it may also be episodic. Sometimes the contact is intense, other times more indirect and casual.

The example below is taken from work we did with a major phone company anxious to improve residential telephone repair. This example focuses on the "phone repair" cycle of service.

Note that the process flow in the sample cycle of service doesn't reflect the telephone company's perspective or detail its internal operations. A cycle of service is about what the *customer* experiences, and examines all Place, Process, or Performance issues from that perspective.

For that reason, mapping a service cycle must include feedback from customers as well as internal employees. Relying only on your staff to craft the cycle will give short shrift to the kind of details or process steps only customers see and experience. The data for this analysis, and the Moment of Truth Impact Assessment that follows, should come from a variety of sources: customer interviews, surveys and observations, employee experiences with customers, knowledge of the service process, and customer complaint data.

The "moment of truth" phrase originated with bullfighting. When a matador faces the bull head-on, it's a moment of truth—a crucial life or death encounter. For customers, a "moment of truth" occurs any time they come into contact with your organization—whether through your advertising, call centers, Web site, or in a physical store—and have an opportunity to evaluate that experience. Because each moment of truth in a service cycle is a discrete encounter, the customer has a specific set of expectations for that encounter. The first moment of truth is a discovery by the customer that his phone isn't working, followed by, "I figured out how to call the phone company." In all, there are 14 such moments in this phone repair cycle—from the customer's point of view.

Let's say you've decided a particular moment of truth in your service cycle is ripe for Service Magic. Perhaps you decide that "I contact the repair answering center" (box 3 in the sample) is a good place to enchant the customer. To better understand the customer's *standard* expectations (actions that would leave them satisfied), the *experience detractors* (actions detracting from a satisfactory experience), and *experience enhancers* (actions exceeding expectations) of that process, you would conduct a Moment of Truth Impact Assessment.

Phase 3: Moment of Truth Impact Assessment™

The Moment of Truth Impact Assessment puts a microscope to *key* moments of truth (not all moments are created equal, as you'll see shortly) to learn what aspects of that experience satisfy the customer, which enhance the experience, and which create negatives in their minds. The sample analysis shows "I contact the repair answering center" broken out into those three categories.

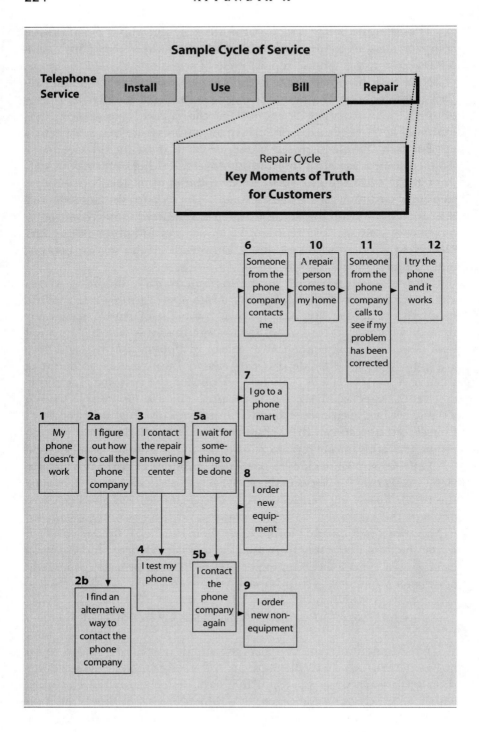

Sample Cycle of Service

Telephone Service

| Install | Use | Bill | Repair |

Repair Cycle
Key Moments of Truth for Customers

6 Someone from the phone company contacts me

10 A repair person comes to my home

11 Someone from the phone company calls to see if my problem has been corrected

12 I try the phone and it works

7 I go to a phone mart

1 My phone doesn't work

2a I figure out how to call the phone company

3 I contact the repair answering center

5a I wait for something to be done

8 I order new equipment

2b I find an alternative way to contact the phone company

4 I test my phone

5b I contact the phone company again

9 I order new non-equipment

Sample
Moment of Truth Impact Assessment™

I contact the repair answering center.

Experience Detractors	Standard Expectations	Experience Enhancers
▪ I had to call an 800 number.	▪ I will only have to call one number.	▪ The operator had a melodious, well-modulated voice.
▪ I can't understand the operator's words.	▪ I will call a local number.	▪ The operator communicated a sense of urgency.
▪ I had to call more than once.	▪ I will be treated fairly.	▪ The operator really understood my problem/situation, had heard it before, and knew just what to do.
▪ I had to listen to a recording that made me feel unwelcome.	▪ The operator will speak clearly.	
▪ While I am on hold, I get silence, which makes me wonder if I am disconnected.	▪ The phone will not be busy.	
	▪ The operator will answer within a reasonable time frame.	▪ The operator apologized sincerely.
▪ The operator sounded like he/she was following a form/ stock or routine questions.	▪ The operator will be a real person.	▪ The operator asked me about medical emergencies or other special situations that may warrant sooner service.
▪ I thought the operator rushed me.	▪ The operator will speak pleasantly.	
▪ I got Mirandized: "Are you sure that there may be a …"	▪ The operator will listen to my problems in a manner that lets me know he/she understands my problems.	▪ The operator made some comment that let me know that he/she was aware of my area (i.e., sounded like a neighbor).
▪ The operator told me to go to the Phone Mart to have my phone tested.	▪ The operator will seem competent, helpful and understanding.	▪ The operator offered to have work done at my convenience.
▪ I was not able to walk into an office and talk to someone personally.	▪ The operator will promise me a solution within a reasonable deadline.	

We've focused on the "phone repair" moment of truth based on its perceived importance to customers and its measured impact on customer retention. Most hotels can tell you that the front desk occupies a similar importance—no matter how good room service, housekeeping, bellman, or concierge, check-in and wake-up call stand apart as memory makers. Some moments of truth are simply more important than others to customers.

Notice that the component descriptions in each category are written in a way to make them specific and actionable rather than generic and forgettable. For instance, under the "Experience Detractors" column is the bulleted point, "I got Mirandized." That is shorthand for this description given by a customer: "I felt like I was being given a Miranda warning when they were telling me what my payment obligations would be if the problem I was reporting was in my phone and not in their wiring."

That specific comment was chosen to represent a class of service performance—being robotic and officious in informing the customer of a potential fiduciary obligation.

Note also that these bulleted points are more behavioral than descriptive, and written strictly from the customer's point of view, not from the organization's perspective.

SELECTING HIGH-IMPACT MOMENTS OF TRUTH

Addressing the following questions can help you choose moments of truth (MOT) where an injection of Service Magic can have a big impact on customer perception and loyalty, and where such a focus might have lesser pay off:

- Is this a MOT where customers have low expectations based on prior reported experience, and where even incremental improvement might have a big effect on customer satisfaction?

- Is this a MOT where "enchantment," rather than mere competence or rote efficiency, has considerable value to the customer?

- Is this a MOT where, if the customer was enchanted by the experience, it would positively impact future dealings with the customer?

- Is this a MOT with any regulatory implications (like safety) that could inhibit or restrain service innovation?

- Is this a MOT where, if Service Magic happened as planned, it might bring joy or increased fulfillment to your associates?

- Is this a MOT where Service Magic would be perceived by customers as an appropriate fit with the culture and vision of your organization, and as authentic rather than contrived?

- Will the Service Magic produce positive long-term effects, such as enhanced customer retention or word of mouth? What about positive short-term impact?

- Will delivering magic at this juncture in the service cycle enhance your brand or decrease the attractiveness of competitive brands?

BENEFITS BEYOND SERVICE MAGIC

Beyond determining where Service Magic might have the biggest positive impact in your operations, the Service Magic Impact Audit provides several additional benefits:

- Decisions about staff procurement, allocation, and development become clearer when you can see, right before you, the kinds and number of people needed to operate and manage your service system.

- Considerations about where automation or technology might save money, and where personalized human contact is a must, can be pinpointed using the blueprint as a discussion focus.

- Competitive service processes can be studied and analyzed by diagramming them and comparing blueprints.

- Used as the focus for productivity improvement discussions, such service blueprints can make employee participation much easier to develop. Employee involvement is a critical issue in decentralizing complex service decisions and in "engineering out" the design problems that characterize new service introductions.

Recommended Resources

MAGIC BOOKS

Gold, Glen David. *Carter Beats the Devil.* New York: Hyperion, 2001.

Jay, Ricky. *Jay's Journal of Anomalies.* New York: Farrar Straus Giroux, 2001.

Nelms, Henning. *Magic and Showmanship: A Handbook for Conjurers.* New York: Dover Publications, 1969.

Pogue, David. *Magic for Dummies.* Chicago: Hungry Minds, 1998.

Randi, James. *Conjuring.* New York: St. Martin's Press, 1992.

Rose, Ed. *Presenting and Training with Magic: 53 Simple Magic Tricks You Can Use to Energize Any Audience.* New York: McGraw-Hill, 1998.

Ross, Barry. *Now You See It, Now Your Don't! Lessons in Sleight of Hand.* New York: Vintage Books, 1976.

Schiffman, Nathaniel. *Abracadabra! Secret Methods Magicians & Others Use to Deceive Their Audience.* New York: Prometheus Books, 1997.

Tyler, Diamond Jim. *Pockets Full of Miracles: Secrets from the Repertoire of a Professional Close-up Magician.* Irving, TX: Diamond Jim Productions, 2000.

MAGIC PERIODICALS

GENII. The International Conjurors Magazine. P.O. Box 36068, Los Angeles, CA 90036.

Magic Magazine. Stan Allen and Associates, 7380 South Eastern Avenue, Suite 124-179, Las Vegas, NV 89123.

M-U-M. The Society of American Magicians Monthly Magazine. P.O. Box 338, 26855 Sanders Meadow Road, Idyllwild, CA 92549.

MAGIC SOCIETIES

The Society of American Magicians
Box 510260
St. Louis, MO 63151
314-846-5659

International Brotherhood of Magicians
1115 South Towne Square
Suite C
St. Louis, MO 63123
314-845-9200

International Magicians Society
581 Ellison Avenue
Westbury, NY 11590
516-333-2377

MAGIC WEB SITES

www.allmagic.com
www.magician.org—International Brotherhood of Magicians
www.magiccastle.com—The Magic Castle—Home of the Academy of Magical Arts
www.hanklee.com—Hank Lee's Magic Factory
www.geniimagazine.com—Web site of GENII magazine
www.service-magic.com—Performance Research Associates, Inc.

SERVICE RESOURCES

Albrecht, Karl and Ron Zemke. *Service America in the New Economy.* Chicago: McGraw-Hill, 2001.

Anderson, Kristin and Ron Zemke. *Knock Your Socks Off Answers.* New York: AMACOM Books, 1995.

Bell, Chip R. *Customers as Partners: Building Relationships That Last.* San Francisco, CA: Berrett Koehler Publishers, 1994.

Bell, Chip R. *Customer Love: Attracting and Keeping Customers for Life.* Provo, Utah: Executive Excellence Publishing, 2000.

Bell, Chip R. *Managers as Mentors: Building Partnerships for Learning.* San Francisco, CA: Berrett-Koehler Publishers, 1996.

Bell, Chip R. and Heather Shea. *Dance Lessons: Six Steps to Great Partnership in Business & Life.* San Francisco, CA: Berrett Koehler Publishers, 1998.

Bell, Chip R. and Ron Zemke. *Managing Knock Your Socks Off Service.* New York: AMACOM Books, 1992.

Berry, Leonard L. *Discovering the Soul of Service: The Nine Drivers of Sustainable Business Success.* New York: The Free Press, 1999.

Connellan, Thomas K. *Bringing Out the Best in Others; 3 Keys for Business Leaders, Educators, Coaches, and Parents.* Austin, TX: Bard Press, 2003.

Connellan, Thomas, K. *Inside the Magic Kingdom: Seven Keys to Disney's Success.* Austin, TX: Bard Press, 1996.

Connellan, Thomas K. and Ron Zemke. *Sustaining Knock Your Socks Off Service.* New York: AMACOM Books, 1993.

Dimitrius, Jo-Ellan, and Mark Mazzarella. *Reading People: How to Understand People and Predict Their Behavior, Anytime, Anyplace.* New York: Ballantine Books, 1999.

Disney Institute. *Be Our Guest: Perfecting the Art of Customer Service.* New York: Disney Enterprises, 2001.

Nierenberg, Gerald. *How to Read a Person Like a Book.* New York: Pocket Books, 1982.

Rafferty, Kevin and Bruce Gordon. *Walt Disney Imagineering: A Behind the Dreams Look at Making the Magic Real.* New York: Disney Editions, 1996.

Zemke, Ron. *Delivering Knock Your Socks Off Service.* 3rd ed. New York: AMACOM Books, 2003.

Zemke, Ron. *The Service Edge: 101 Companies That Profit from Customer Care.* New York: New American Library, 1989.

Zemke, Ron, and Kristin Anderson. *Tales of Knock Your Socks Off Service.* New York: AMACOM Books, 1998.

Zemke, Ron, and Kristin Anderson. *Coaching Knock Your Socks Off Service.* New York: AMACOM Books, 1996.

Zemke, Ron, and Chip Bell. *Knock Your Socks Off Service Recovery.* New York: AMACOM Books, 2000.

Zemke, Ron, and Tom Connellan. *E-Service: 24 Ways to Keep Your Customers— When the Competition Is Just a Click Away.* New York: AMACOM Books, 2001.

CHAPTER 1. The Art and Craft of the Stage Magician

1. Leonard L. Berry, Valarie Zeithaml, and A. Parasuraman, "Five Imperatives for Improving Service Quality," *Sloan Management Review* (Summer 1990): 29–38.

2. "Delivering Knock Your Socks Off Service: The Seminar," available through Performance Research Associates, American Management Association, and National Seminars.

3. Timothy Keiningham and Terry Vavra, *The Customer Delight Principle* (New York: McGraw-Hill, 2001).

4. Robert A. Peterson, "Measuring Customer Satisfaction: Fact and Artifact," a working paper.

5. Christopher Hart, "Growing the Trust Relationship," *Marketing Management Magazine* (Spring 1999).

6. Chip R. Bell, *Customer Love: Attracting and Keeping Customers for Life* (Provo, Utah: Executive Excellence Publishing, 2000).

CHAPTER 2. The Service Magic Method

1. Karl Albrecht and Ron Zemke, *Service America in the New Economy* (Chicago: McGraw-Hill, 2002), 33–47.

2. Ron Zemke, *The Service Edge* (New York: New American Library, 1990), 35–36.

3. Robert A. Stebbins, *Career, Culture, and Social Psychology in a Variety Art: The Magician* (Malabar, Fla.: Krieger, 1993), 51–52.

CHAPTER 3. Place, Process, Performance

1. Ron Zemke, "Give Customers Royal Treatment to Encourage Retention, Referrals," *The Business Journal* (16 August 2002).

2. Ron Zemke and Tom Connellan, *E-Service: 24 Ways to Keep Your Customer When the Competition Is Just a Click Away* (New York: AMACOM, 2000).

3. Ibid.

4. Edward Shenton, "The Happy Storekeeper of the Green Mountains," *Saturday Evening Post* (15 March 1952).

5. Roger Dow and Sue Cook, *Turned On: Eight Vital Insights to Engaging Your People, Customers, and Profits* (New York: HarperBusiness, 1996), 16.b.

6. Ron Zemke and Kristin Anderson, *Tales of Knock Your Socks Off Service* (New York: AMACOM, 1997), 35.

7. Leonard L. Berry, *Discovering the Soul of Service: The Nine Drivers of Sustainable Business Success* (New York: The Free Press, 1999), 27.

8. Leonard L. Berry, *Discovering the Soul of Service*, 124.

9. Steve Rushin, "A lark in the park," *Sports Illustrated* (10 June 2002).

10. Leonard L. Berry, *Discovering the Soul of Service*, 123.

CHAPTER 5. Man-Made Place Magic

1. Martin Sklar, *Walt Disney Imagineering* (New York: Hyperion, 1996).

2. Ibid.

3. Disney Institute, *Be Our Guest: Practicing the Art of Customer Service* (New York: Hyperion, 2001). Reprinted by permission of Hyperion Books for Children.

4. Sharon Hori, "Zany Servers at Ed Devebic's Dish Out Attitude to Diners," *UCLA Daily Bruins* (1 December 1999).

CHAPTER 6. Applying Little Magics in Big Places

1. Author interview with Carl Sewell.

2. Kendall Anderson, "Alzheimer's Patients Find Homes in Past," *Dallas Morning News*, 15 April 2002.

3. Frequently, customer place feedback will be about shortcomings, things that disappoint them—too hot, too cold, too bright, too dark, too smelly, too small, too big, too noisy. Those basic place attributes, particularly the negative ones, detract from the experience, but when remedied will not likely lead to magic—or discernible positive difference. They do, however, need to be dealt with so their distraction value doesn't impinge on the positive place impression you want the customer to take away. A department store with cramped, poorly lit dressing rooms with inadequate hooks and handles will annoy customers to the point of abandonment. Simply fixing the dressing room problems will not, however, lead to customers racing back. On the other hand, making the dressing rooms the height of posh and pampering could become a point of Place Magic—if the products you offer are at least price and style competitive. Only your customers and their behavior can tell you for certain.

CHAPTER 7. Third Place Magic

1. Raymond Oldenburg, *The Great Good Place* (New York: Marlowe and Company, 1999).

CHAPTER 8. Process Magic

1. John Goodman and Cindy Grimm, "Making Delight a Part of Your Marketing Strategy," TARP, April 2002.

2. Chip R. Bell and Ron Zemke, *Managing Knock Your Socks Off Service* (New York: AMACOM, 1992), 72.

3. Andrew Quinn, "Service with a smile—dangerous for workers?" Reuters, 2 September 1998.

4. Fred Weirsema, *Customer Service: Extraordinary Results at Southwest Airlines, Charles Schwab, Lands' End, American Express, Staples, and USAA.* (New York: Harper Business, 1998), 202.

5. Ron Zemke and Dick Schaaf, *The Service Edge* (New York: New American Library 1990).

6. Susan Greco, "Fanatics!", *Inc.* magazine, April 2001.

CHAPTER 9. Magical Scripts

1. Cathy A. Enz and Judy A. Siguaw, "Best Practices in Service Quality," *Cornell Hotel and Restaurant Administration Quarterly* (October 2000).

2. Chip R. Bell and Ron Zemke, *Managing Knock Your Socks Off Service* (New York: AMACOM, 1992), 72.

3. Brenda Paik Sunoo, "How Fun Flies at Southwest Airlines," *Personnel Journal* (June 1995).

4. Ron Zemke and Chip R. Bell, *Service Wisdom: Creating and Maintaining the Customer Service Edge* (Minneapolis: Lakewood Books, 1989), 87.

5. Ron Zemke and Chip R. Bell, *Knock Your Socks Off Service Recovery* (New York: AMACOM, 2000), 40.

6. Kristin Anderson and Ron Zemke, *Knock Your Socks Off Answers: Solving Customer Nightmares & Soothing Nightmare Customers* (New York: AMACOM, 1995), 17–18.

7. Ibid., 3.

8. Ibid., 33–34.

CHAPTER 10. The Six Secrets of Magical Service Recovery

1. "Increasing Customer Satisfaction: Through Effective Corporate Complaint Handling," a study conducted by TARP, Arlington, Virginia, for the United States Office of Consumer Affairs Professionals with Chevrolet Motor Division General Motors Corporation, 1987.

2. Ron Zemke and Chip R. Bell, *Knock Your Socks Off Service Recovery* (New York: AMACOM, 2000).

3. Ron Zemke and Kristin Anderson, *Tales of Knock Your Socks Off Service* (New York: AMACOM, 1997), 62.

4. Kathleen Seiders and Leonard L. Berry, "Service fairness: What it is and why it matters," *Academy of Management Executive* 12, no. 4 (1998): 8–20.

SECTION 4. Performance Magic

1. Stephen C. Lundin, Harry Paul, and John Christensen, *Fish! A Remarkable Way to Boost Morale and Improve Results* (New York: Hyperion, 2000), 29–31.

2. John Yokoyama and Jim Bergquist, "The world famous Pike Place Fish story: A breakthrough for managers," *Retailing Issues Letter* 13, no. 6 (November 2001): 2.

CHAPTER 11. Reading Your Audience

1. B. Joseph Pine III and James H. Gilmore, *The Experience Economy: Work Is Theatre & Every Business a Stage* (Boston: Harvard Business School Press, 1999), 133.

2. Gerard I. Nierenberg and Henry H. Calero, *How to Read a Person Like a Book* (New York: Simon & Schuster, 1971), 34.

3. Ibid., 47–50.

4. Ibid., 67–68.

5. Ibid., 32.

6. Ron Zemke, "Put Your Best Foot Forward with Individual Service," *City Business Journal,* 29 March 2002.

7. Chip R. Bell and Ron Zemke, *Managing Knock Your Socks Off Service* (New York: AMACOM, 1992), 52.

8. J. Goodman et al., "Setting Priorities for Satisfaction Improvement," in *Service Wisdom: Creating and Maintaining the Customer Service Edge,* eds. Ron Zemke and Chip R. Bell (Minneapolis: Lakewood Books, 1990). First published in *Quality Review* (Winter 1987).

CHAPTER 12. Magical Rapport

1. Leonard L. Berry. *Discovering the Soul of Service: The Nine Drivers of Sustainable Business Success* (New York: The Free Press, 1999), 211.

2. Daniel Goleman, *Working with Emotional Intelligence* (New York: Bantam Books, 1998), 136.

3. Ibid., 139.

4. Kristin Anderson and Ron Zemke, *Knock Your Socks Off Answers: Solving Customer Nightmares & Soothing Nightmare Customers* (New York: AMACOM, 1995), 57.

5. MidAmerican Energy uses the LIST model through arrangement with Sigma International, Inc., of Herndon, Virginia.

6. "Words to say; words to avoid" is part of a training module from "Achieving Stellar Service Experiences," a training program owned and distributed by AchieveGlobal, Inc., of Tampa, Florida.

7. Ibid.

8. Ron Zemke and Chip R. Bell, *Knock Your Socks Off Service Recovery* (New York: AMACOM, 2000), 180–81.

9. "Words to say; words to avoid" is part of a training module from "Achieving Stellar Service Experiences," a training program owned and distributed by AchieveGlobal, Inc., of Tampa, Florida.

CHAPTER 13. Delivering Magical Dialogues

1. Kristin Anderson and Ron Zemke, *Knock Your Socks Off Answers: Solving Customer Nightmares & Soothing Nightmare Customers* (New York: AMACOM, 1995), 44–45.

CHAPTER 14. The Tenants of Performance Magic

1. Henning Nelms, *Magic and Showmanship: A Handbook for Conjurors* (Toronto, Can.: General Publishing Company, Ltd., 1995), 34.

2. Ron Zemke, "Call Centers: Powerful Economic Engines," *Training* magazine, February 2003.

CHAPTER 15. Virtual Place Magic

1. Ron Zemke and Tom Connellan, *E-Service: 24 Ways to Keep Your Customers When the Competition Is Just a Click Away* (New York: AMACOM, 2001).

2. "Shopping the Internet: The Good, the Bad and the Ugly," a study conducted by Minneapolis-based Performance Research Associates, Inc., February 2000.

CHAPTER 16. Virtual Performance Magic

1. Ron Zemke and Tom Connellan, *E-Service: 24 Ways to Keep Your Customers When the Competition Is Just a Click Away* (New York: AMACOM, 2001).

CHAPTER 18. Romano's Macaroni Grill

1. Margaret Sheridan, "Choice in Chains: Italian," *Restaurants & Institutions,* 1 March 2003.

2. Paul Frumkin, "And the survey says: Dining for less turns out to be more," *Nation's Restaurant New,* 19 June 2000.

3. Patricia Sharpe, "Phil Romano," *Texas Monthly,* September 2000, 153.

4. Scott Gross, *Positively Outrageous Service* (New York: Warner Books, 1994), 5.

5. Rick Ramsey, "Just like mama used to make?", *Restaurant Business,* 15 July 2002.

CHAPTER 19. Von Maur

1. John Ewoldt, "Von Maur power: An Iowa-based department store is betting that exclusive merchandise and old-fashioned customer service will woo customers to its new Twin Cities store," *Minneapolis Star Tribune,* 9 August 2001, 1E.

CHAPTER 23. Place Pocket Service Magic

1. Maria Puente, "Mall of Them All Turns 10," *USA Today,* 9 August 2002.

2. "301 Great Customer Service Ideas," *Inc.* magazine, 1 January 1997.

3. Jonathan Barsky, *World Class Customer Satisfaction* (New York: McGraw-Hill, 1996), 28.

4. Joseph Pine and James Gilmore, *The Experience Economy* (Boston: Harvard Business School Press, 1999), 36.

CHAPTER 24. Process Pocket Service Magic

1. Joseph Pine and James Gilmore, *The Experience Economy* (Boston: Harvard Business School Press, 1999), 70.

2. Polly LaBarre, "Leader—Feargal Quinn," *Fast Company,* issue 52, 88.

3. Ibid.

4. Ibid.

5. Susan Greco, "Fanatics!", *Inc.* magazine, April 2001.

6. Joseph Pine and James Gilmore, *The Experience Economy,* 71.

7. "301 Great Customer Service Ideas," *Inc.* magazine, 1 January 1997.

8. Susan Greco, "Fanatics!"

9. Peppers & Rogers Group, "A Midsized Retailer Goes One to One," Inc.com, 1 October 2001.

10. Adapted from Drive-you-nuts.com, © *Quality Talk.* Used with permission.

11. "301 great customer service ideas," *Inc.* magazine, 22 September 2000.

12. Ron Zemke, *The Service Edge* (New York: New American Library,1990), 186.

13. Ibid., 254.

14. Ibid., 255.

15. Ibid., 105.

16. Ibid., 147.

CHAPTER 25. Performance Pocket Service Magic

1. Author personal experience.

2. John Yokoyama and Jim Bergquist, "The world famous Pike Place Fish story: A breakthrough for managers," *Retailing Issues Letter* 13, no. 6 (November 2001): 2.

3. Carl Sewell and Paul B. Brown, *Customers for Life* (New York: Doubleday Currency, 1990), 11.

4. Susan Greco, "Fanatics!", *Inc.* magazine, April 2001.

5. Adapted from Drive-you-nuts.com, © *Quality Talk.* Used with permission.

6. Betsy Sanders, *Fabled Service* (San Francisco: Pfeiffer and Company, 1995), 27.

7. Jayne Clark, "Eddy Garza, a grand hotel, 'door de force'," *USA Today,* 26 August 2002.

8. Ibid.

9. Ibid.

10. Ibid.

11. Ron Zemke and Dick Schaaf, *The Service Edge* (New York: New American Library, 1990), 146.

CHAPTER 26. Magical Recovery

1. Jonathan Barsky, *World Class Customer Satisfaction* (New York: McGraw-Hill, 1996), 130.

2. Ron Zemke and Kristin Anderson, *Tales of Knock Your Socks Off Service* (New York: AMACOM, 1997), 34.

3. Adapted from Drive-you-nuts.com, © *Quality Talk.* Used with permission.

4. Ibid.

5. Ibid.

6. *The Supervisor's Guide to Improved Customer Service and Retention Newsletter* Gary Henderson, "Ben & Jerry's Euphoric Service Makes Customers More Confectionale," (sample issue, 2002): 3.

7. Adapted from Drive-you-nuts.com, © *Quality Talk.* Used with permission.

8. Ron Zemke and Kristin Anderson, *Tales of Knock Your Socks Off Service,* 153–54.

Ron Zemke is one of the pioneers of the American customer service revolution. His writings and research on the organizational impact of customer service are considered landmark. As president of Minneapolis-based Performance Research Associates, he has consulted with Fortune 500 corporations and professional service organizations such as General Motors, Giant Eagle Inc., Turner Broadcasting System, Inc., Best Buy, General Mills, Microsoft, Sun Microsystems, DaimlerChrysler Services, and PricewaterhouseCoopers. He is coauthor of the best-selling *Service America: Doing Business in the New Economy,* the *Knock Your Socks Off Service* series, and *Generations at Work.* He is a highly sought after keynote speaker and seminar facilitator.

Chip Bell is a senior principal of Performance Research Associates, Inc., and manages the firm's Dallas office. Chip has advised such corporations as Universal Studios, Merrill Lynch, USAA, Pfizer, MBNA, Bank of America, Marriott, Victoria's Secret, and Ritz-Carlton Hotels. He is the author of such best-selling books as *Customer Love, Customers as Partners,* and *Managers as Mentors.* Dr. Bell holds graduate degrees in organizational psychology and human resource development from Vanderbilt University and George Washington University. He was a highly decorated infantry unit commander with the elite 82nd Airborne Division in Vietnam. Chip is a renowned keynote speaker on customer loyalty, mentoring, and partnerships.

Performance Research Associates, Inc.—founded in 1972—consults with large and medium-sized corporations and nonprofits on service quality, customer loyalty, and creating a customer-driven culture. PRA conducts organizational effectiveness and customer retention studies and creates customer retention strategies for a who's who of clients including GlaxoSmithKline, First Wachovia, American Express Financial Advisors, Prudential Insurance, Harley-Davidson, Depository Trust Clearing Corporation, Dun & Bradstreet, CUNA, Wachovia Bank & Trust, Roche Diagnostic Systems, Oppenheimer Funds, Microsoft, General Reinsurance, Motorola, Deluxe Corporation, and Ford Motor Company.

The firm currently has offices in Minneapolis, Minnesota; Dallas, Texas; Orlando, Florida; and Ann Arbor, Michigan. In addition to the company's consulting work, the firm's principals are heavily involved in writing, publishing, conducting seminars, and public speaking. Several of the principals make in excess of 100 paid presentations a year to business groups around the globe.

As a group, the PRA team has written more than 50 business books and several thousand articles. They have developed a dozen commercially successful, proprietary seminars, 13 commercially available training films, and several proprietary organizational assessment instruments. The work of PRA partners literally touches hundreds of thousands of people a year in corporate America and beyond. To inquire about how PRA might assist your organization, please call 800-359-2576 or visit us at <www.service-magic.com>.

Ron Zemke
PRA
821 Marquette Ave.
Suite 1820
Minneapolis, MN 55402
612-338-8523
PRA@socksoff.com

Chip Bell
PRA
25 Highland Park #100
Suite 374
Dallas, TX 75205
214-522-5777
chip@chipbell.com